# Teaching General Chemistry: A History and Philosophy of Science Approach

# TEACHING GENERAL CHEMISTRY: A HISTORY AND PHILOSOPHY OF SCIENCE APPROACH

## MANSOOR NIAZ

Nova Science Publishers, Inc.
*New York*

KH

For permission to use material from this book please contact us:
Telephone 631-231-7269; Fax 631-231-8175
Web Site: http://www.novapublishers.com

**NOTICE TO THE READER**

The Publisher has taken reasonable care in the preparation of this book, but makes no expressed or implied warranty of any kind and assumes no responsibility for any errors or omissions. No liability is assumed for incidental or consequential damages in connection with or arising out of information contained in this book. The Publisher shall not be liable for any special, consequential, or exemplary damages resulting, in whole or in part, from the readers' use of, or reliance upon, this material.

Independent verification should be sought for any data, advice or recommendations contained in this book. In addition, no responsibility is assumed by the publisher for any injury and/or damage to persons or property arising from any methods, products, instructions, ideas or otherwise contained in this publication.

This publication is designed to provide accurate and authoritative information with regard to the subject matter covered herein. It is sold with the clear understanding that the Publisher is not engaged in rendering legal or any other professional services. If legal or any other expert assistance is required, the services of a competent person should be sought. FROM A DECLARATION OF PARTICIPANTS JOINTLY ADOPTED BY A COMMITTEE OF THE AMERICAN BAR ASSOCIATION AND A COMMITTEE OF PUBLISHERS.

LIBRARY OF CONGRESS CATALOGING-IN-PUBLICATION DATA

Niaz, Mansoor.
 Teaching general chemistry : a history and philosophy of science approach / Mansoor Niaz.
   p. cm.
 ISBN 978-1-60456-105-0 (hardcover)
 1. Chemistry--Study and teaching. I. Title.
QD40.N53 2007
540.71--dc22
                          2007044155

*Published by Nova Science Publishers, Inc.* ✤ *New York*

10/13/09

# DEDICATION

*For Magda and Sabuhi*

*For their love, patience, and understanding*

# CONTENTS

**Preface**    **ix**

**Acknowledgements**    **xi**

**Chapter 1**    An Introduction to the History and Philosophy of Science    **1**

**Chapter 2**    Framework to Understand Conceptual Change    **9**

**Chapter 3**    A Methodology for Science Instruction Based on the History and  Philosophy of Science    **19**

**Chapter 4**    Understanding Mole    **23**

**Chapter 5**    Understanding Stoichiometry: Conflicts, Lacunae, and Perturbations    **27**

**Chapter 6**    Understanding Atomic Structure: Baroque Tower on a Gothic Base    **37**

**Chapter 7**    Understanding Gases: From 'Algorithmic Mode' to 'Conceptual Understanding'    **59**

**Chapter 8**    Understanding Heat Energy and Temperature: How Students Resist Conceptual Change from Caloric to Kinetic Theory?    **73**

**Chapter 9**    Understanding Chemical Equilibrium: Facilitating Conceptual Change    **85**

**Chapter 10**    Epistemological Beliefs of Students and Teachers about the Nature of Science    **117**

**Chapter 11**    Conclusion    **133**

**References**    **141**

**Index**    **161**

# PREFACE

If one could subscribe to Kuhn's thesis of revolutions interspersed with periods of 'normal science', science education has indeed gone through a revolutionary period in the last few decades. Delamont (1990) narrates an incident that in retrospect is quite revealing. She relates how at the end of the 1970s a paper was submitted to an educational research journal, which used the theoretical debate between Kuhn and Lakatos as its central 'motif.' The editor was so perplexed that he exclaimed: "Who on earth are Kuhn and Lakatos?" The interesting point is that the editor was a distinguished professor of science education.

In 1952, Gerald Holton's *Introduction to concepts and theories in physical science*, provided a glimpse for students and teachers as to how science evolves through the interactions of theories, experiments, and actual scientists, within a history and philosophy of science perspective. Looking back after almost 50 years, Holton (2003) considered that the textbook facilitated understanding of science as a coherent story based on the thoughts and work of living scientists. More recently, a new edition of this textbook presents science as an human adventure, from Copernicus to Einstein and beyond (Holton & Brush, 2001). The importance of history and philosophy of science was generally recognized by science educators in the 1960s (Klopfer, 1969; Robinson, 1969a; 1969b), and in the last few years there has been a worldwide sustained effort to provide a rationale for its inclusion in the science curriculum (Matthews, 1994; Scheffler, 1992).

The main objective of this monograph is to incorporate history and philosophy of science in the chemistry curriculum in order to provide students an overview of the dynamics of scientific research, which involves controversies, conflicts and rivalries among scientists, that is the humanizing aspects of science.

A major thesis of this book is the parallel between the construction of knowledge by the students and the scientists. In looking for this relationship, it is not necessary that ontogeny recapitulate phylogeny, but rather to establish that students can face similar difficulties in conceptualizing problems as those faced by the scientists in the past. Given the vast amount of literature on students' alternative conceptions (misconceptions) in science, it is plausible to suggest that these can be considered not as mistakes, but rather as tentative models, leading to greater conceptual understanding, similar to what Lakatos (1970) in philosophy of science has referred to as progressive 'problemshifts'. Just as scientists resist changes in the 'hard-core' of their beliefs by offering 'auxiliary hypotheses', students may adopt similar strategies. Conceptual change, in science education can thus be conceptualized as building of tentative models that provide greater explanatory power to students' understanding.

Chapter 1 of the book provides a brief introduction to the history and philosophy of science, with a discussion of the theory-ladenness of observation and the scientific method. This is followed, in Chapter 2 by a framework to understand conceptual change in science education. Chapter 3 provides a methodology based on history and philosophy of science that provides a rationale for the rest of the chapters and can facilitate guidelines for future research in different content areas. Chapters 4, 5, and 9, dealing with the mole concept, stoichiometry, and chemical equilibrium respectively, may be of interest primarily to chemistry teachers. The remaining chapters dealing with atomic structure (6), gases (7), heat and temperature (8), and the epistemological beliefs of students and teachers about the nature of science (10) can be of interest to science teachers in general. Although, the application of history and philosophy of science is based on a domain-specific content, an effort has been made to provide a rationale and guidelines for application to other topics. In order to facilitate the flow of ideas and emphasize the narrative, I have reduced the number of references in the text and provided more details in the Reference section.

# ACKNOWLEDGMENTS

My institution, Universidad de Oriente (Venezuela) has been the major sponsor of most of my research activities for the last 20 years, through various grants provided by the Consejo de Investigación.

I am indebted to Juan Pascual-Leone (York University, Toronto) and Richard F. Kitchener (Colorado State University) for having introduced me not only to philosophy of science but also to the philosophical aspects of Piaget's genetic epistemology.

Over the years I have been fortunate in having received the following awards that helped me to study and reflect on various issues related to science education and the history and philosophy of science: a) Research Award, International Council for Canadian Studies, 1988 at York University, Toronto; b) Senior Fulbright Research Fellowship, 1988-89 at Purdue University; and c) British Council Research Award, 1992 at University of Aberdeen, Scotland.

Thanks are due to the following publishers for extensive reproduction of materials from my publications:

a) John Wiley and Sons, Inc., New York (chapters: 4, 5, 6 & 7).
b) Springer, The Netherlands (chapters 4, 7, 8, 9 & 10).
c) Taylor and Francis, London (chapters 7 & 9).

*Chapter 1*

# AN INTRODUCTION TO THE HISTORY AND PHILOSOPHY OF SCIENCE

Recent research in science education has shown considerable interest in the history, philosophy of science and epistemological issues. This, relatively new approach to teaching and research in science education requires a brief recapitulation of the debates and controversies in history and philosophy of science.

History of science shows that positivism was the dominant philosophy from about the end of the 19th century to about the middle of the 20th century. Positivism has many faces and philosophers tend to characterize it in different ways: 1) *Classic positivism* can be traced to Comte (1798-1857), who emphasized that science focuses upon observation and hence scientific knowledge consisted of only in the description of observed phenomena and not inferred theoretical entities; 2) *Logical positivism* associated with the Vienna Circle which was very active during the 1930s and introduced the Verifiability Principle, according to which something is meaningful if and only if it is verifiable empirically, or in other words, 'if it can't be seen or measured, it is not meaningful to talk about'; 3) *Behaviorism* for their hostility to abstract theorizing and metaphysics; and 4) *Empiricism* which again emphasizes that our knowledge is wholly or partly based on experience through the senses and introspection. According to Phillips (1983) although logical positivism is a type of empiricism not all varieties of empiricism are positivistic. Although most philosophers these days would perhaps agree that positivism is dead (at least in academic circles), there seems to be some debate as to who was responsible for this. For science teachers it is important to note that prominent scientists, such as E. Mach (physicist, 1838-1916) and W. Ostwald (founder of physical chemistry, 1853-1932) were positivists, who opposed the introduction of atomic theory in physics and chemistry. Ostwald, for example, even tried to derive fundamental laws in chemistry (constant and multiple proportions) without the use of the atomic theory. The philosophical outlook of these scientists contrasts sharply with later developments in the history of science and has been summarized by Elkana (1971):

An important group of scientists led by Wilhelm Ostwald and Georg Helm developed in the 1870's and 1880's a metatheory of science, which later turned into an almost religious cult with the following hard-core metaphysics: all hypotheses should be banned from science and all observable phenomena should be reduced to one fundamental principle, namely the principle of energy. Its programme was to develop all scientific fields deductively from this unitary principle. It combined in its core the phenomenology of Kirchhoff, Mach and other great philosophers-scientists who all tried to eliminate untestable speculations from science ... " (p. 265).

The influence of Mach and Ostwald was checked by L. Boltzmann (1844-1906) and M. Planck (1858-1947), which led to many controversies. It is of interest to note that many of these controversies centered around the atomic theory. In his address at the annual meeting of the National Academy of Sciences (Washington, D.C., 1914), Rutherford summarized the development of atomic theory within a historical perspective:

> ... the great majority of scientific men now regard the atomic theory not only as a working hypothesis of great value but as affording a correct description of one stage of the subdivision of matter. While this is undoubtedly the case to-day, it is of interest to recall that less than 20 years ago there was a revolt by a limited number of scientific men against the domination of the atomic theory in chemistry. The followers of this school considered that the atomic theory should be regarded as a mere hypothesis, which was of necessity unverifiable by direct experiment, and should, therefore, not be employed as a basis of explanation of chemistry ... This tendency advanced so far that textbooks of chemistry were written in which the word atom or molecule was taboo, and chemistry was based instead on the law of combination in multiple proportion (Rutherford, 1915, p. 176).

This passage, coming from an exceptional witness, such as Rutherford (an experimentalist *par excellence* himself) is illustrative of the tension between those who wanted scientific theories to be verifiable by direct experiment (it is not difficult to guess who led the revolt) and those like Rutherford and Bohr who forged ahead with hypothetic (speculative) models. Interestingly, as late as 1886, French schools were not permitted to teach atomic theory as it was a 'mere hypothesis' by decision of the Minister of Education, the well-known chemist Berthelot.

From about the middle of the 20th century the work of the positivists has been questioned by the new philosophers of science (cf. Feyerabend, Hanson, Kuhn, Lakatos, Laudan, Newton-Smith, Polanyi, Popper, & Toulmin). In spite of the continuous debate among these philosophers, they agree (to a fair degree) upon at least one criticism of the positivists, which refers to the *theory-ladenness* of observation, viz., our observations depend on our formation, previous experience and conceptual framework that we invoke in order to solve a problem.

## 1.1. THE ROLE OF OBSERVATION IN PHILOSOPHY OF SCIENCE

The dilemma of the philosophers with respect to the theory-ladenness of observation has been expressed in truly picturesque terms by Hanson (1958):

> Let us consider Johannes Kepler: imagine him on a hill watching the dawn. With him is Tycho Brahe. Kepler regarded the sun as fixed: it was the earth that moved. But Tycho followed Ptolemy and Aristotle in this much at least: the earth was fixed and all other celestial bodies moved around it. *Do Kepler and Tycho see the same thing in the east at dawn?*" (p. 5, original emphasis).

Hanson's (1958) thesis, of course has not gone unchallenged in the philosophy of science literature. An important aspect of the positivist philosophy was the inductive generalizations of scientific laws based on observations. Lakatos (1971) has explained cogently: "According to inductivism only those propositions can be accepted into the body of science which either describe hard facts or are infallible inductive generalizations from them" (p. 92). The main paradigms of inductivist/positivist historiography were: Kepler's generalizations from Tycho Brahe's careful observations, Newton's discovery of his law of gravitation, Ampere's discovery of his law of electrodynamics, Lavoisier's experiments which refuted the phlogiston theory, and Boyle's law of gases.

According to Hanson scientists rarely find laws by enumerating and summarizing observables, that is, by induction, and nor do they start from hypotheses; but rather start from data. Thus, the inductive view is wrong in suggesting that the law is, but a summary of the data, instead of being what it must be, an explanation of the data. On the other hand, the hypothetico-deductive (H-D) account obscures the initial relationship between data and laws by suggesting that the fundamental inference is from higher-order hypotheses to observation statements. Galileo, for example, struggled for 34 years before advancing his constant acceleration hypothesis with confidence and Darwin went through a similar process.

Hanson argues that a physical theory is not pieced together from observed phenomena, but rather provides patterns within which data appear intelligible, that is, a sort of 'conceptual gestalt', which provides an explanation of the data. Interestingly, Leibniz had remarked: "What a pity that, for all his hundreds of experiments, [Boyle] provides no general ideas for the interpretation of nature" (*Die Philosophischen Schriften*, reproduced in Hanson, 1958, p. 205). It is quite clear that Leibniz is alluding to the fact that Boyle did not provide an explanation of the data (cf. 'conceptual gestalt'). Actually, it took almost 200 years and the work of many theorists, before a satisfactory explanation of the data was provided by the kinetic theory of Maxwell and Boltzmann.

Lakatos takes even a more critical stance with respect to the positivist / inductivist interpretation of the history of science by pointing out that Boyle's and his successors' labors to establish pv = RT were irrelevant for the later theoretical development (except for developing some experimental techniques), just as Kepler's three laws may have been superfluous for the Newtonian theory of gravitation. Brush (1978) has explained cogently that:

> ... as soon as you start to look at how chemical theories developed and how they were related to experiments, you discover that the conventional wisdom about the empirical nature of chemistry is wrong. The history of chemistry cannot be used to indoctrinate students in Baconian methods" (p. 290).

Another episode from the history of science that illustrates the difference between the inductivist and the new philosophers' understanding of science is the explanation of wavelengths of hydrogen's line emission spectrum, based on Bohr's 1913 paper. As the Balmer series (1885) and the Paschen series (1908) of the hydrogen spectrum were known before 1913, the inductivist account presents the story as an example of what Lakatos refers to as the Baconian 'inductive ascent', viz., observation of the spectrum lines led to Balmer's empirical law, for which Bohr provided a theoretical explanation. This episode illustrates the crux of the debate between the inductivists and the new philosophers, as Bohr's major problem was not to explain Balmer's and Paschen's series, but to explain the paradoxical stability of the Rutherford atom. Interestingly, Bohr had not even heard of Balmer and Paschen's formulae before he wrote the first version of his paper. In a letter dated January 31, 1913, addressed to Rutherford, Bohr had clarified:

> I do not at all deal with the question of calculation of the frequencies corresponding to the lines in the visible spectrum. I have only tried, on the basis of the simple hypothesis, which I used from the beginning, to discuss the constitution of the atoms and molecules in their 'permanent' state (Reproduced in Jammer, 1966, p. 77).

Studies about the philosophical background of Bohr have clarified that he did not have any specific philosophical guide line. The main goal was to reconcile the Rutherford atom with the claim of stability. Bohr was, in a way forced into the acceptance of stationary states and discontinuous energy-transitions. It was the inner logic of the problems that determined step by step what he had to accept. In tracing the genesis of the Bohr atom, Heilbron and Kuhn (1969) have shown that: "... Bohr had developed a detailed, non-spectroscopic, quantized version of Rutherford's atom some time before he saw the relevance of the Balmer formula" (p. 255).

It is important to note the similarity between the inductivist interpretation of Bohr's work and a freshman level chemistry textbook:

> The relationship, proposed by J.J. Balmer in 1885, was derived from experimental observations and was not based on any theory of atomic structure.... In 1913, Niels Bohr proposed a theory for the electronic structure of hydrogen atom that explained the line spectrum of this element (Mortimer, 1983, pp. 84-85).

The Baconian flavor of this historical account is remarkable and also reveals how the scientific enterprise is presented to the students. Another freshman chemistry textbook is even more revealing: "In 1913, Niels Bohr developed a model for the atom that accounted for the *striking regularities seen in the spectrum of the hydrogen atom*" (Oxtoby, Nachtrieb & Freeman, 1990, p. 680, emphasis added). Apparently, for most textbook writers and positivist historians the most important contribution of Bohr's theory was the explanation of the hydrogen atom line spectrum. Lakatos in contrast, would consider such historical accounts as, caricatures of actual history. At this stage, it is important to note that most general chemistry topics are based on a historical reconstruction of the events and this inevitably leads to a philosophical interpretation. In other words, while teaching general chemistry we impart knowledge with respect to not only the content but also the dynamics of progress in science. Most general chemistry textbooks provide a Baconian vision of progress in science, while ignoring the fact that there are alternative interpretations.

The *Chemical Revolution* in the 18th century associated with A. Lavoisier (1743-1794) provides another interesting episode in the history of science. According to the positivist/inductivist interpretation before Lavoisier did his experiments the scientists accepted G. Stahl's (1660-1734) theory, who sustained that a burning substance emitted phlogiston and hence should decrease in weight. Thus, according to the phlogiston theory, metals on being burnt in air must decrease in weight due to the loss of phlogiston. Lavoisier's experiments in 1772 showed that when phosphorus was burned in a volume of air confined over water, the volume of air was reduced, and the product of combustion weighed more than the original. According to the positivist interpretation this decisively refuted phlogiston theory. Many chemistry textbooks follow this interpretation (cf. Brown & Le May, 1987, p. 5 as an illustration). In spite of the popularity of this interpretation, the history of chemistry shows that as early as 1630 (i.e., long before Lavoisier came on the scene) J. Rey (1630) had reported that it was common knowledge that metallic oxides weigh more than the metals from which they were prepared. According to Musgrave (1976), who gives a detailed account of this episode, "... if Lavoisier's 1772 experiment refutes phlogiston theory, then phlogiston theory was *born* refuted" (p. 183, original emphasis). For somewhat different interpretations of the Chemical Revolution see Perrin (1988) and Thagard (1990). This episode is discussed again in chapter 2.

## 1.2. FROM THEORY-LADENNESS OF OBSERVATION TO: IS THERE A SCIENTIFIC METHOD?

Although there seems to be considerable consensus among philosophers of science with respect to the thesis that all observation is theory-laden, there seems to be considerable debate with respect to 'the scientific method'. It appears that the acceptance of the theory-ladenness of observations has led some philosophers to sustain that there is no specifiable 'method of science', and thus empirical testing cannot objectively (impartially) arbitrate between rival theories. One of the extreme views is that of Feyerabend (1975): "There is only one principle that can be defended under *all* circumstances ... It is the principle: *anything goes*" (p. 28, original emphases). The stark difference and the gulf that separates positivism and the new philosophers of science can be understood from the following quotations:

> Hempel (1970): "Science strives for objectivity in the sense that its statements are to be capable of public tests with results that do not vary essentially with the tester" (p. 695).
> Phillips (1990): "A person does not have to read very widely in the contemporary methodological or theoretical literature pertaining to research in social sciences and related areas, such as education, in order to discover that objectivity is dead" (p. 19).

A critique of the new philosophy of science has concluded: "Since the 1960s, the theory-ladenness of observation has become so entrenched that it has been referred to as one of the two dogmas of contemporary philosophy of science" (Hunt, 1994, p. 134). According to Kitcher (1995): "... the once popular idea that the natural sciences make progress and that scientists make their decisions in accordance with objective standards is regarded as a myth" (p. 611). In a nut-shell we have a new cult: 'theory-ladenness of observation dooms objectivity', perhaps quite similar to what Elkana (1971) has referred to as 'all hypotheses should be banned from science', which had become a cult in the late 19th century. Given the force of some of the critiques, one might wonder why the new philosophy of science view has become so popular, much less become dogma. One explanation is that theories in philosophy of science, as in science proper, can only be overthrown by rival theories.

The conceptualization of scientific progress through competition between rival theories is perhaps one of the most significant contribution of modern history and philosophy of science to science education, and constitutes the 'leit motif' of this book. Papineau (1979) after Lakatos, has made an important contribution towards the understanding that although observation is theory-laden and science does not proceed by reasoning inductively to generalizations, and yet acknowledge the role of observation in the following terms:

> The role of observation is not to provide a firm basis from which generalizations can then be inductively extrapolated but, if anything, to provide some check on whether the promise of previously made theoretical commitments has been fulfilled. And it is no essential bar to observation playing this role that the significance we attach to observation reports should depend on our having certain generalizations about human observers. Provided the scientist does not have *carte blanche* to discard such generalizations at will, the check provided by observation reports so construed will be real enough (Papineau, 1979, p. 100, original emphasis).

Lakatos (1970) recognizes that: "Even then experience still remains, in an important sense, the 'impartial arbiter' of scientific controversy. We cannot get rid of the problem of the 'empirical basis' if we want to learn from experience ..." (p. 131). From a Lakatosian point of view, the absence of a specifiable 'scientific method' does not signify the abandonment of the processes of science, but rather provides an opportunity to shift from one method (problem-solving approach) to another. Similarly, Laudan, Laudan and Donovan (1988) have pointed the close relationship between theory and observation: "... scientific practice shows, the soundness of theoretical claims and the significance of empirical data can be determined only by constantly moving back and forth between theory on the one hand and observation and experiment on the other" (pp. 7-8). Thus, the proliferation of different approaches to science can be both an asset and an opportunity to advance science through competition between different research programs. A review of the literature in science education shows that the controversy regarding, 'Is there a scientific method' has attracted considerable attention. More recently, Niaz (2005) has shown that despite the popularity of the quantitative imperative (i.e., studying something scientifically means measuring it), progress in science has frequently involved a confrontation between this view and the imperative of presuppositions.

## 1.3. A BRIEF INTRODUCTION TO LAKATOS' METHODOLOGY OF SCIENTIFIC RESEARCH PROGRAMS

For an introduction to the history and philosophy of science, the beginning reader in science education can find the following sources useful: Duschl, 1990, 1994; Duschl & Gitomer, 1991; Giere, 1988; Gilbert & Swift, 1985; Loving, 1991; Matthews, 1994; Niaz (1995a) and Phillips, 1987. A general introduction to Lakatos' methodology can be found in: Brown, 1990; Hacking, 1979; and Papineau, 1979. In what follows an overview of a Lakatosian framework is presented. For details the reader is referred to the original sources: Lakatos (1970, 1971, 1974, 976).

According to Lakatos, the basic unit of appraisal must not be an isolated theory or conjunction of theories but rather a 'research program,' with a conventionally accepted *'hard core'* and with a *'positive heuristic'* which defines problems, outlines the construction of a belt of auxiliary hypotheses, foresees anomalies and turns them victoriously into examples, all according to a preconceived plan. The *negative heuristic* represents the *'hard core'* of the program, consisting of basic assumptions considered 'irrefutable' by the methodological decision of its protagonists, and does not allow *modus tollens* to de directed at this hard core. The *positive heuristic* represents the construction of a 'protective belt' consisting of a partially articulated set of suggestions or hints on how to change, develop the 'refutable variants' of the program. The positive heuristic saves the scientist from becoming confused in the 'ocean of anomalies' by directing the *modus tollens* at the 'auxiliary hypotheses'. The scientist lists anomalies, but as long as his research program sustains its momentum, he may freely put them aside, and it is primarily the positive heuristic of the program, not the anomalies, which dictate the choice of problems.

There is no such thing as crucial experiments, in the sense that a theory is falsified (refuted) when a statement that expresses the result of an observation is in contradiction with a statement of the theory – that is, naive falsificationism. A theory is refuted, by a rival research program which explains the previous success of its rival and supersedes it by a further display of heuristic (explanatory) power, and not by a crucial experiment. Lakatos considers this to be his sophisticated falsificationism.

A research program is progressing if it frequently succeeds in converting anomalies into successes, that is, explainable by the theory – referred to as *'progressive problemshifts'*. The classic example of a successful research program is Newton's gravitational theory. Lakatos also deals extensively with Bohr's atomic theory in order to illustrate various aspects of his philosophy. According to Lakatos, Bohr's famous postulates constitute the *negative heuristic* of his research program, which helped me to develop his theory. On the contrary, most general chemistry and physics textbooks consider the postulates in themselves as Bohr's theory. The textbook presentations lack the appreciation of how scientists face difficulties and resort to various methodological strategies.

*Chapter 2*

# FRAMEWORK TO UNDERSTAND CONCEPTUAL CHANGE

Following Galileo's method of idealization, scientific laws, being epistemological constructions, do not describe the behavior of actual bodies. As philosophers, psychologists and science educators generally think that they should emulate physics, which is the paradigm-case of science, it would be interesting to consider Newton' law of gravitation, as summarized by Feynman (1967): "... two bodies exert a force between each other which varies inversely as the square of the distance between them, and varies directly as the product of their masses" (p. 14). At the turn of this century a leading historian of science conceptualized it in the following awe inspiring terms:

> ... the Newtonian gravitation formula has been generally accepted, and it still stands there as almost the only firmly established mathematical relation, expressive of a property of all matter, to which the progress of more than two centuries has added nothing, from which it has taken nothing away (Merz, 1904, p. 384).

According to Lakatos (1970), Newton's law of gravitation is one of the "... best-corroborated scientific theory of all times ... " (p. 92) and Feynman (1967) endorses the view that it is, "... the greatest generalization achieved by the human mind" (p. 14). In spite of such impressive credentials, Cartwright (1983) asks: Does this law (gravitation) truly describe how bodies behave?" (p. 57) and responds laconically: "Assuredly not" (p. 57). Cartwright (1983) explains further:

> For bodies which are both massive and charged, the law of universal gravitation and Coulomb's law (the law that gives the force between two charges) interact to determine the final force. But neither law by itself truly describes how the bodies behave. No charged objects will behave just as the law of universal gravitation says; and any massive objects will constitute a counterexample to Coulomb's law. These two laws are not true: worse they are not even approximately true" (p. 57).

This would perhaps be quite a surprise to many students and even teachers. This, however, is not the whole story. Feynman's version of the law of gravitation, given above has an implicit *ceteris paribus* modifier or clause. According to Cartwright (1983) with the modifier the law would read:

> *If there are no forces other than gravitational forces at work, then* two bodies exert a force between each other which varies inversely as the square of the distance between them, and varies directly as the product of their masses (p. 58, modifier in italics).

The law with the modifier can explain in only very simple or ideal circumstances, and may even be considered as, "... irrelevant to the more complex and interesting situations" (Cartwright, 1983, p. 58).

*Ceteris paribus* clauses play an important role in scientific progress, enabling us to solve complex problems by introducing simplifying assumptions (idealization). Lakatos (1970) has endorsed this position in the following terms: "Moreover, *one can easily argue that ceteris paribus clauses are not exceptions, but the rule in science*" (p. 102, original italics). Application of the Lakatosian methodology, to Bohr's research program, as an example of how scientists progress from simple to complex models (simplifying assumptions) is provided in the next section. This illustrates quite cogently the research methodology of idealization utilized for studying physical laws in particular and complex problems in general. According to Matthews (1987):

> The gas laws, inheritance laws, Newton's laws, Piagetian stages, etc. – all of these describe the behaviour of ideal bodies, they are abstractions from the evidence of experience. The laws are true only when a considerable number of disturbing factors (itemized in the *caeteris paribus* clauses) are eliminated ... The art of experimentation is to progressively try to do so (p. 295).

This research methodology of idealization, that is, building of models is an important characteristic of modern non-Aristotelian science. Another example of idealization familiar to science educators is Piaget's genetic epistemology, who has emphasized that the whole history of physics is about decentration, which reduced to a *minimum* the deformations introduced by an egocentric subject and based this science to a maximum on the laws of an epistemic subject. The role of the epistemic subject is an important aspect of Piaget's genetic epistemology and Niaz (1991a) has shown its importance for science education. Similarly, Kitchener (1987) considers Piaget's genetic epistemology as a philosophy of science in which Piaget attempts to explain the growth of knowledge in ways similar to those of Popper and Lakatos, namely, as being a rational reconstruction of the course of epistemic change in which epistemic transitions occur by virtue of certain normative principles.

More recently, as an extension of the positions of Cartwright (1983) and Lakatos (1970), Klee (1992) has shown: "There really isn't the categorical difference between the way *ceteris paribus* clauses work in the physical domain and the way they work in the psychological domain ..." (p. 398). This interpretation opens the possibility of new alternatives in educational practice.

## 2.1. APPLICATION OF LAKATOSIAN METHODOLOGY TO HISTORY OF SCIENCE

With this background it is instructive to compare Lakatos' rational reconstruction of Bohr's research program. The most important aspect of this reconstruction is that Bohr's main objective was not to explain the emission spectrum of the hydrogen atom (see discussion in Chap. 1) but to understand the paradoxical stability of the Rutherford atom:

> The background problem was the riddle of how Rutherford atoms (that is, minute planetary systems with electrons orbiting round a positive nucleus) can remain stable; for according to the well-corroborated Maxwell-Lorentz theory of electromagnetism they should collapse. But Rutherford's theory was well corroborated too (Lakatos, 1970, p. 141).

Next, Lakatos outlines Bohr's five postulates as the *hard core* of his program and points out how Bohr's theory based on Planck's quantum hypothesis was inconsistently grafted on to classical electrodynamics. It is important to note that even some of the textbooks (cf. Mahan & Myers, 1990) note the paradox, however, without elaborating on it. What makes Lakatos' methodology useful for the science teacher is the understanding that such inconsistencies/grafts are fairly common in the history of science:

> Indeed, *some of the most important research programmes in the history of science were grafted on to older programmes with which they were blatantly inconsistent.* For instance, Copernican astronomy was 'grafted' on to Aristotelian physics, Bohr's programme on to Maxwell's. Such 'grafts' are irrational for the justificationist and for the naive falsificationist, neither of whom can countenance growth on inconsistent foundations" (Lakatos, 1970, p. 142, original emphasis).

Furthermore, as the young grafted program strengthens, the symbiosis becomes competitive and finally the old program is displaced. These aspects of Lakatos' philosophy will be helpful in designing a methodology for science instruction in the next chapter. Margenau (1950) has summarized Bohr's predicament in truly picturesque terms:

> ... it is understandable that, in the excitement over its success, men overlooked a malformation in the theory's architecture; for *Bohr's atom sat like a baroque tower upon the Gothic base of classical electrodynamics* (p. 311, emphasis added).

Finally, Lakatos shows how Bohr used the methodology of idealization (i.e., simplifying assumptions) and developed the *positive heuristic* of Bohr's program by progressing from simple to complex models, that is, from a fixed proton-nucleus in a circular orbit, to elliptical orbits, to removal of restrictions (fixed nucleus and fixed plane), to inclusion of spin of the electron, and so on until the program could ultimately be extended to complicated atoms. Similarly, Lakatos considers Newton's gravitational theory as a research program based on a sequence of evolving models (degree of idealization) that finally led Newton to incorporate interplanetary forces, perturbations, bulging planets rather than round planets, etc.

Another example of progressing from simple to complex models is provided by Piaget's genetic epistemology (Kitchener, 1986; Vuyk, 1981). Piaget's problem was much more difficult and thus he focused on: How is the development of knowledge (competence) possible in an ideal epistemic subject by ignoring variables, such as cognitive styles, studies of variables that detract from correct reasoning, and memory limitations. There is of course no limit to the number of variables that can affect performance of the real subjects. In this respect Pascual-Leone's (1987) theory of constructive operators has played a crucial role in the integration of these variables to Piaget's epistemological framework. Furthermore, Niaz (1992) has demonstrated a progressive 'problemshift' in the Lakatosian sense between Piaget's epistemic subject and Pascual-Leone's metasubject, which leads to the development of a theory with greater explanatory power.

## 2.2. RELATIONSHIP BETWEEN ONTOGENESIS AND PHYLOGENESIS

The above reconstruction from the history of science shows that if scientists adopt the methodology of idealization (simplifying assumptions) in order to solve complex problems, it is plausible to hypothesize that students adopt similar strategies by building models that facilitate conceptual understanding. The relationship between the process of theory development by scientists and an individual's acquisition of knowledge has been recognized in the literature. In spite of the commonalities between psychogenesis and the history of science, it is important to point out that ontogenesis is not an exact and detailed recapitulation of phylogenesis (cf. Piaget, 1971a). Nevertheless, according to Vonéche and Bovet (1982):

> ...the link between phylogenesis and ontogenesis is very strong indeed, since individual variations are always concomitant with species variations. So much so, that the only way for Piaget to understand the missing links between historical and prehistorical men is the study of today's children (p. 88).

Actually, Piaget's position with respect to Haeckel's biogenetic law ('Phylogenesis is the mechanical cause of ontogenesis', cf. Gould, 1977, p. 78) is quite complex. It appears that although Piaget believed in parallels between ontogeny and phylogeny, he denies Haeckelian recapitulation as their mechanism. Interestingly, when Gould wrote to Piaget asking about his view of the biogenetic law, Piaget responded:

> I have done very little work in psychology on the relationships between ontogenesis and phylogenesis because, psychologically, the child explains the adult more than the reverse (p. 146).

More recently, Garcia (1987) has clarified the Piagetian position:

> There are common mechanisms underlying both individual development and the development of science. However, let us say very strongly that this hypothesis has nothing to do with the classic idea of a relationship between ontogenesis and phylogenesis (p. 128).

Similarly, Kitchener (1985) considers that Piaget does not endorse the biogenetic law (p. 6). Furthermore, it is important to understand that ontogeny does not refer to the psychogenesis of individual persons but rather about what Piaget calls *the epistemic subject*, that which is common to all subjects at the same level of development.

There have been various attempts at a critical appraisal of this subject and the following critique is helpful in understanding the issues:

> ... phylogeny is not a sufficient causal or mechanical explanation for ontogeny. Rather, phylogeny is best characterized as an historical description of progressive variations in ontogenesis" (Lickliter & Berry, 1990, p. 357).

Interestingly, Lakatos (1976) mentions very briefly the biogenetic law by referring to its endorsement by Poincaré (1908) and Pólya (1962). However, what is of interest to the science teacher is that Lakatos uses it to emphasize that history of science should be our guide and presents the historical development of mathematics through a continuous dialogue between the teacher and various students, and often attributes the views of mathematicians in the past to some of the students, in order to provide a rational reconstruction. For example, one of the students (Delta) considers that once a theorem has been established in mathematics, there is nothing conjectural about it any more. Then in the footnote Lakatos provides the information that this view was shared by many mathematicians in the 19th century. Similar examples can be found throughout the book. Brown (1990) has provided a gist of the main ideas of Lakatos (1976) and concluded:

> Lakatos thinks mathematics would be much easier to learn if textbooks were written historically. Definitions, theorems, etc. would all be more readily grasped if only they were presented to the learner within the problem situation in which they first arose (p. 118).

The parallel between students' development of scientific concepts and history of science has been of interest to science educators. Pomeroy (1993) considers the growing awareness of and commitment to constructivism as providing a philosophical foundation for science teachers, as the construction of knowledge by children echoes Piaget's notion of genetic epistemology, which proposes that evolution of science is recapitulated in cognitive development. Thus, after having discarded the biogenetic law, it can be concluded that ontogenesis (psychogenesis of knowledge in the child) follows principles similar to those in the scientist (phylogenesis, history of collective knowledge) and there exist various commonalities between psychogenesis and the history of science.

## 2.3. CONCEPTUAL CHANGE: WEAK/RADICAL RESTRUCTURING

Research in science education has shown considerable interest as to how children acquire knowledge about the physical world and how they come to understand the currently accepted scientific explanations of concepts such as matter, weight, density, force, gravity, day/night cycle, heat and temperature. A review of the literature on knowledge acquisition and conceptual change shows that it may be more useful to replace Piagetian global restructuring by an approach based on domain-specific restructuring. Carey (1986), for example, approves of most of Piaget's descriptive work and the argument seems to center on Piaget's interpretations, within his metatheory:

It is only when Piaget sought to further explain the differences between young children and adults in terms of domain-general limitations on the child's representational or computational abilities that his interpretations have come under fire. However, the question is still very much open (p. 1129).

Indeed, there has been considerable controversy between domain-specific/domain-general restructuring (Niaz, 1994a; Sternberg, 1989). It is important to note that domain-specific restructuring can be of two kinds: a) *Weak restructuring*: Based on the finding that knowledge representation of experts is different from that of novices (Chi, Feltovich & Glaser, 1981). Experts represent more and/or different relations between concepts than do novices. Similarly, experts organize their knowledge in terms of abstract relational schemata that are not easily accessible to novices. b) *Radical restructuring*: Based on the finding that the novice does not simply have an impoverished knowledge base but rather has a different theory (Carey & Smith, 1993; Vosniadou & Brewer, 1987). Furthermore, the radical restructuring view postulates a relationship between theory changes in the history of science and an individual's acquisition of knowledge (Chinn & Brewer, 1993; Niaz, 1995a). The following statement represents this point of view very succinctly:

> As we have searched the literatures on the history of science and on education and psychology for instances of people responding to anomalous data [presenting students with evidence that contradicts their preinstructional theories], we have been struck by the similarities in the descriptions of the responses of scientists, nonscientist adults, and science students. The fundamental ways in which scientists react to anomalous data appear to be identical to the ways in which nonscientist adults and science students react to such data (Chinn & Brewer, 1993, p. 3).

## 2.4. CONCEPTUAL CHANGE: MISCONCEPTIONS AS PARADIGMS

One of the most well known conceptual change model in science education was proposed by Posner, Strike, Hewson and Gertzog (1982). A recent study considers that this is the most widely accepted conceptual change model and has 250 literature citations (Institute for Scientific Information) between 1998-2003, which is at least five times more than for any other model (Piquette & Heikkinen, 2005). A major contribution of this model was the condition (as a pre-requisite for conceptual change) that the new conception must appear initially plausible to the students. This is based on a major insight of Kuhn (1962), viz.; scientists will not give up a theory unless there is a plausible alternative theory available. Posner et al. seem to consider Kuhn's 'paradigms' to be the same as the Lakatosian hard core. Similarly, Duschl and Gitomer (1991 consider alterations during Kuhn's 'normal science' as similar to changes to the soft core of a Lakatosian research program, and Kuhn's 'revolutions' as similar to abandonment of Lakatosian research program's hard core. This comparison between the Kuhnian and the Lakatosian frameworks seems to be inappropriate as Kuhnian paradigms are considered to be incommensurable, whereas two or more competing research programs in the Lakatosian framework may engage in a permanent struggle and competition (cf. phlogiston and oxygen theories) and what is more important they may even share some parts of their hard cores. A recent example of such sharing is provided by the research programs of Piaget and Pascual-Leone in both cognitive psychology and science education. Niaz (1993a) has shown, for example, that:

> ... Pascual-Leone's theory extends Piaget's negative heuristic [hard core] by introducing antecedent variables, and at the same time enriches the positive heuristic [soft core] by introducing metasubjective task analysis, which leads to a progressive problemshift (p. 757).

A reconstruction of the events associated with the Chemical Revolution in the history of science (late 18th century), clarify the underlying issues even more. According to the standard historical account Lavoisier's 1772 experiments were supposed to have refuted the phlogiston theory of combustion (Musgrave, 1976). From a Kuhnian point of view (cf. McCann, 1978), the paradigmatic shift from phlogiston to oxygen was an all-or-nothing gestalt switch. On the other hand, according to Perrin (1988):

> My purpose in reviewing its conceptual and methodological dimensions is not only to make explicit what the chemical revolution was about, but to emphasize its complex and multi-layered nature. Such a system did not spring fully developed from Lavoisier's brow, but was laboriously conceived and articulated over a period of more than twenty years. Lavoisier published no full and systematic exposition of his views until 1789 (p. 107).

Interestingly, the chemist J.B.M. Bucquet, a chief ally of Lavoisier in his last complete chemistry course in 1778-1779, was offering phlogistic and Lavoisian explanations side-by-side, clearly favoring the latter (Perrin, 1988, p. 112). According to Laudan, Laudan and Donovan (1988):

> The slow and gradual conversion to Lavoisier's approach raises grave doubts whether community-wide change is a rapid process.... acceptance of this new paradigm was not an 'all-or-nothing' affair. Furthermore, ... there was extensive discussion between phlogistonists and oxygen theorists; these exchanges exhibit none of the incommensurability often assumed to make inter-paradigmatic communication exceedingly difficult ... (p. 27).

Reference to this episode in the history of science is important for the following reasons: a) This episode has been often used as an example by theorists of scientific change and, "... it looms large in Kuhn's treatment of revolutions, as it had earlier in Conant's ..." (Laudan et al., 1988, p. 42); b) Conceptual change for Kuhn represents a break with the tradition which leads to displacement of the old paradigm by a new one. On the other hand, for Lakatos rival research programs can work together for years; c) For science educators, the crux of the issue is that according to Kuhn (1970) different paradigms are incommensurate because their core beliefs are resistant to change and that paradigms do not merge over time, rather they displace each other after periods of chaotic upheaval or scientific revolution (cf. Hoyningen-Huene, 1993 where Kuhn maintains his views on most of the important issues).

With this background we would like to go back to the Posner et al. (1982) conceptual change model and show that it draws quite heavily on Kuhn's philosophy of science and hence is problematic. The authors recognize the importance of anomalies for conceptual change and point out that if taken seriously by students, anomalies provide the sort of cognitive conflict (like a Kuhnian state of crisis) that prepares the student's conceptual ecology for an accommodation. This shows that Posner et al. foresee a 'crisis' in student's thinking before conceptual change is accomplished, quite similar to the crises that precede Kuhn's scientific revolutions. The role of cognitive conflict has been recognized in science education (see chap. 5 for details), but it does not necessarily produce a state of 'crisis' in the Kuhnian sense.

In contrast Lakatos has emphasized that the history of science has been and should be a history of competing research programs, but it has not been and must not become a succession of periods of normal science. Similarly, an alternate account of conceptual change (Niaz, 1997, see chap. 9 for details) would rather emphasize students' alternative conceptions (misconceptions) as rival theories that compete with the present scientific theories and at times recapitulate theories scientists held in the past. Strike and Posner (1992) in an attempt to revise the Posner et al. (1982) model have reinforced the Kuhnian thesis even more explicitly:

> ... a misconception is not merely a mistake or a false belief. Either it must also play the kind of organizing role in cognition that paradigms play, or it must be dependent on such organizing concepts ... A misconception, thus, may become a candidate for change (pp. 152-153).

One could, of course, agree that misconceptions are not simply mistakes. However, instead of considering them as paradigms (which are resistant to change and do not foster debate) it would be more helpful to consider them as alternative theories that compete with the scientific theories. Clement, Brown, and Zietsman (1989) have emphasized that, "... misconceptions should be respected as creative constructions of the individual" (p. 555). Furthermore, these authors differentiate between preconceptions that are detrimental to learning, from those that are largely in agreement with accepted physical theory and are considered as 'anchoring conceptions.' For example, even many physics students refuse to believe that static objects can exert forces. However, most students do believe that when you press down on a spring and hold your hand still, the spring pushes up on your hand. These authors have reported results suggesting that such preconceptions can be used as 'anchors' that have potential for use in instruction.

## 2.5. PROGRESSIVE TRANSITIONS: BUILDING OF MODELS BY STUDENTS AND SCIENTISTS

Most high school and freshman science courses emphasize the application of algorithms to solve routine (plug-and-chug) problems (cf, Nurrenbern & Pickering, 1987). It appears that for most teachers solving numerical problems that require algorithmic solution strategies in contrast to conceptual understanding, is a major behavioral objective of science courses. According to Sawrey (1990):

> Many instructors, myself included, have believed (or hoped) that teaching students to solve problems is equivalent to teaching the concepts. If, as is now being proposed, the axiom is not true, then we all must rethink our approach to chemical education (p. 253).

Educators in other areas of science face a similar dilemma. What, however, makes the problem more difficult is the fact that this has been an unquestioned axiom of freshman chemistry teaching for the last many decades. Furthermore, textbooks generally do not emphasize conceptual understanding. According to De Berg (1989): "... if text books are a guide to what students learn in classroom, it is no wonder that the 'algorithmic' mode of problem solving in gas law problems predominates ..." (p. 119). More recently, Chiappetta et al. (1991) have shown that high school chemistry textbooks not only deemphasize science as a way of thinking, but also do not stress the importance of how chemists discover ideas and experiment, historical development of chemistry concepts, cause-effect relationships, and self-examination of one's thinking in the pursuit of knowledge.

Interestingly, recent research has also shown that for physical theories in general and for the ideal gas law in particular, one should not expect training or experience with algorithmic problems to develop the understanding required to solve conceptual problems. These findings pose considerable problems for science educators and they seem to be on the threshold of a crucial turn in their pedagogical frameworks. Given this state of affairs, the contribution of history and philosophy of science to the improvement of science education can be even more crucial. At this stage it is important to have an idea as to what is happening in the science classroom, which in my opinion is not very different in most parts of the world (in spite of the debate about multiculturalism in science education). The opinions of the following students show how our students are perhaps more aware of the problems than most of the teachers:

> *Eric a student of introductory physics*: "The class consisted basically of problem solving and not of any interesting or inspiring exchange of ideas. The professor spent the first 15 minutes defining terms and apparently that was all the new information we were going to get on kinematics. Then he spent 50 minutes doing problems from Chapter 1. He was not particularly good at explaining why he did what he did to solve the problems ..." (Tobias, 1993, p. 299).

> *Tom a student of introductory chemistry*: "It would be better not to waste the expertise of the professor on working problems hour after uncomfortable hour. We need to know more of the back-ground of Dalton's laws in ancient atomic theory and of the work done on gas laws during the 18th century. As chemistry students we should know the evolution of Avogadro's concept from the point at which he conceived it up to the determination of the size of the constant named after him. The periodic table, how it was intuited, filled in, and gave clues to the understanding of the electron configuration of atoms ... We spent more time on Avogadro's number than on Avogadro's insight" (Tobias, 1993, p. 300).

According to Tobias, the 'tyranny of technique' robbed them of the profound intellectual experience they had expected from science. The clarion call for change could not be, more timely. Again the history and philosophy of science come to our rescue if we care to listen:

> ...definitions, are rather the last than the first step in each advance. In the progress of real knowledge, these definitions are always the results of the laborious study of individual cases, and are never arrived at by a pure effort of thought... (Whewell, 1856, p. 9).

Although, this was pointed out almost 150 years ago, we still force our students to memorize algorithms. According to Brown (1990):

> ...we do not start with the right concepts at the beginning of an inquiry, but rather ... we arrive at them as a *result* of the inquiry. Whewell and Lakatos are equally and vehemently opposed to that spirit of inquiry that says define your terms before you start (pp. 126-127, original emphasis).

It seems that if we had learnt our history and philosophy of science adequately, we would have been better off in differentiating the role of algorithms and conceptual understanding. In our quest for new pedagogical frameworks, Shulman (1986) has proposed 'pedagogical content knowledge' and Schwab (1974, 1978) has proposed the 'structure of a discipline' (see chap. 6 for more details). According to Shulman (1992): "We need a literature that focuses on the intersection of content and pedagogy, that brings together the wisdom of practice on a topic-by-topic, idea-by-idea basis" (p. 18).

The above reconstruction from the history and philosophy of science shows that if scientists adopt the methodology of idealization (simplifying assumptions) in order to solve complex problems, it is plausible to hypothesize that students adopt similar strategies in order to facilitate conceptual understanding. It can be further hypothesized that as scientists build models of increasing complexity, which lead to epistemic transitions (i.e., increase heuristic/explanatory power of their models), similarly students build a series of evolving models (progressive transitions) that increase in conceptual understanding. Linn and Songer (1991a) have summarized this transition in the following terms:

> Essentially, students could base their first prediction on conceptions they brought to science class but would construct their second prediction by integrating the results of their first experiment. Thus students would use observation and prediction as a key component of their student reports to engage in a progressing research program as described by Lakatos (1970, 1976) (p. 904).

# Chapter 3

# A METHODOLOGY FOR SCIENCE INSTRUCTION BASED ON THE HISTORY AND PHILOSOPHY OF SCIENCE

A methodology in this context is considered to be a set of guidelines (GL) based on previous research in science education, related to the history and philosophy of science. The objective of this methodology is to present a series of guidelines that are flexible and can be adapted by science educators in different science content domains in order to design teaching strategies. The degree to which the guidelines can be implemented in a particular domain will depend, among other factors, on previous research on the topic, students' views on the nature of science and the previous educational training of the students (e.g., emphasis on rote learning and solving problems based on formulae, algorithms). Presentation of the guidelines in this chapter is brief as complete details can only be presented in the context of a domain. The following chapters will illustrate in detail the application of the methodology in different topics.

## 3.1. GUIDELINES (GL)

GL1 A reconstruction of students' and teachers' understanding of a science topic, based on a historical development of the subject. The main objective is to ascertain students' and teachers' views of the nature of science, scientific progress, how theories/laws develop, and the role of experiments with respect to theory (cf. Niaz, 1994a).

GL2 Construction of models based on strategies students use to solve science problems and to show that these models form sequences of 'progressive transitions,' similar to what Lakatos (1970) in the history of science refers to as 'progressive problemshifts' that increase the explanatory / heuristic power of the models (cf. Niaz, 1995a). Furthermore, the sequences of evolving models generally vary in the degree to which students' manifest algorithmic or conceptual understanding. According to Hanson (1958), in spite of the differences between the algorithmic and the conceptual approaches, the two are compatible: "A law might have been arrived at by enumerating particulars; it could then be built into an H-D (hypothetico-deductive) system as a higher order proposition" (p. 70).

GL3   Some of the most important scientific research programs in the history of science progressed on inconsistent foundations. For example, Copernican astronomy was 'grafted' on to Aristotelian physics and Bohr's program on to Maxwell's (cf. Lakatos, 1970, p. 142). Similarly, Laudan (1977) has recognized: "... the historical fact that *a scientist can often be working alternately in two different, and even mutually inconsistent, research traditions*" (p. 110, original italics). In the case of students this state of affairs may even be more common as the introduction of new theories in the classroom does not necessarily imply that students would abandon their previous frameworks.

GL4   Looking for core beliefs (cf. hard core / negative heuristic, Lakatos, 1970) of the students in a topic could be the next appropriate step for the teaching strategy. It is plausible to suggest that just as the scientists resist changes in their hard core of beliefs, similarly students offer more resistance to change in core beliefs than the soft core beliefs (cf. positive heuristic, Lakatos, 1970). Criteria for classification of students' responses as part of a Lakatosian hard core are provided later in this chapter.

GL5   Exploration of the relationship between core beliefs and student alternative conceptions (misconceptions) could be the next step. Given the considerable amount of research that has been conducted in this area in almost all science domains, this step could be particularly useful. A detailed review of the literature on alternative conceptions is beyond the scope of this book. Nevertheless, some important reviews and sources are presented in chapter 2.

GL6   It is essential that students' alternative conceptions be interpreted not as mistakes, but within an epistemological perspective, that is models, perhaps in the same sense as used by scientists to simplify the complexity of a problem. Strike and Posner (1992) consider alternative conceptions as 'paradigms' in the Kuhnian sense, whereas our model considers them to be alternative theories that compete with the scientific theories (details about the two models are provided in chapter 2).

GL7   The cognitive complexity of the core belief can be broken down into a series of related and probing questions, through the design of 'teaching experiments' or 'cognitive conflicts' or 'anomalous data', that is presenting students with evidence that contradicts their preinstructional theories (cf. Chinn & Brewer, 1993). As a pre-requisite for conceptual change it is important that students be provided with alternative views that apparently contradict their previous thinking. This is based on the Lakatosian thesis that the, "... history of science has been and should be a history of competing research programmes ..." (Lakatos, 1970, p. 155). Furthermore, the new / alternative framework must appear initially plausible to the students. Classification of students' beliefs as belonging to hard core/soft core provides insight for this task. Examples of such strategies will be provided in subsequent chapters.

GL8   Students resist changes in their core beliefs more strongly than those in other related aspects (soft core) of a topic. Just as scientists use 'auxiliary hypotheses' (cf. Lakatos, 1970, p. 153) to protect the hard core of their research programs students also use similar strategies. Based on Lakatosian methodology it is suggested that: "... the individual can add or abandon auxiliary theoretical hypotheses, change beliefs about how experiments in the theoretical domain should be conducted, adjust the definition of a theoretical construct, or alter the domain of the theory. In all of these cases, however, the changes leave the theory's central hypotheses intact" (Chinn & Brewer, 1993, p. 11). 'Auxiliary hypotheses' used by students to defend their core beliefs can themselves provide clues and guidance for the construction of new teaching strategies.

GL9    Cognitive conflicts used in the design of teaching strategies, in order to be convincing, must have been engendered by the students themselves in trying to cope with different problem solving strategies. According to Mischel (1971): "The cognitive conflicts which the child himself engenders in trying to cope with his world, are then what motivates his cognitive development; they are his motives for reconstructing his system of cognitive schemas ..." (p. 332).

GL10    Teaching strategies based on these guidelines assume an interactive approach on the part of the teacher within an intact classroom. According to Rowell and Dawson (1985) most of the researchers have worked with individuals or very small groups, thus ignoring the importance of, "... classroom practice which is premised on teaching classes as units" (p. 331).

## 3.2. CRITERIA FOR CLASSIFICATION OF STUDENTS' RESPONSES AS PART OF A LAKATOSIAN CORE BELIEF

1.    *Deletion criterion.* An analogy to Piagetian theory will help to understand the issues involved. Piaget's theory of cognitive development has been considered to be a research program in the Lakatosian sense. The anomalous nature of Piagetian stages is considered to be the most controversial aspect of his research program, leading to the rejection by some researchers of the whole research program (cf. Brainerd, 1978). According to Lakatos (1971): "The scientist lists anomalies, but as long as his research programme sustains its momentum, he may freely put them aside" (p. 99). Most critics would agree that these anomalies did not curtail the momentum of Piaget's research program. Piaget's research program by studying the epistemic subject (cf. Niaz, 1991a), followed Lakatos' advice in that it ignored the psychological subject, "... the *actual* counterexamples, the available 'data'" (Lakatos, 1970, p. 135, original emphasis). Against this background, it is understandable that Piaget's concept of equilibration (1985) has been considered as part of the hard core of his research program by most researchers (Beilin, 1985; Gilbert & Swift, 1985; Niaz, 1993a; Rowell, 1983). On the other hand, Piaget's stages can be considered to be part of the positive heuristic of the research program (Niaz, 1993a; 1998a). If the function of the positive heuristic within a Lakatosian framework is precisely to 'operationalize' the hard core (i.e., means to an end), it is plausible to suggest that *deletion* of Piagetian stages will not alter the theory irreparably. It was faced with such problems that Beilin (1985) proposed the deletion criterion in the following terms: "If a construct in the theory can be deleted without apparent damage to the identification of the theory as Piaget's, then it is not part of the hard core. If on the other hand, deletion detracts materially

from the theory or alters it in irreparable ways, then it is part of the hard core" (pp. 109-110).

2.  *Hard core and protective belt propositions.* According to Chinn and Brewer (1993): "Lakatos (1970) has distinguished between two types of propositions within a theory: *hard core* propositions and *protective belt* [soft core] propositions. Hard core propositions cannot be altered without scrapping the entire theory, but protective belt propositions can be altered while preserving the key central hypotheses" (p. 10, original emphasis).

3.  *Auxiliary hypotheses.* Given the opportunity for conceptual change, students invariably tend to accept changes in their soft core of beliefs but resist changes to the hard core by offering 'auxiliary hypotheses'. In the history of science Lakatos (1970, p. 153), for example, considers Pauli's 'exclusion principle' as an 'auxiliary hypothesis', that protected the hard core of Bohr's theory.

Application of these criteria in concrete problem situations will illustrate their usefulness in subsequent chapters. It is possible that in a given domain-specific context only some of the guidelines presented above may apply. At this stage it is important to note that according to Holton and Brush (2001) textbooks must emphasize:

... nature of discovery, reasoning, concept-formation and theory-testing in science as a fascinating topic in its own right. This means that the historical and philosophical aspects of the exposition are not merely sugar-coating to enable the reader to swallow the material as easily as possible, but are presented for their own inherent interest (pp. xiii-xiv).

# Chapter 4

# UNDERSTANDING MOLE

Most high school and college students have difficulty with the mole concept and considerable amount of research has been done on the topic. According to Staver and Lumpe (1993):

> The mole concept, then, is a cornerstone to building a successful understanding of domain-specific knowledge in chemistry. If students fail to understand the mole concept, and many do fail it is likely that their chemical problem-solving ability will be severely limited (p. 322).

The main objective of this chapter is to construct models based on strategies students use to solve mole problems and to show that these models form sequences of progressive transitions similar to what Lakatos (1970) in the history of science refers to as progressive 'problemshifts' (cf. GL2, chap. 3). Guideline GL2, suggests that students' strategies in solving problems can be considered as sequences of evolving models, varying in the degree to which students manifest algorithmic or conceptual understanding.

## STUDY 1

Twenty-seven freshman students enrolled in a section of Chemistry I for chemistry majors at the Universidad de Oriente, Venezuela were asked to solve the following problem based on the mole concept:

If we have equal number of moles of $P_2O_5$ and $P_2O_3$, it can be concluded that:

*Item 1a*: Number of atoms of oxygen in the two compounds is different.
*Item 1b*: The mass of phosphorus in the two compounds is the same.

Results based on strategies used by students in solving Items 1a and 1b show the following aspects:

1. Number of students who responded correctly to Item 1b (33%) increased considerably as compared to those who solved Item 1a correctly (11%).

2.  Apparently, the stoichiometric relation between the two elements (phosphorus and oxygen) forming two different compounds misleads the students.

3.  The fact that the moles of oxygen in the molar formula of the two compounds is different and the number of moles of the two compounds is the same (that the students were asked to consider), produces a conflict for the students and is partially responsible for the low performance on Item 1a.

4.  On the other hand, in Item 1b both pieces of information coincide, that is, the number of moles of the two compounds are the same and the moles of phosphorus in the molar formula of the two compounds is also the same, leading to a better performance.

5.  It was observed that performance on Item 1a correlated significantly ($r = 0.40$; $p < .05$) with functional mental capacity $M_f$ (i.e., ability to process information – a cognitive variable. Cf. Pascual-Leone, 1987, Rojas de Astudillo & Niaz, 1996 for details). A step-wise multiple regression analysis produced a model based on the test of prior knowledge in chemistry and $M_f$, explaining 28% of the variance in performance. Interestingly, performance on Item 1b did not correlate significantly with any of the cognitive variables.

## Study 2

Eighty-three freshman students enrolled in Chemistry I at the Universidad de Oriente, Venezuela were asked to solve the following problems, which formed part of a monthly exam. Students were encouraged and given credit for providing justification for their answers (cf. Niaz, 1995a for complete details).

## Item 1A

Calculate the moles of the following quantities of nitrogen:
a) 79 molecules  b) $56 \times 10^{23}$ atoms

## Item 1B

How many moles of the atoms B (Boron) are present in a sample having $2 \times 10^{23}$ molecules of $B_4H_{10}$?

a) 1.3 moles          b) 4.0 moles
c) 8.0 moles          d) None of the previous

Item 1B requires conceptual understanding and Item 1A can be solved by the use of algorithms. Results obtained show that 57% of the students solved Item 1A correctly, whereas 22% solved Item 1B correctly. Of the 47 students who solved the algorithmic Item 1A correctly, 12 (26%) solved the conceptual Item 1B correctly. On the other hand, of the 18 students who solved the conceptual Item 1B correctly, 12 (67%) solved Item 1A correctly. It was also observed that students who solved conceptual Item 1B correctly used one of the following strategies:

Strategy A (two-step solution)
     Step 1:   $6.023 \times 10^{23}$ molecules $\rightarrow$ 1 mole of $B_4H_{10}$
               $2.0 \times 10^{23}$ molecules $\rightarrow$ X = 0.33 moles of $B_4H_{10}$
     Step 2:   1 mole of $B_4H_{10}$ has $\rightarrow$ 4 moles of B
               0.33 moles of $B_4H_{10}$ $\rightarrow$ X = 1.3 moles of B
Strategy B (one-step solution)
     $6.023 \times 10^{23}$ molecules of $B_4H_{10}$ have $\rightarrow$ 4 moles of B
     $2.0 \times 10^{23}$ molecules of $B_4H_{10}$ have $\rightarrow$ X = 1.3 moles of B

Strategy A, goes from the number of molecules provided to the moles of the compound ($B_4H_{10}$), and from there to the moles of the atoms of B. On the other hand, students using Strategy B show greater conceptual understanding by establishing a direct relationship between the number of molecules provided to the moles of the atoms of B, and in the process also obviate one step. It is plausible to suggest that students using Strategy B are capable of 'chunking' information (cf. Herron, 1990; Niaz, 1989a; White, 1988), that is, process information more efficiently. In other words, what may be held as separate bits of information to begin with, later with greater expertise and conceptual understanding may be 'chunked' as a single larger unit of information. This suggests the importance of information processing in student reasoning processes (cf. Niaz, 1991b, Pascual-Leone, 1970). Furthermore, the progressive nature (increase in explanatory power) of the strategies used by the students can be observed from the following: the 13 students, who solved Item 1B partially correct, used Step 1 of Strategy A and missed precisely Step 2, which involved greater understanding.

# 4.1. Progressive Transitions (Models) Leading to Greater Conceptual Understanding of the Mole Concept

Based on strategies used in solving Items 1A and 1B it is plausible to suggest that students go through the following process of progressive transitions (models) that facilitate different degrees of conceptual understanding, quite similar to what Lakatos (1970) has referred to as progressive 'problemshifts:

Model 1: Strategies used to solve the algorithmic Item 1A partially correctly (N=25).
Model 2: Strategies used to solve the algorithmic Item 1A correctly (N=47).
Model 3: Strategies used to solve the conceptual Item 1B partially correctly, that is, using Step 1 of Strategy A (N=13).
Model 4: Strategies used to solve the conceptual Item 1B correctly, using the two-step Strategy A (N=11).
Model 5: Strategies used to solve the conceptual Item 1B, using the one-step Strategy B (N=7).

# CONCLUSION

This reconstruction of various strategies (progressive transitions) can provide the teacher a framework to anticipate as to how student understanding could develop from being entirely algorithmic to conceptual. An important educational implication of this methodology is that student ability to conceptualize the underlying complexity of a topic can increase, if they are progressively given an opportunity to build models with increasing heuristic/explanatory power. At this stage it is important to point out that students with different academic and social backgrounds need not follow the same sequence of models as outlined here. It is suggested that the methodology used here can be applied in different problem-solving situations and contexts. Details of the application of this methodology to a problem of dilution of chemical solutions, is provided in Niaz (1995a).

Studies reported in this chapter illustrate how strategies used by students to solve mole problems represent models that evolve from being algorithmic to conceptual. Study 1, for example, shows that even a fairly simple problem (Item 1a) which requires students to think at the atomic (micro) level represents a conflicting situation. Performance could improve if we let the students tackle first problems of the type represented by Item 1b (no conflict) and furthermore requires thinking at the macro (mass) level. Similarly, Study 2 explicitly demonstrates the progressive nature of students' strategies (models) that lead to greater conceptual understanding of the mole concept.

# Chapter 5

# UNDERSTANDING STOICHIOMETRY: CONFLICTS, LACUNAE, AND PERTURBATIONS

Stoichiometry is another topic which presents considerable difficulty for the students, especially the understanding of the concept of a limiting-reagent. The main objective of this chapter is to construct a teaching strategy (cf. GL7, chap. 3) based on 'cognitive conflict' and 'teaching experiments' within a dialectic-constructivist framework, and is based partially on the study by Niaz (1995c). Guideline GL7, suggests that the cognitive complexity of the core belief of the students can be 'broken' down by presenting alternative views that contradict their previous thinking. Before going into the details of the teaching strategy it is essential to briefly describe the following concepts:

## 5.1. COGNITIVE CONFLICT

The importance of cognitive conflict in human development has been recognized in the literature (Festinger, 1957; Piaget, 1980; Vygotsky, 1978). A cognitive conflict can be produced by various situations: a) surprise produced by a result which contradicts a students' expectations, resulting in the generation of perturbations (von Glasersfeld, 1989); b) experience of puzzlement, feeling of uneasiness, a more or less conscious conflict, or a simple intellectual curiosity (Furth, 1981); c) experiencing a cognitive gap, as if the person involved were vaguely aware that something within his knowledge structure was missing (Furth, 1981); d) disequilibria – that is, questions or felt lacunae that arise when the students attempt to apply their schemas to a given problem situation (Mischel, 1971). Within the constructivist framework the development of conflicts or contradictions is essential to facilitate conceptual change and has been summarized by von Glasersfeld (1989):

> The learning theory that emerges from Piaget's work can be summarized by saying that cognitive change and *learning* take place when a scheme, instead of producing the expected result, leads to perturbation, and perturbation, in turn, leads to accommodation that establishes a new equilibrium (p. 128, original emphasis).

Adey and Shayer (1994) have provided a somewhat different perspective:

Cognitive conflict is a feature both of Piaget's account of the impact of environmental stimulus and children's constructivist response on cognitive growth, and of cognitive acceleration programmes which are effective in raising levels of thinking (p. 62).

## 5.2. DIALECTIC-CONSTRUCTIVIST FRAMEWORK

The dialectic approach is an attempt to understand reality within the context of complex interrelationships. According to Bidell (1988): "Rather than backgrounding conflict, the dialectic approach seeks to foreground it as the most salient feature of processes grasped in their complexity"(p. 332). The dialectic perspective emphasizes the understanding of psychological phenomena in their interrelationship to one another, rather than as isolated and separate processes characterized by a Cartesian reductionist approach to science. Interestingly, according to Ernest (1994), Lakatos (1976) in his *Proofs and Refutations*, not only adopted a dialogical form but explicitly appropriated the Hegelian dialectic. However, "Under the sway of Popper and his followers at LSE in the 1960s Lakatos increasingly repudiated the Hegelian origins of his work" (p. 46). Another important aspect of this study is the constructivist perspective, which presupposes that subjects construct their own world of experience (objects, events, transformations) by means of cognitive structures and organismic regulations/factors. This constructed world, however, is valid only if it epistemologically *reflects* distal objects, distal events, and transformations actually occurring in the environment (Pascual-Leone, 1987). Furthermore, Pascual-Leone (1976) conceptualized a constructive theory to "... model or reflect the subject's internal functional organization (i.e., his psychological system) in order to rationally reconstruct the genesis of the subject's performance" (pp. 90-91), similar to what Lakatos (1971) referred to as the rational reconstruction of scientific theories and models in the history of science. At this stage it is important to point out that in spite of the similarity of our framework to that of radical constructivism (von Glasersfeld, 1989, who also draws quite heavily on Piagetian theory), the two are different. The existence of many forms of constructivism in science education has been recognized and a critique of von Glasersfeld's constructivism can be found in the literature (cf. Niaz et al. 2003).

## 5.3. TEACHING EXPERIMENTS

'Teaching experiments' used in this study are based partially on the framework outlined earlier, and adapted from Cobb and Steffe (1983). According to D'Ambrosio and Campos (1992) the instructor's role in the 'teaching experiment' is to generate questions or changes in the learner's experiential field that lead the learners into situations in which they experience conflicts or contradictions between their representations and those needed to interpret those situations.

## Details of the Study

The study is based on two intact sections of freshman students who had registered for Chemistry I at the Universidad de Oriente, Venezuela. One of the sections (N=39) was randomly designated as the control group and the other (N=33) as the experimental group. The two teaching experiments were conducted during the 3rd and the 5th week of the semester and dealt with the topic of stoichiometry involving problems based on the limiting-reagent. Students in the control group were exposed to the same problems at the same time – however, without the cognitive conflict teaching experiment format.

## Application of Teaching Experiment 1

During the 3rd week of the semester, students in the experimental group were presented the following problem:

Barium oxide contains 10.46% of oxygen. How many grams of this compound can be obtained from 2.541 g of barium and 0.444 g of oxygen? Calculate the grams of barium and oxygen that reacted completely.

After the students read the problem, they were asked to consider the following problem-solving strategy as a possible solution to the problem:

Step 1:  g of Ba = 100 - 10.46 = 89.54
Step 2:  89.54 g of Ba = 10.46 g of $O_2$
         2.541 g of Ba = X = 0.2968 g of $O_2$
Step 3:  10.46 g of $O_2$ = 89.54 g of Ba
         0.444 g of $O_2$ = X = 3.80 g of Ba
Step 4:  g of Barium oxide = g of Ba and $O_2$ that reacted = 3.80 + 0.2968 = 4.09 g.

The problem used in this teaching experiment formed part of, two previous studies (Niaz, 1988, 1996) based on students with a similar background at the same university. The problem solving strategy presented here as a possible solution was used by a group of 32 students in a sample of 109 in the previous study (Niaz, 1996). The crucial step in the problem-solving strategy is Step 3, which shows that students fail to take account of a crucial piece of information: *Reaction of 3.80 g of Ba means that they are using more Ba than is available.* The fact that 29% (32 of 109) of the students in the previous study used this strategy indicates that the students find it convincing. This aspect of the problem-solving strategy is important as it complies with the guidelines (cf. GL9, chap. 3). Furthermore, it appears that students' theoretical framework for stoichiometric problems is primarily based on establishing equivalent relations between different chemical elements or compounds, while ignoring the fact that a limiting-reagent limits the amount of a product.

After the students had read the problem and the problem-solving strategy, they were taken through the following sequence of steps: a) Students were asked to discuss among themselves the problem-solving strategy and encouraged to ask any questions. This lasted about 15 min. b) Students were asked whether they considered the possible solution presented in the problem-solving strategy to be correct. Of the 33 students, 13 considered the solution to be correct. These students were asked to explain their response. At this stage, some of the students who considered the strategy to be incorrect were seen to smile. c) Students were asked and encouraged to discuss the possible errors in the four steps of the strategy. Some of them pointed out Step 3 as problematic. On further discussion, some were seen to discuss and point out to their neighbors the fact that 3.80 g of Ba could not have reacted, as only 2.541 g was available. d) One of the students (who had the correct answer) was asked to solve the problem on the chalkboard. e) Students were asked to compare the problem-solving strategy presented previously to that on the chalkboard. It was found that 10 of the 33 students had solved the problem correctly. f) A general discussion took place in which the importance of the limiting reagent concept was emphasized. The total time taken by the experiment was about 40 min.

It is important to note that the conflicting situation was produced not by simply giving them a problem-solving strategy, but by slowly drawing their attention (sequence of steps) to the conflicting situation (using more Ba than was available), which contradicted the students' expectations. Another important aspect of this study is that it was conducted in an intact classroom (cf. GL10, chap. 3), which included students with varying degrees of understanding. Most teachers would agree that it would be extremely difficult to design a teaching strategy that could provide a conflicting situation to the same degree for all students.

## Application of Teaching Experiment 2

During the 5th week of the semester, students in the experimental group were presented with the following problem:

In a vessel 10 g of $N_2$ is made to react with 1 g of $H_2$, according to the following equation:

$$N_2(g) + H_2(g) \leftrightarrow NH_3(g)$$

Calculate: a) g of $N_2$ that reacted; b) g of $H_2$ that reacted; c) g of $NH_3$ produced. [Molar masses were provided].

After the students had read the problem, they were asked to consider the following problem-solving strategy as a possible solution to the problem:

Step 1:     Balance the equation: $N_2(g) + 3 H_2(g) \leftrightarrow 2NH_3(g)$
Step 2:     Moles of $N_2$ = 10/28 = 0.36; moles of $H_2$ = 1/2 = 0.5
Step 3:     3 moles of $H_2$ = 1 mole of $N_2$
             0.5 moles of $H_2$ = X = 0.17 moles of $N_2$
                                = 0.17 X 28 = 4.76 g of $N_2$
Step 4:     1 mole of $N_2$ = 3 moles of $H_2$
             0.36 mole of $N_2$ = X = 1.08 moles of $H_2$
                                = 1.08 X 2 = 2.16 g of $H_2$
Step 5:     1 mole of $N_2$ = 2 moles of $NH_3$
             0.36 mole of $N_2$ = X = 0.72 mole of $NH_3$
                                = 0.72 X 17 = 12.24 g of $NH_3$

Once again the problem used in this strategy is based on the concept of a limiting-reagent, with the difference that it involves a chemical equation, which the students generally consider to be more difficult than the problem used in Teaching Experiment 1. The premise for producing cognitive conflict in this experiment, however, remains the same. The crucial step in the problem-solving strategy is Step 4, as the amount of $H_2$ that reacted is more than what is available. After the students had read the problem and the problem-solving strategy they were taken through a similar sequence of steps as in Teaching Experiment 1, whose details are not presented here.

At this stage, it is important to mention that the control group received the same two problems during the 3rd and the 5th weeks of the semester. Control group students were encouraged through an interactive approach to help solve the problems, and one of them was called to solve the problems on the chalkboard. Every effort was made to involve the control and experimental groups in the problem-solving activity. The only difference was that the control group was not exposed to cognitive conflict through the teaching experiments.

## Evaluation of the Teaching Experiments

To evaluate the effectiveness of the teaching experiments, both the experimental and the control groups were tested on five different problems at different intervals of time, referred to as posttests, according to the following schedule: Posttests 1 and 2 as part of a monthly exam (7 weeks); Posttests 3 and 4 as part of a semester exam (9 weeks); and Posttest 5 as part of the final exam (17 weeks). All 5 posttests formed part of the regular evaluation of the students. Posttest 1 was a problem similar to that used in the Teaching Experiment 1 and control group during the 3rd week, and was designed as an immediate posttest. Posttest 2 was different and was designed to evaluate transfer of problem-solving strategies. Posttests 3 and 4 were familiar to the students and were designed to be slightly delayed posttests. Posttest 5 was designed to be a delayed posttest. The five posttests are presented below:

*Posttest 1 (7 weeks)*
  Chromic oxide contains 68.4 % chromium. How many grams of this compound can be obtained from 1.17 g of chromium (purity 80%) and 0.63 g of oxygen? Calculate the grams of chromium and oxygen that reacted completely.

*Posttest 2 (7 weeks)*
  In methane the mass relationship between carbon and hydrogen is 3:1. In carbon dioxide, for every 2.2 g of dioxide there are 0.6 g of carbon present. In water, the percentage of the mass of hydrogen is 11.12%. Demonstrate the law of equivalent proportions.

*Posttest 3 (9 weeks)*
  In a vessel, 8 g of sulfur is made to react with $3.01 \times 10^{23}$ atoms of oxygen. If the mass relationship in the product ($SO_3$) between sulfur and oxygen is 2:3, the mass of $SO_3$ obtained is: a) 5 g; b) 20 g; c) 13.33 g; d) None of the previous. (Explain your answer).

*Posttest 4 (9 weeks)*
  In a vessel, 4 g of CaO is made to react with 100 mL of 0.36M $H_2SO_4$, according to the following equation:

$$CaO + H_2SO_4 \rightarrow CaSO_4 + H_2O$$

Calculate: a) grams of $CaSO_4$; b) moles of $H_2O$ produced.

*Posttest 5 (17 week)*

In a vessel, 77 mL of HCl (density = 1.3 g/mL and 37% purity) is made to react with 20 g of Mg (60% purity), according to the following equation:

$$Mg\ (s) + HCl\ (aq) \rightarrow MgCl_2\ (aq) + H_2\ (g)$$

Calculate the moles of $H_2$ produced.

## Results and Discussion

Posttest 1 results showed that 13% of the control group students solved the problem correctly as compared with 33% of the experimental group. It was observed that 6 students (18%) from the experimental group and 2 (5%) from the control group used the following strategy:

Step 1:   g of $O_2 = 100 - 68.42 = 31.58$

Step 2:   g of pure Cr = 80/100 X 1.17 = 0.936

Step 3:   68.42 g of Cr = 31.58 g of $O_2$

       0.936 g of Cr = X = 0.43 g of $O_2$

Step 4:   31.58 g of $O_2$ = 68.42 g of Cr

       0.63 g of $O_2$ = X = 1.36 g of Cr

Step 5:   g of chromium oxide = g of Cr and $O_2$ that reacted

               = 1.36 + 0.43 = 1.79 g

Apparently, these students ignored the fact that reaction of 1.36 g of Cr means that they would be using more Cr than was available. That these students ignored the limiting reagent is even more significant as they calculated the amount of pure Cr in Step 2 of the strategy presented above. However, what makes this result interesting and somewhat counterintuitive is the fact that it was precisely the experimental group (18%) rather than the control group (5%) who adopted this strategy. A possible interpretation, based on the philosophy of science literature is offered (cf. GL3 and GL8 in chap. 3). Guideline GL3 suggests that introduction of new theories in the classroom does not necessarily imply that students would abandon their previous frameworks, whereas Guideline GL8 suggests that students resist changes in their core beliefs more strongly than those in other related aspects (soft core).

According to philosophers of science, conflicting (anomalous) data do not necessarily convince a scientist to abandon a particular theory (cf. Duhem, 1914/1954; Kitchener, 1993; Quine, 1951). Furthermore, according to Lakatos (1970) the hard core of a research program consists of basic assumptions considered to be irrefutable by the methodological decision of its protagonists, whereas the protective belt serves the dual purpose of operationalizing and protecting the hard core (cf. chap 1 and 2 for details).

Taking their cue from Lakatos, Chinn & Brewer (1993) suggested that, "... another response to anomalous data is for the individual to make a relatively minor modification in his or her current theory" (p. 10). For example, Lawson and Worsnop (1992) investigated the effect of science instruction on students' beliefs about evolution. The 3-week instructional unit on evolution included a section on fossil evidence for evolution. Before instruction, only

1% of the students agreed with the statement, "Fossils were intentionally put on the earth to confuse humans." After instruction, however, 6% agreed with the same statement. Chinn and Brewer (1993) considered this to be a Peripheral Theory Change: "... some of the creationist students who were confronted with compelling fossil evidence for evolution adjusted their peripheral beliefs in order to protect their core belief in special creation" (p. 11). In the light of this discussion, we suggest that in the present study the 6 students (18%) from the experimental group (mentioned earlier) protected their core belief in stoichiometry (establishing equivalent relations between different chemical elements or compounds, independently of the limiting reagent) by ignoring the conflicting (anomalous) data. This provides an indication of the deep entrenchment of the students' hard core of beliefs in stoichiometry.

Posttest 2 (adapted from Mahan & Myers, 1990) requires an understanding of stoichiometric relations (equivalent proportions) but not the concept of limiting reagent and was included to evaluate transfer of problem-solving strategies in a different context. Results obtained show that once again the experimental group (45%) had better performance than did the control group (21%). Apparently, the absence of the limiting-reagent helped both groups to improve their performance as compared with Posttest 1. This shows that the limiting-reagent concept is an alternative theory for the students and hence poses considerable difficulty as it constitutes a different framework from that of the students, which is based on the reaction of equivalent proportions between different elements or compounds. Interestingly, of the 15 students in the experimental group who solved correctly Posttest 2, 9 (60%) also correctly solved Posttest 1.

Posttests 3 and 4 (9th week) were designed to be slightly delayed posttests – - that is, 6 weeks after Teaching Experiment 1. Once again, on Posttest 3, performance of the experimental group (64%) was considerably better than that of the control group (26%). It was also observed that the percentage of students who scored 100% on Posttests 1, 2, and 3 increased progressively for both, the control (13, 21, and 26) and experimental (33, 45, and 64) groups. Performance of both groups on Posttest 4, however, was extremely poor. How do we explain the difference in performance on Posttests 3 and 4? Both of these posttests were part of the same semester exam. A possible explanation is the use of stoichiometric relations based on a chemical equation in Posttest 4, which is cognitively more complex than Posttest 3.

Posttest 5 was designed to be a delayed posttest (17 week) as part of the final exam. According to university rules, only students who maintain an average performance of at least 50% during the semester (monthly and semester exams) are allowed to sit for the final exam. For this reason Posttest 5 results are based on 17 students for the control group and 16 students for the experimental group. Surprisingly, the experimental (38%) and the control (29%) groups improved their performance considerably on Posttest 5, as compared to Posttest 4. Two possible explanations could be that: a) students presenting the final exam represented a better than average part of their respective sections; and b) the final exam requires the preparation of all the course material, and this could have helped the students to go back and study some of the difficult topics once again.

## 5.4. Conclusions and Educational Implications

Results obtained in this study seem to indicate that although the experimental treatment was effective in improving performance on the immediate posttests, perhaps its effect was not long enough to produce changes in the core belief of students, viz., establishing equivalent relations between different reactants, which could facilitate conceptual change (cf. GL8 in chap. 3). Guideline GL8, precisely points out that students resist changes in their core beliefs.

The research methodology used and the results obtained can be questioned on two grounds: a) The study seems to be based on the assumption that as the conflicting information is out there and the teacher or other students explained it to those who had difficulty with the problem, all would have seen the conflict. This line of argument misses the point that even if the students can see the conflict they resist changes in their preinstructional beliefs (cf. Lakatos, 1970, hard core of beliefs). According to Chinn and Brewer (1993): "Instead of abandoning or modifying their preinstrucional beliefs in the face of new conflicting data and ideas, students often staunchly maintain the old ideas and reject or distort the new ideas" (pp. 1-2). b) Alternative explanations, such as lack of conceptualization or increasing the demands on working memory capacity (cf. Niaz & Logie, 1993) of the students cannot be ruled out. Postulation of alternative explanations in science education is extremely important from a philosophy of science perspective (cf. Niaz, 1993b).

## 5.5. Hard Core and Soft Core of Students' Understanding of Stoichiometry

Although more research needs to be done, tentatively it is plausible to suggest that students' understanding of stoichiometry is based on the following:

### Hard Core

Establishing of equivalent relations between different reactants (elements or compounds) while ignoring the possibility of a limiting reagent. Following two pieces of evidence substantiate this claim: a) Performance of both groups of students increased considerably on Posttest 2 (no limiting reagent) as compared to Posttest 1 (limiting reagent); b) More students from the experimental group ignored or resisted the acceptance of a limiting reagent in Posttest 1 (cf. Steps 3 and 4 of the teaching strategy).

### Soft Core

You cannot produce more atoms than you started with.

Finally, it appears that the hard core is strengthened by epigrammatic versions of the Law of Definite Proportions, found in most text books: "In a given chemical compound, the proportions by mass of the elements that compose it are fixed, independent of the origin of the compound or its mode of preparation" (Oxtoby, et al. 1990, p. 9). Similarly, the soft core seems to be sustained by the following definition of the Law of Conservation of Mass: "In every chemical operation an equal quantity of matter exists before and after the operation" (Oxtoby et al., 1990, p. 9).

This chapter illustrates the presence and functioning of students' hard core and soft core of beliefs in stoichiometry, which is considered to be a difficult topic in high school and freshman chemistry. It is suggested that the hard/soft cores are reinforced by classroom emphasis on rote memorization of laws and textbook presentation of laws as scientific knowledge that has been firmly established. The role of scientific laws in the classroom will be discussed further in chapter 10.

*Chapter 6*

# UNDERSTANDING ATOMIC STRUCTURE:
# BAROQUE TOWER ON A GOTHIC BASE

In our quest for new pedagogical frameworks, in this chapter we show the importance of understanding the students' and teachers' conceptualization of science content and how it relates to the history and philosophy of science. This part of the chapter is a reconstruction of students' and teachers' understanding of structure of the atom (cf. GL1, chap. 3) based partially on the study conducted by Blanco and Niaz (1998). Guideline GL1, suggests a rational reconstruction of students' and teachers' understanding of structure of the atom, based on the experiments and atomic models of Thomson, Rutherford and Bohr, that constitute progressive transitions. Given the importance of pedagogical content knowledge (Shulman, 1986) and the structure of a discipline (Schwab, 1974) for the teachers' instructional approach and its close relationship to students' understanding of science, this study was based on a domain-specific topic of considerable interest to science educators, viz., structure of the atom. Lederman (1992) has emphasized this aspect for future research: "The research on students' and teachers' conceptions of the nature of science can and should inform research on pedagogical content knowledge" (p. 353).

There seems to be some controversy among science educators as to how a pedagogical approach based on science content could be implemented in the classroom. Millar and Driver (1987), for example, have strongly endorsed a problem-solving approach based on the learner's content specific knowledge. Although Millar and Driver (1987) point out explicitly that their approach does not lead to rote learning of content, it would be interesting to see as to how such an approach would be implemented. For example, Hodson (1985), who is generally in agreement with the Millar and Driver thesis, has suggested that:

> The pupil's first priority is to *learn* currently accepted theories and to apply them to appropriate phenomena and in appropriate situations ... Much of the laboratory work in school should concentrate on theory illustration and investigation, rather in the manner of Kuhn's normal science (p. 43, original emphasis).

This raises an important question: "Is the goal of science education simply to produce competent normal scientists?" (Siegel, 1978, p. 303). Based on a critical evaluation of Kuhn and Schwab, Siegel has shown that emphasizing 'normal science' is incongruous with the actual nature of scientific research. According to Schwab (1962), science cannot be taught as an, "... unmitigated *rhetoric of conclusions* in which the current and temporary constructions of scientific knowledge are conveyed as empirical, literal, and irrevocable truths" (p. 24, original emphasis).

As an example, let us consider the Kuhnian and the Lakatosian approaches to teaching the structure of the atom. Most physics and chemistry textbooks refer to the work on the subject by scientists such as Thomson, Rutherford, and Bohr. According to Kuhn (1970) textbooks are pedagogic vehicles for the perpetuation of 'normal science'. For the Kuhnian approach (normal science), what is important in Thomson's experiments is that they have contributed to the development of the currently accepted theory in the field, viz., that the charge-to-mass ratio for cathode rays is a constant independent of the gas used in the discharge tube. On the other hand, for the Lakatosian approach, it is essential to point out there were competing frameworks of understanding that clash in the face of evidence, viz., a determination of the charge-to-mass ratio for the cathode ray particles would help identify it either as an ion or some other charged particle.

Similarly, the experimental work of Rutherford is important from a Kuhnian point of view as it postulated the existence of a positively charged nucleus and surrounding electrons. On the contrary, a Lakatosian point of view would emphasize the fact that Rutherford's experiments provided evidence against a competing framework, viz., Thomson's model of the atom.

Once again, from the Kuhnian point of view, perhaps it is important that Bohr developed a model of the hydrogen atom, which allowed him to explain the fact that the frequencies emitted were in agreement with the experimental work of Balmer's and Paschen's series. On the contrary, Lakatos has emphasized that Bohr's major concern was to explain the paradoxical stability of the Rutherford atom, that is, a competing framework that was not entirely consistent. The Kuhnian approach is problematic and Siegel (1985) has shown its contradictory nature: "Kuhn, however, recommends that science education seek to dogmatically (his word) inculcate the reigning paradigm, on the grounds that a student is more likely to further the progress of science by doing competent 'normal science'" (p. 102).

It appears then that at least for some science educators (Hodson, 1985, 1988; Millar & Driver, 1987) emphasizing content would lead to the acceptance of a Kuhnian perspective of 'normal science', in which the students, for example, '*learn*' variously about the charge-to-mass ratio of the cathode ray particles, existence of a positively charged nucleus and the surrounding electrons, a model of the hydrogen atom which explained the experimentally observed frequencies, and so on. However, it appears that this picture leaves out what really happens, that is the 'how' and 'why' of scientific progress. On the other hand, the Lakatosian perspective would enable students to understand that scientific progress is subsumed by a process involving conflicting frameworks, based on processes that require the elaboration of rival hypotheses and their evaluation in the light of new evidence (cf. Niaz, 1994a). Similarly, Burbules and Linn (1991) have utilized this insight from modern philosophy of science to foster, "... multiple avenues of investigation ...", that provide, "competing frameworks of understanding that clash in the face of evidence" (p. 237).

It is interesting to observe how science educators, after having drawn inspiration from the same philosophical sources, arrive at quite different conclusions. According to Siegel (1978) science textbooks:

... are not to be regarded as tools for inculcating in science students the principles and methods of the paradigm of the day. Rather, textbooks are to function as challengers to students. They should be designed and utilized so as to impart to the student the fallible, improvable, and non-permanent character of scientific knowledge" (p. 309).

## 6.1. FRAMEWORK FOR THE RECONSTRUCTION OF STUDENTS' AND TEACHERS' UNDERSTANDING OF STRUCTURE OF THE ATOM

1. History of science can be conceived as that of competing rival research programs (Lakatos, 1971, p. 103).
2. Scientists do not abandon a theory on the basis of contradictory evidence alone, and "There is no falsification before the emergence of a better theory" (Lakatos, 1970, p. 119).
3. Some of the greatest scientific research programs progressed on inconsistent foundations (Lakatos, 1971, p. 113).
4. In actual scientific practice, Popper's *dramatic* counter examples would be considered as *mere* anomalies (Lakatos, 1971, p. 112). Furthermore, the scientist lists anomalies but as long as his research program (positive heuristic) sustains its momentum, he may freely put them aside (p. 99).
5. J.J. Thomson's experiments with cathode ray tubes were conducted to test rival hypotheses, viz., a determination of the charge-to-mass ratio for the cathode ray particles would help to identify it as an ion or some other charged particle (Niaz, 1994a, p. 420).
6. E. Rutherford's alpha-particle scattering experiments provided evidence against a competing framework, viz., J.J. Thomson's model of the atom (Niaz, 1994a, p. 420).
7. N. Bohr's experiments were designed to explain the paradoxical stability of the Rutherford atom, i.e., a competing framework based on inconsistent foundations (Lakatos, 1970, p. 147).

### Details of the Study

The study (Blanco & Niaz, 1998) is based on 171 freshman students enrolled in Chemistry I at the Instituto Universitario de Tecnología, El Tigre, Venezuela and 7 chemistry teachers at the same institution. All 7 teachers were either giving the course in the same semester or had given it previously. All the teachers had the equivalent of a 'Licenciatura' degree, which requires 5 years of academic work including a thesis, after high school. One of the teachers had a teaching experience of 16 years, five teachers from 8-14 years and one teacher of 2 years. *University Chemistry* by Mahan & Myers (1990) was the main text used by most of the teachers. Some of the teachers used the following as supplementary texts: *Chemical Principles* by Masterton, Slowinski & Stanitski (1985), and *General Chemistry* by Whitten, Gailey & Davis (1992). All the students and teachers were asked to respond to an 11-item questionnaire and encouraged to explain their responses in writing.

## The Questionnaire

*Part A: Thomson.* A brief description of Thomson's experiments was presented in order to facilitate Ss recall of what they had already seen during class.

*Item 1*

In your opinion what was most important in Thomson's experiments?

*Item 2*

Why did Thomson determine the charge to mass (e/m) relation?

*Item 3*

How do you interpret the finding that on using different gases in the cathode-ray tube, the relation (e/m) remained constant?

*Item 4*

How would you have interpreted, if on using different gases in the cathode-ray tube, the relation (e/m) would have resulted different?

*Item 5*

Based on his experiments Thomson proposed a model of atom as a uniform sphere of positive electricity with the electrons embedded in this sphere, much as raisins in a pudding. (students were provided an illustration of the model, similar to that found in most text-books). The following question was asked: Would you agree that this model represents the information that Thomson had at that time?

*Part B: Rutherford.* A brief description of Rutherford's experiments was presented.

*Item 6*

In your opinion what was most important in Rutherford's experiments.

*Item 7*

How would you interpret the finding that most of the alpha-particles passed undeflected through the thin metal foil?

*Item 8*

How would you have interpreted, if most of the alpha-particles would have deflected through large angles?

*Item 9*

A brief description of Rutherford's model of the atom was presented along with an illustration as found in most text-books. It was pointed out that Rutherford's model of the nuclear atom was entirely different from that of Thomson. The following question was asked: If Rutherford's experiments changed Thomson's model of the atom entirely, in your opinion did Thomson make mistakes while doing his experiments?

*Part C: Bohr.* A brief description of how Rutherford's model of the atom violates one of the classical principles of physics was presented. If the electrons were stationary, there was nothing to keep them from being drawn into the nucleus; and if they were in circular motion, the well known laws of electrodynamics predicted that the atom should radiate light until all electronic motion ceased. Bohr attempted to resolve this apparent paradox by analyzing atomic structure in terms of the quantum theory. Bohr's four postulates, as found in most text-books were presented.

*Item 10*

In your opinion what was most important in Bohr's experiments.

*Item 11*

If Bohr's experiments changed Rutherford's model of the atom, in your opinion did Rutherford make mistakes while doing his experiments?

## 6.2. CRITERIA FOR CLASSIFICATION OF STUDENTS' AND TEACHERS' RESPONSES

a) *Positivist*: Responses included in this category emphasized experimental observation, demonstration and description of an absolute reality that has little to do with the hypotheses and theoretical framework of the scientist. According to Lakatos (1971) for an inductivist/positivist: "...only those propositions can be accepted into the body of science which either describe hard facts or are infallible inductive generalisations from them" (p. 92).

b) *Transitional*: These responses indicated a partial understanding with respect to the existence of alternative/competing models for explaining the experimental observations and that no knowledge is ever absolutely established (cf. Phillips, 1994).

c) *Lakatosian*: These responses indicated that scientific progress is subsumed by a process involving conflicting frameworks, based on processes that require the elaboration of rival hypotheses and their evaluation in the light of new evidence (cf. Lakatos, 1970).

In order to facilitate the application of the above criteria, responses of 25 students (selected randomly) were classified into the three categories mentioned above, separately by both authors. Both authors coincided in their classification of positivist, transitional and Lakatosian responses in almost 60% of the cases. All differences were resolved by discussion. Based on this experience, responses of another 10 students (selected randomly) were classified into three categories. There was an agreement on 75% of the responses. Based on this experience, both authors classified responses of rest of the students separately. There was an overall agreement of almost 80% in the classification of all responses. All differences were resolved once again by discussion.

Classification of responses within subcategories was relatively more difficult. For example, in Item 1, in order to classify the different types of positivist responses, both authors looked together for conceptual themes referred to by the students in order to explain what was most important in Thomson's experiments. We came up with the following tentative list: (e/m relation), (cathode rays could be deflected), (positive and negative charges are neutralized), (cathode-rays are negatively charged), etc. With this tentative list we assigned students' responses to these subcategories, and left open the possibility of finding other response patterns. Similar procedure was followed in other items. Both authors coincided in almost 70% of the sub-classifications. All differences were once again resolved by discussion.

## Results and Discussion

An important aspect of this study is that Item 1 of the questionnaire started with a fairly general question (What was most important in Thomson's experiments?) to see if based on their content knowledge students could go beyond the simple repetition of experimental details found in most textbooks. Item 2 is more specific and gives a clue with respect to the fact that what was most important in Thomson's experiments had something to do with the charge to mass (e/m) relation. Item 3 is even more specific, asking about their opinion with respect to the constant value of e/m. Item 4 is based on a hypothetical experimental finding and Item 5, based on the Thomson model of the atom completes the sequence of items based on Thomson's work.

Table 1 shows that the positivist responses decrease from Item 1 to 5, transitional responses increase from Item 1 to 4, Lakatosian responses increase from Item 1 to 3 – clearly a progressive transition indicative of greater conceptual understanding. It is important to note that as the questions became more specific, ambiguous responses increased from Item 1 to 3 and those who did not respond increased from Item 1 to 4 – indicative of the complexity of the issues involved. Item 6 once again starts with a fairly general question (What was most important in Rutherford's experiments?), followed by Item 7 providing information about an important aspect of the experiment. Item 8 is based on a hypothetical experimental finding and Item 9 completes the sequence of items based on Rutherford's experiments by comparing the work of Thomson and Rutherford.

Positivist responses decreased from Item 6 to 8 (see Table 1), transitional responses increased from Item 6 to 9, and the Lakatosian responses do not show any clear trend. Similar to the first sequence, as the items became more specific, ambiguous responses increased from Item 6 to 8, and those who did not respond increased from Item 6 to 9. The last two items based on Bohr's work show a similar trend. In the following sections students' responses to 11 items of the questionnaire are presented:

## What Was Most Important in Thomson's Experiments? (Based on Item 1)

It is important to note that these freshmen students had studied Thomson's cathode-ray experiments as part of their chemistry program and also in their textbooks, where it is given considerable importance. Given the empiricist orientation of our textbooks and teaching practice it is not surprising that 155 (91%) students gave a positivist response and following are some of the examples: determine the charge/mass (e/m) relation, demonstrate that cathode rays could be deflected, positive charge in the atom is neutralized by electrons, cathode rays consist of negatively charged particles, discovery of the electrons, determine the nature of cathode rays, and determine e/m by the scientific method. Responses to all items are paraphrased from students' actual written answers. See Table 1 for complete details.

In contrast to the positivist responses only 8 (5%) students gave a transitional response and following are two examples: establish a new model of the atom – that of a cotton ball; demonstrate that the relation (e/m) is the same, i.e., independent of the gas used in the tube. It is interesting to note that positivist responses simply mentioned the relation (e/m), whereas a transitional response goes beyond by emphasizing that e/m was independent of the gas used in the tube. Transitional responses represented thinking that went beyond the simply 'observable' and highlighted those aspects that facilitated the formulation of alternative /competing atomic models.

For most teachers around the world it must be a cause for concern that only 2 (1%) students responded in a manner that approximated a Lakatosian framework and following is an example: Reach the conclusion that the cathode-rays consisted of a universal particle, which was later named as the electron. Leaving aside the Lakatosian framework, most teachers would agree that Thomson's experiments were particularly helpful in establishing the universal nature of the cathode rays, which in turn helped to formulate an alternative model of the atom. Such responses captured the essence of what was at stake. Thomson was questioned by his peers not for his method for determining the relation (e/m) but rather the conclusion / interpretation that cathode rays were universal particles. Once again, most teachers would perhaps agree that this is what they would like their students to learn, and not simply the experimental / empirical details.

### Table 1. Distribution of students' responses on all items (N=171)

| Item | Positivist | Transitional | Lakatosian | Ambiguous | No |
|------|-----------|--------------|------------|-----------|-----|
| 1 | 155 | 8 | 2 | 4 | 2 |
|   | (91)* | (5) | (1) | (2) | (1) |
| 2 | 106 | 14 | 4 | 12 | 35 |
|   | (62) | (8) | (2) | (7) | (20) |
| 3 | 78 | 11 | 16 | 25 | 41 |
|   | (46) | (6) | (9) | (15) | (24) |
| 4 | 71 | 16 | 5 | 11 | 68 |
|   | (42) | (9) | (3) | (6) | (40) |
| 5 | 39 | 2 | 2 | 18 | 46 |
|   | (23) | (1) | (1) | (11) | (27) |
| 6 | 134 | 12 | - | 5 | 20 |
|   | (78) | (7) | - | (3) | (12) |
| 7 | 63 | 16 | 30 | 24 | 38 |
|   | (37) | (9) | (18) | (14) | (22) |
| 8 | 46 | 5 | - | 77 | 43 |
|   | (27) | (3) | - | (45) | (25) |
| 9 | 62 | 45 | 4 | 13 | 47 |
|   | (36) | (26) | (2) | (8) | (27) |
| 10 | 87 | 13 | 6 | 29 | 36 |
|   | (51) | (8) | (4) | (17) | (21) |
| 11 | 47 | 51 | 9 | 12 | 52 |
|   | (27) | (30) | (5) | (7) | (30) |

* Figures in parentheses represent percentages. Note: No= No response.

## Why did Thomson Determine the Charge to Mass (e/m) Relation? (Based on Item 2)

As compared to Item 1, Item 2 was more specific and was designed to guide the students towards the understanding that the importance of Thomson's experiments had something to do with the determination of the relation (e/m). In spite of this, 106 (62%) students gave a positivist response and following are some of the examples: cathode-rays were deflected by electric and magnetic fields; obtain a value for the relation (e/m); verify that the electron was extremely small; helped in the calculation of the charge or mass of the electron; determine the number of electrons in the atom. It is interesting to note that of those students who reasoned in Item 1 that what was most important in Thomson's experiments was the determination of the e/m, many responded to Item 2 by reasoning that he wanted to obtain a numerical value – a hard infallible fact. This shows once again the hold of positivist / empiricist ideas among students.

Only 14 (8%) students gave a transitional response and following are some of the examples: magnitude of the relation (e/m) being small; led to the conclusion that there was a subatomic particle; to determine if the relation (e/m) varied by changing the experimental conditions. As compared to the positivist responses, the transitional responses move away from the value of e/m and instead suggest a relationship between the value and the experimental conditions.

Only 4 (2%) students grasped the essence of the issue at stake by giving a Lakatosian response and following are two examples: hypothesized that if a universal particle constituted all matter then the relation (e/m) should remain constant; help to identify cathode rays as ions or some other charged fragments. Indeed, this is important if we want our students to understand that it is not the experiments that provide new insights, but rather the interpretations based on conflicting hypotheses.

## How to Interpret the Finding that on Using Different Gases the Relation (e/m) Remained Constant? (Based on Item 3)

As compared to Items 1 and 2, Item 3 was designed to be much more specific and guide the students towards the understanding that what was most important in Thomson's experiments was the finding that on using different gases in the cathode-ray tube the relation (e/m) remained constant. Predictably, positivist responses decreased to 78 (46%) and following are some of the examples: on using different gases the relation (e/m) did not change because the charge and the mass also changed; because of the effects produced by the applied fields; because of the influence of the gases used; because of the dependence between charge and mass; due to the application of the law of conservation of mass. The first response, namely on using different gases the relation (e/m) did not change because the charge and the mass also changed, is interesting and was paraphrased from the responses of 21 students. It is plausible to suggest that these students found an alternative way of justifying an experimental finding, which is quite common among scientists in the history of science.

Only 11 (6%) students gave a transitional response and following are some of the examples: because the gases acted independently and this did not alter the relation (e/m);

because the properties of cathode rays do not depend on the gases or the materials used. Interestingly, 16 (9%) students gave a Lakatosian response and following are some of the examples: because if they were the same particles present in different types of gases the relation (e/m) should be constant; because cathode rays contain a fundamental / universal particle charged negatively and found in all atoms.

As compared to Items 1 and 2, in Item 3 (see Table 1) the positivist responses decreased, the transitional responses remained about the same and the Lakatosian responses increased considerably. It is plausible to suggest, that students' interaction with the Items 1, 2 and 3 provided an opportunity to think and reflect about Thomson's cathode ray experiments, which resulted in a better appreciation of the issues involved.

## How would you have Interpreted, if on Using Different Gases in the Cathode Ray Tube, the Relation (e/m) would have Resulted Different? (Based on Item 4)

Item 4 was designed to evaluate students' responses to a hypothetical experimental finding (if e/m for different gases would have resulted different), which would have led to the postulation of a different atomic model and thus reflect the tentative nature of science. Given this difficulty, 68 (40%) students did not respond to this item (see Table 1), and 71 (42%) students gave a positivist response and following are some of the examples: the relation (e/m) could not have been a constant, as it was dependent on the type of gas; only if the substances used in the tube were not gases; it could not have been different as Thomson reached his conclusion by varying the gases and found that all atoms contained electrons; if that would have been the case, Thomson could not have discovered the relation (e/m); that is a poor interpretation, as we already know that the relation (e/m) is independent of the gas used; this could be attributed to inadequate techniques that would alter the structure and composition of matter or even due to calculation errors; Thomson did not use cathode rays. This wide range of responses shows that on the one hand some students simply did not respond, while others did not understand that Thomson designed his experiments to determine precisely if the relation (e/m) would be constant or not. Accordingly, his model of the atom would have adjusted to his experimental findings. Most of these responses consider Thomson's model as an absolute reality, a law or even perhaps predetermined. In other words, Thomson perhaps already knew what he was going to find. Classroom practice and textbooks simply ignore the dynamics of scientific progress based on historical reconstructions that can provide students with a much clearer picture of the relationship between the scientists' expectations (presuppositions / hypotheses) and the experimental findings.

Transitional responses were provided by 16 (9%) students and following are some of the examples: the types of gases used would have different types of electrons with different mass and charge; the non-existence of electrons in the atoms; we would not have an atomic structure as the present, and the constitution of the different elements would have been unstable. These responses show an understanding beyond that of the positivist responses by recognizing that either electrons did not exist in the atoms, or different types of electrons existed and hence atomic structure would have been different.

Lakatosian responses were provided by 5 (3%) students and following are some of the examples: different gases do not have the same relation (e/m), with respect to the electrons that constitute them; each gas has a different mass and charge, in other words the electron is not a fundamental particle of a gas; gases vary in the charge and mass of their electrons, and hence other models will have to be made. These responses go beyond the transitional responses by explicitly recognizing that under these circumstances electrons would not be considered as a fundamental particle and hence other models will have to be constructed. In comparison to Item 3, positivist and transitional responses remained about the same, Lakatosian responses decreased considerably and those who did not respond also increased considerably.

## Did Thomson's Model Represent the Information he Had at that Time? (Based on Item 5)

Before responding to this item students were provided an illustration of Thomson's model of the atom, similar to that found in most textbooks. We considered this to be a fairly straightforward question but still most students had difficulty responding to it. Furthermore, it is important to note that students are never asked or expected to discuss such issues in class. In a typical general chemistry classroom in most parts of the world, the teacher expounds and the students take notes, with almost no room for discussions and much less discussions based on the origin, construction, and development of models, hypotheses and theories. Thus it is not surprising that only 2 (1%) students gave a Lakatosian response and following is an example: Thomson's model was an advance for the discovery of the atom which created anxiety among other scientists, leading to further discoveries.

Positivist responses were provided by 39 (23%) students and following are some of the examples: yes, because at that time science was not so advanced with respect to instruments and techniques; no, because Thomson did not know how were the electrons and other particles distributed within the atom. He only knew that they existed; no, because Thomson considered the atom to be a sphere of uniform charge density; no, because Rutherford later with his experiments demonstrated that all the mass was concentrated in a small region, called the nucleus; no, because he should have taken into account the attraction and repulsion between the electric charges found in the atom. These responses show how students fail to recognize that Thomson could not have postulated a model by taking into consideration experimental findings later to his own work. It appears that students conceive science as providing information about an absolute, unchanging conception of the atom. It is interesting to note that 32 students, of the 39 who gave a positivist response, did not agree that Thomson's model represents the information he had at that time. Science teachers must be aware as to how our students construe progress in science. It is a cause for concern that students considered that Thomson only knew that electrons existed and not their distribution within the atom and that Thomson considered the atom to be a sphere of uniform charge density. This lack of a historical perspective with respect to the progressive construction of theories is a stumbling block in our efforts to facilitate not only scientific literacy but also the formation of new scientists.

Another feature of this item was that many students responded affirmatively or negatively, without giving much information, so as to classify the response within a philosophy of science perspective. Following are some of the examples of affirmative responses: Thomson based his model on the information obtained from his experiments (N=31), hypothesized the atom as a fruit cake, with positive and negative fruits (N=12), for Thomson, the atom was a sphere of uniform charge density with positive and negative particles (N=10).

## What Was Most Important in E. Rutherford's Experiments? (Based on Item 6)

Rutherford's alpha particle deflection experiments constitute an important part of the chemistry curriculum and textbooks in most parts of the world. Before responding to the four items (6, 7, 8 & 9) in the questionnaire students were provided a brief description of Rutherford's experiments, which they had already studied as part of the Chemistry I program. Similar to Thomson's experiments, 134 (78%) students provided a positivist response and following are some of the examples: to establish a small and massive region in the center of the atom, having a positive charge, called the nucleus; to propose that the atom was for the most part empty space, having a positively charged nucleus in the center with surrounding electrons; discovery of the concentration of positive charge in the atoms of gold foils; demonstrate that deflection of alpha particles was caused by a positively charged center; to demonstrate that the great majority of the alpha particles passed through the gold foil, and only a small number were deflected with large angles. Most of the positivist responses emphasized the hard empirical findings. It is not farfetched to suggest that such experimental details were important, but there was something even more important, namely Rutherford's interpretation that led to a confrontation with Thomson, due to the competition between two rival models of the atom.

Transitional responses were provided by 12 (7%) students and following are some of the examples: Rutherford formulated his hypothesis based on the previous work of Thomson; Rutherford demonstrated that Thomson's model was not correct and that the mass of the atom was concentrated in an extremely small region called the nucleus; propose an atomic model comparable to the planetary system, in which the nucleus has the positive charge and the electrons surrounding it. Transitional responses indicate a greater understanding by emphasizing the relationship between Rutherford and Thomson's models. Nevertheless, these responses represent more of a Popperian refutation (Popper, 1962) of Thomson's model by Rutherford's experimental findings rather than the conceptualization of the two models as competing research programs in the Lakatosian sense (cf. point 6 of Framework). The difference between Popper and Lakatos is important, as according to the latter, theories are not right or wrong and hence refutations are not important. Within the Lakatosian framework, Rutherford's model is better and hence more important, as it provides greater heuristic power, namely explains the experimental findings to a greater extent. Interestingly, there were no Lakatosian responses on this item. The essential point here is that scientific models are not right or wrong. In other words, it is not very helpful, if we really want to understand scientific progress, to say that Thomson was right so long as Rutherford did not appear on the scene. Very few textbooks explain that Thomson's model was good enough for his time, and Rutherford provided us with a greater understanding of the atom.

## How would you Interpret the Finding that Most of the Alpha Particles Passed Undeflected through the Thin Metal Foil? (Based on Item 7)

The idea behind this item was to explore students' ability to study experimental findings (emphasized by most textbooks) and the degree to which it can facilitate the ability to interpret and thus enhance understanding. Positivist responses were provided by 63 (37%) students and following are some of the examples: due to the fact that alpha particles have a greater mass than the electrons; alpha particles were attracted by the negative particles in the gold foil; due to the high energy of the alpha particles; due to the fact that the metal foil was very thin. Transitional responses were provided by 16 (9%) students and following are some of the examples: as very few alpha particles were deflected through large angles he proposed that the atom has a very small positively charged nucleus in the center; through mathematical calculations he demonstrated that the large deflections were produced by a positively charged center whose mass was approximately equal to that of the atom. Interestingly, Lakatosian responses were provided by 30 (18%) students, a considerable increase as compared to Item 6. Surprisingly, 38 (22%) students did not respond, which shows the complexity of the issues involved. Following is an example of a Lakatosian response: as most of the alpha particles passed undeflected through the metal foil, he proposed that most of the atom is empty space with a small positively charged region called the nucleus.

Positivist responses to Item 7 are particularly illustrative of the fact that even if the students are given the experimental findings and asked to interpret, they insist on highlighting the experimental and concrete details, that is empirically verifiable facts. On the other hand, the transitional responses go beyond by relating the deflection through large angles to a model of the atom. The Lakatosian responses are even more explicit with respect to the experimental evidence (passing of alpha particles undeflected) and the model postulated by Rutherford. It appears that students consider the objectivity of science (or the scientific method) and the empirically observable and verifiable experimental facts to be closely interrelated. The interpretations, on the other hand, constitute the very essence of scientific practice and still are generally ignored by textbooks and teachers. In the positivist tradition, perhaps interpretations are too subjective and hence not an important part of science. Thus students are deprived of experiences that can show the difficulties and vicissitudes faced by the scientists.

## How would you have Interpreted, if Most of the Alpha Particles would have Deflected through Large Angles? (Based on Item 8)

The main idea behind this item was to provide students with hypothetical experimental evidence (quite different from what they had studied), and observe the degree to which students can assimilate conflicting evidence and go beyond by formulating alternative models. Positivist responses were provided by 46 (27%) students and following are some of the examples: assuming that a repulsive force would impede penetration of the atom; due to the fact that a majority of the alpha particles were heavy; magnitude of the positive charge density would be much greater; as if the nucleus of the gold atom would not be in the center but on the surface; they would be deflected because on colliding with the nucleus all of them would not be able to enter; as if the nucleus had a greater mass and the number of electrons much greater; size of the nucleus would be relatively big and hence the electrons would have greater mass and positive charge. It is interesting to note that these students do make an effort to provide an explanation of the hypothetical experimental finding. These explanations are, however, based entirely on some other experimental property not taken into consideration preciously, such as repulsive forces, greater positive charge density, bigger size of the nucleus, etc. There is no attempt to formulate an alternative model.

Transitional responses were provided by 5 (3%) students and following are some examples: as if the atoms in the gold foil would not have any empty space; could be attributed to various zones of positive charge existing in the gold foil; as if the mass of the nucleus were much greater or the majority of positive charges could be found outside the nucleus. These responses did make an effort towards a partial understanding of the need for alternative models in the light of conflicting evidence. There were no Lakatosian responses to this item, and surprisingly 77 (45%) students gave an ambiguous response, which shows the difficulty of the issues involved. Interestingly, in Item 4 (which also presented hypothetical experimental evidence) 68 students (40%) did not respond and the Lakatosian responses were also few.

Results obtained in this item show the need for discussing various aspects of an experiment including hypothetical findings so that students can discuss and debate and thus familiarize themselves with the dynamics of conflicts and controversies, and their significance in scientific practice.


## If Rutherford's Experiments Changed Thomson's Model of the Atom Entirely, did Thomson Make Mistakes while Doing his Experiments? (Based on Item 9)

The idea behind this item was to pursue further students' ideas (based on positivist philosophy) that scientific progress consists of replacing wrong theories with right ones. Before responding to the question students were provided a brief description of Rutherford's model of the atom as found in most textbooks. Positivist responses were provided by 62 (36%) students and following are some of the examples: no, Rutherford did not do the same experiments as Thomson – he only served as a guide; no, Thomson did not have the equipment and the knowledge necessary to demonstrate what Rutherford could demonstrate later; no, they tell us what they see through their experiments; no, at least he demonstrated that there were charged particles. However, he failed to find the orbitals; yes, because Thomson mixed all the charges, whereas Rutherford studied them separately; yes, because Thomson could not discover the nucleus; yes, the proof lies in the fact that Rutherford demonstrated contrary to what Thomson had proposed; yes, many of Thomson's experiments had problems and were not of much use to Rutherford; yes, it is something that requires a lot of observation in order to deduce and then propose a model based on convincing proofs. For any one teaching or doing science, these responses must be a cause for concern. In other words, many students considered Thomson to have made mistakes in his experiments as he could not find the orbitals, nucleus or simply lacked experimental finesse, which shows quite cogently the importance of precise empirical observations within the positivist framework. Of the 62 students who gave positivist responses, 24 explicitly responded in the affirmative, that is, Thomson made mistakes while doing his experiments.

Transitional responses were provided by 45 (26%) students and following are some of the examples: no, because each scientist performed different experiments, leading to different conclusions but both had their validity; no, because one was the continuation of the other; no, because Thomson achieved what he was looking for and so did Rutherford; no, Thomson did not make mistakes. His experiments were good for his time. With the passage of time new theories are discovered, which does not mean that the previous theories did not serve a function. It is important to note that all the transitional responses did not agree that Thomson made mistakes. Furthermore, these students made an attempt to understand the progressive nature of science.

Lakatosian responses were provided by 4 (2%) students and following is an example: no, because Rutherford could improve upon the model postulated by Thomson by giving additional explanations. The idea of 'additional explanations' or increase in 'heuristic power' as Lakatos would put it, is essential in order to understand that theories / models are not right or wrong.

Some of the positivist responses to this item could also be considered as refutation of Thomson's theory by Rutherford in the Popperian sense. Students and teachers may find it interesting that philosophers of science do not necessarily agree in their historical reconstructions. Popper emphasized refutations, whereas Lakatos provided the insight that theories are difficult to refute, and what actually happens is a progressive increase in heuristic power. Transitional responses basically emphasized the continuation of Thomson's work by Rutherford, without grasping the Lakatosian interpretation that Rutherford's experiments do not refute Thomson's theory (unlike Popper) but rather provide a model with greater heuristic power. Complexity of the issues involved in this item is apparent from the fact that 47 (27%) students did not respond.

## What Was Most Important in Bohr's Experiments? (Based on Item 10)

Before responding to this item students were provided a brief description of how Rutherford's model of the atom violates one of the classical principles of physics, as presented in most textbooks. Positivist responses were provided by 87 (51%) students and following are some of the examples: to suggest that according to quantum mechanics, electrons in an atom possess certain well defined amounts of energy; to suggest that an accelerated electron circling around a nucleus emits electromagnetic radiation, which leads to a loss in energy of the electron; postulation of stationary states for the movement of the electrons in which no radiation is emitted; demonstrate by the application of quantum theory the true structure of the atom; demonstrate that the frequencies emitted in the spectrum of the hydrogen atom obeyed simple laws; Bohr's four postulates.

Transitional responses were provided by 13 (8%) students and following are some of the examples: modify Rutherford's model by constructing the first model that correctly predicted atomic spectra; propose an atomic model in order to amplify some of the questions raised by Rutherford's model; demonstrate that classical physics principle, according to which an electron moving around a nucleus would lose energy and thus destroy itself, was false.

Lakatosian responses were provided by 6 (4%) students and following are two examples: based on the quantum theory Bohr demonstrated the stability of the Rutherford atom;

resolved the paradox that existed in Rutherford's model, by clarifying the instability produced by the movement of the electrons around the nucleus.

Most of the responses to Item 10 were positivist and 36 (21%) students did not respond. It is important to note that their is a difference between the use of quantum theory by Bohr and the students' response that what was most important in Bohr's theory was the use of quantum theory in order to study the energy of the electrons. Bohr's work went beyond positivism (hence his difficulties with many influential physicists), whereas students' conceptualization of quantum theory is very similar to a positivist approach as it anticipates, '... the true structure of the atom', that is, an absolute reality.

According to Lakatos (1970), the fact that the Balmer and Paschen series in the hydrogen's line emission spectrum were experimentally observed before Bohr presented his 1913 paper, has led some positivist historians to present the story as an example of a Baconian 'inductive ascent', viz., chaos of spectrum lines (before 1885) → Balmer's 'empirical law' (1885) → Bohr's theoretical explanation (1913). Balmer presented his empirical law in 1885 and work on atomic spectra was already known for many years and hence the chaos. The interesting (and perhaps amusing) part of the story is that in the first version of his famous article, Bohr (1913) stated explicitly that his primary concern was the paradoxical stability of the Rutherford atom and made no mention of atomic spectra or Balmer's law. There is evidence to show that at this stage Bohr had not heard of the Balmer formula! This episode has been well recorded in the history of chemistry and physics, which is generally ignored by teachers. It is extremely relevant to note that some of the students also reasoned along positivist lines by pointing out that what was most important in Bohr's theory was the explanation of hydrogen's line spectrum. In contrast to the above interpretation, according to Lakatos (1970): "... Bohr's problem was not to explain Balmer's and Paschen's series, but *to explain the paradoxical stability of the Rutherford atom*" (p.147, emphasis added). Interestingly, some of the Lakatosian responses in this study came quite close to this conceptualization. Transitional responses, on the other hand simply refer to the problems faced by the Rutherford atom, without referring to its 'paradoxical stability'.

## If Bohr's Experiments Changed Rutherford's Model of the Atom, did Rutherford Make Mistakes while Doing his Experiments? (Based on Item 11)

The idea behind this item (similar to Item 9) was to make students think and reflect with respect to progress in science, namely we do not necessarily replace wrong theories with right ones, but rather look for greater explanatory power. Positivist responses were provided by 47 (27%) students and following are some of the examples: no, what happened was that Rutherford only limited himself to the existence of the nucleus; no, he only made mistakes with respect to the orbitals of each electron; no, in reality he made deductions from what he observed.; yes, because he established that the electrons circled around the nucleus and according to the laws of classical physics the electron would have lost energy, and ultimately destroyed the atom; yes, some phenomenon did not permit him to observe the real model of the atom; yes, at least he made some mistakes, otherwise Bohr would not have taken the care to present a good model; yes because he based his model on suppositions. It is interesting to note that as compared to Item 9 (which compared Rutherford with Thomson) the number of positivist responses decreased. However, the number of students who considered Rutherford to have made mistakes was 19 (Item 11), which is about the same as in Item 9. Again, the number of students who did not respond remained about the same in both Items 9 and 11, which shows that students continued to have the same difficulties in both items.

Transitional responses were provided by 51 (30%) students and following are some of the examples: no, Rutherford's experiments served as a base for Bohr to carry out his experiments; no, each experiment contributes towards the perfection of a previously obtained result; no, each one of them made his postulations according to their knowledge and the progress in the field at that time. Both of them worked in different periods of time and scientific progress tends to improve with the passage of time; no, both experiments had their importance and contributed ideas towards the development of the structure of the atom. Lakatosian responses were provided by 9 (5%) students and following is an example: no, actually Bohr solved the problem of the stability of the Rutherford model of the atom, which could not explain as to how the electron could stay outside the nucleus in spite of the electrostatic force of attraction.

Positivist responses to this item seem to emphasize that Rutherford based his model on suppositions and not hard facts, and hence the need for Bohr's model. This makes interesting reading, as Bohr's four postulates were not only based on suppositions but also speculations, which according to Lakatos is perfectly justifiable. Transitional responses highlighted the fact that Rutherford's experiments served as a base for Bohr, whereas the Lakatosian responses emphasized that Bohr by solving the paradox of the stability of the Rutherford atom was postulating a rival research program.

## Teachers' Responses

Teachers' responses were also classified as positivist (P), transitional (T), or Lakatosian (L). Each of the teachers' response was compared to that of the students. On Item 1, only teacher 2 had a Lakatosian response, whereas all the other teachers had a positivist response. Teacher 7 had the following response: "Thomson explained the relation between the electrons and the atomic structure and showed clearly the dependence of the periodic properties of the elements on the number of electrons". This response is quite similar to some of the other positivist responses of students and teachers, as it considers the establishment of a concrete relationship, between the periodic properties and the number of electrons, as the most important thing in Thomson's experiment.

Four of the teachers had a positivist response on Item 2, one transitional and two Lakatosian. Item 3 had the maximum number (5) of Lakatosian responses. Four of the teachers responded affirmatively on Item 5, without giving an adequate justification for the response to be classified as P, T, or L. Only teacher 2 had a Lakatosian response on Item 6: "Rutherford's experiments led to the elimination of the basic idea on which Thomson's model of the atom was based. In contrast to Thomson's model, Rutherford's model led to the postulation of a positively charged nucleus and what is most important – the atom for the most part is empty space." It is important to note that on Item 6 none of the students or the other teachers expressed the Lakatosian idea that Rutherford's experiments provided evidence against a competing framework, viz., Thomson's model of the atom (cf. point 6 of Framework). Responses on Item 8 show that two of the teachers clearly tried to resist changes in their core belief by invoking 'auxiliary hypotheses' and following is an example: "Of all the alpha particles that were deflected, the majority did so through large angles, which shows that the positive charge must be concentrated in a small part of the atom". These responses show the inability to visualize/construct alternative models of the atom and hence represent a defense of a core belief, viz., most of the positive charge is concentrated in a small part of the atom. Six of the teachers had a transitional response on Item 9. Teacher 1 gave the following response: "Thomson's experiments served as a stepping-stone for other scientists, so that their investigations could either refute or verify the model postulated by Thomson". This response is quite representative of a Popperian approach (Popper, 1962) and was classified as transitional.

## 6.3. BAROQUE TOWER ON A GOTHIC BASE: CONCLUSIONS

The following response on Item 11 by teacher 2 is quite representative of most teachers' and students' thinking in this study:

> We do not have to ignore the importance of the work of previous investigators. Each one of them proposed an explanation for the phenomenon observed. For example, in the case of Rutherford the angles of deflection. Rutherford's experiments served as a basis for the development of other models. We cannot be 100% certain even of the most advanced models. In general all the models are a product of the necessity to explain experimental facts. Each of these models (conceptions) had their validity so far as they could explain those facts. Each of these conceptions is a hypothesis and the hypotheses, just as the theories, undergo modifications. These modifications are implemented progressively, to the extent that these hypotheses do not interpret correctly the discovery of new phenomena based on observations and experimentation. For example, the theory of phlogiston was opposed by the theory of oxidation. This is how science advances and in the field of chemistry this evolution is even more patent.

This response is complex and shows how teachers (and perhaps students) have been exposed to different influences. Furthermore, it is quite surprising that teacher 2 should have expressed these positivist views, as she/he had responded with a clearly Lakatosian approach on Items 1, 2, 3, 4, and had the only Lakatosian response among teachers and students, on Item 6. In spite of the positivist 'flavor' of this response or what Lakatos would refer to as Baconian 'inductive ascent', it has certain elements which can be helpful for teachers in order to facilitate conceptual change. For example, the following sentences are indicators of change in thinking: "We do not have to ignore the importance of the work of previous investigators", "Rutherford's experiments served as a basis for the development of other models", and "We cannot be 100% certain even of the most advanced models". These sentences are quite inconsistent with respect to the rest of the response which represents positivist thinking. Similarly, except for teacher 4 (who did not have any Lakatosian response), all the other teachers switched back and forth between Lakatosian, transitional and positivist responses. Students' responses also showed an inconsistent pattern, in which they changed their approach from one extreme (positivist) to another (Lakatosian). None of the Ss maintained a single response pattern in all the 11 items. These results are somewhat unexpected, in view of the fact that all items in this study are closely related and based directly on students'/teachers' course activities.

Looking for a cue to the history of science, it is important to note that, "... *some of the most important research programmes in the history of science were grafted on to older programmes with which they were blatantly inconsistent*. For instance, Copernican astronomy was 'grafted' on to Aristotelian physics, Bohr's programme on to Maxwell's" (Lakatos, 1970, p. 142, original italics). The importance of a relationship based on a Lakatosian framework, between the research methodology used by scientists and the construction of models by students that facilitate conceptual understanding, has been recognized in the literature (Linn & Songer, 1991a; Niaz, 1995b). According to Margenau (1950, p. 311): "... it is understandable that, in the excitement over its success, men overlooked a malformation in the theory's architecture; for Bohr's atom sat like a baroque tower upon the Gothic base of classical electrodynamics" (cited in Lakatos, 1970, p. 142).

A major thesis of this study is that students' and teachers' also go through a process similar to that of the scientists in which some 'progressive' parts of their thinking is inconsistently 'grafted' on to a base that represents positivist thinking. According to Lakatos (1971), such inconsistent 'grafts' are important for the development of science, for otherwise from a Popperian perspective, Bohr's 1913 paper should never have been published, as it was, "... inconsistently grafted on to Maxwell's theory" (p. 113). In spite of the parallel between the work of the scientists and students, we do want to point out a difference. For example, in the case of Bohr, the 'malformation' was not 'overlooked' by the scientists: everybody was aware of it, only they ignored it during the progressive phase of the program. On the other hand, in the case of students and teachers, we hypothesize that they are perhaps not aware of the 'inconsistencies' in their thinking. This has implications for classroom instruction: should the teachers explicitly design strategies in order to make use of these 'inconsistencies' or let the students grapple with such issues on their own.

Studies based on cognitive conflict as a teaching strategy in the science education literature (cf. Chinn & Brewer, 1993; Hewson & Hewson, 1984; Zohar & Aharon-Kravetsky, 2005) would perhaps provide a rationale for the design of teaching strategies based on students' philosophical and epistemological issues. Even in the present study we speculate that there was an interaction with the sequences of items used in the questionnaire, which helped the students (and why not the teachers) to improve their understanding of the underlying issues. For example, in general within a sequence of items the positivist responses decreased, whereas the transitional and Lakatosian responses increased both for the students and the teachers.

In spite of the inconsistencies in students' thinking this study also found some consistent trends based on a particular philosophical stance. For example, Item 1 showed that for many students the most important thing in Thomson's work was the determination of the charge to mass (e/m) relation – a hard infallible experimental fact, thus indicating a positivist/inductivist thinking. In Item 2, students were specifically asked as to why did Thomson determine (e/m) relation. Most of those who had responded, determination of the (e/m) relation, now responded to obtain a value for (e/m). Item 3 was much more specific and students were given the feedback that the constant value of the (e/m) relation was important to Thomson's work. Interestingly, most of those who had responded because he wanted to obtain a value, now responded that the relation (e/m) was constant because the absolute values of charge and mass changed. This clearly shows that students resist changes in their thinking by invoking 'auxiliary hypotheses' in order to protect a core belief.

In general, it appears that students consider the experimental details as the most important part of a scientist's work, and not the hypotheses on which they were based or the interpretations that could be derived from them. For example, in Thomson's experiments it was the determination of the charge to mass (e/m) relation, in Rutherford's it was the deflection of the alpha particles / discovery of the nucleus, and in Bohr's it was the frequencies emitted in the hydrogen spectrum. Schwab (1974) has emphasized this important difference between the experimental details (emphasized in the classroom) and the 'heuristic principle' required to 'structure inquiry' very explicitly: "In physics, we did not know from the beginning that the properties of particles of matter are fundamental and determine the behavior of these particles, their relations to one another. It was not verified knowledge but a heuristic principle, needed to structure inquiry, that led us to investigate mass and charge and, later, spin" (p. 165).

Some of the important findings and salient features of this study are summarized below:

1.  Both students' and teachers' have a very similar positivist/inductivist understanding of structure of the atom. This is all the more important as this topic formed part of their course content and the study is based on intact classrooms. The teachers who participated in this study were either giving this course in the same semester or had given it previously. Furthermore, most of the students and teachers responded with a positivist approach, some were transitional and a few had a Lakatosian perspective.

2.  Most of the students and teachers were inconsistent in their responses by switching from a positivist response on one item to a Lakatosian, on another item.

3.  Students and teachers also showed consistent response patterns by resisting changes in some of their core beliefs by invoking 'auxiliary hypotheses' (Lakatos, 1970).

4.  For most students and teachers the empirically observable hard experimental facts give science its objective status, whereas the interpretations being subjective perhaps go beyond the fold of science.

5.  Students and teachers resist the idea of changing models / tentativeness of science, even when explicitly asked to consider a different experimental situation that would lead to the 'construction' of an alternative model.

6.  If a scientist's model is changed / modified by a subsequent scientist, students in retrospect generally consider the first scientist to have made mistakes in his experiments.

## 6.4. UNDERSTANDING PHOTOELECTRIC EFFECT

This section of the chapter investigates student understanding of the photoelectric effect, which is an important part of the topic of atomic structure. The main objective is to construct models based on strategies students use to solve algorithmic and conceptual problems, and to show that these models form sequences of progressive transitions similar to what Lakatos (1970) has referred to as progressive 'problemshifts' (cf. GL2, chap. 3). Guideline GL2, suggests that the sequences of evolving models constructed by students increase in heuristic power, similar to what happens in the history of science. Results reported here are obtained from Niaz (1995a).

## Details of the Study

Freshman students (N=44) enrolled in Chemistry I at the Universidad de Oriente, Venezuela were asked to solve the following problems, which formed part of a monthly exam. Students were encouraged and given credit for providing justification for their answers.

*Item A*
> Calculate the wave length in Angstrom of an electron transition in the spectrum of hydrogen, from n = 4 to n = 2.
> (Note: Ss were provided values of the constants and the relevant formula in terms of the wave number).

*Item B*
> Which of the following statements about the photoelectric effect are correct?
>
> a. The surface of a metal does not emit electrons, until the frequency of the impinging light is greater than the threshold value;
> b. Above the threshold frequency, greater the intensity of light, the lower the velocity of the emitted electrons;
> c. Above the threshold frequency, the greater the wave length of light, the greater the velocity of the emitted electron;
> d. Above the threshold frequency, the lower the intensity of light, the greater the number of electrons emitted per second.
>
> (Note: Students were asked to justify all responses, whether correct or incorrect).

*Item C*
> A metal having a threshold wavelength of 5900 Angstrom is irradiated with light having a wave length of 3500 Angstrom.
>
> a) Would there be emission of electrons.
> b) If electrons are emitted, calculate their velocity.
> (Note: Students were provided with values of all the constants)

Item B requires conceptual understanding. Items A and C were adapted from Oxtoby, Nachtrieb, and Freeman (1990) and can be solved by the use of algorithms. Results obtained show considerable difference in student performance on the algorithmic and conceptual problems. For example, 45% and 55% of the students solved correctly the algorithmic problems A and C, respectively. On the other hand, the conceptual problem B was solved correctly by only 7% of the students. Based on strategies used in solving Items A, B, and C it is plausible to suggest that students go through the following process of progressive transitions (models) that facilitate different degrees of conceptual understanding:

## 6.5. PROGRESSIVE TRANSITIONS (MODELS) LEADING TO GREATER CONCEPTUAL UNDERSTANDING OF THE PHOTOELECTRIC EFFECT

Model 1: Strategies used to calculate the wave number of an electron transition (Item A), given the relevant constants and the formula in terms of the wave number (N = 22)

Model 2: Strategies used to calculate the wave length of an electron transition, Item A (N = 20).

Model 3: Strategies used to predict if there would be emission of electrons (Item C), given the threshold wave length of the metal and the wave length of the impinging light (N = 24).

Model 4: Strategies used to conceptualize that the surface of a metal does not emit electrons, until the frequency of the impinging light is greater than the threshold value, based on a correct response to part (a) of Item B (N = 21).

Model 5: Strategies used to conceptualize beyond Model 4, that is, above the threshold frequency, the velocity of the emitted electrons increases as the frequency of impinging light increases, based on a correct response to part (b) or part (c) of Item B (N = 13).

Model 6: Strategies used to conceptualize beyond Models 4 and 5, that is, above the threshold frequency, increasing the light intensity increases the number of electrons emitted per unit time, based on a correct response to part (d) of Item B (N = 3). Students with this Model responded correctly to all 4 parts of Item B.

Results obtained in this section show once again the great difference between student ability to apply memorized algorithms and formulae and the inability to comprehend the underlying principles, which according to Stinner (1992) forms part of our 'post-Whewellian' tradition.

## 6.6. CONCLUSION

Studies reported in this chapter show how frequently the traditional classroom fosters a view of science that leads to a 'rhetoric of conclusions' and ignores what Schwab (1974) refers to as the 'heuristic principle' required to structure inquiry. For example, students can easily be misled into believing that the experimental details related to a scientist's work, is all that matters. The 'heuristic principle' facilitates students' understanding as to how Thomson's determination of the charge-to-mass ratio was important and also how Thomson's model constituted a progressive transition by providing greater conceptual understanding. Similarly, the studies reported emphasize the 'heuristic principles' of Rutherford and Bohr models.

# Chapter 7

# UNDERSTANDING GASES: FROM 'ALGORITHMIC MODE' TO 'CONCEPTUAL UNDERSTANDING'

The main objective of this chapter is to reconstruct student understanding of the behavior of gases within a history and philosophy of science perspective. However, before doing that it is important to present a brief account of the early experiments that studied the behavior of gases and the developments that led to the formulation of the kinetic theory of gases.

## 7.1. EXPERIMENTAL STUDIES OF THE BEHAVIOR OF GASES

It was the early work by Torricelli, Pascal, and Boyle related with 'air pressure' that later led to the formulation of the gas laws. For example, Boyle (1627-91) wanted to prove that air has elasticity ('spring') and can exert a mechanical pressure great enough to support a column of water or mercury. Although Boyle did publish data in 1662 in response to the criticism of Franciscus Linus (1661) which confirmed the hypothesis that the product pressure x volume = constant, he had not been able to see any simple relation between the pressures and volumes of a gas before he received a paper written by Richard Townley, in which this hypothesis was proposed. Interestingly, contrary to most textbooks, Boyle's theory was cast into a simple mathematical form by Newton, and provided perhaps one of the first explanations of Boyle's law in his *Principia* (1687), which stated: "If a gas is composed of particles that exert repulsive forces on their neighbors, the magnitude of force being inversely as the distance, then the pressure will be inversely as the volume" (Brush, 1976, p. 13). This led to the well known 'Newton's hypothesis' that gas pressure is due to static repulsion between particles, and Newton's vast authority ensured that the static model of gases was widely adopted and accepted by most scientists till almost 1860.

Contrary to what has been suggested, Boyle in 1660 was not only an empiricist trying to establish relations between observable quantities (also see chap. 1), but also proposed that the atoms behaved as if they were clock springs, and drew figures showing the springs tightly coiled under high pressure and loosely coiled at low pressure, arranged in a regular lattice. Indeed, according to Kuhn (1970): "Boyle's experiments were not conceivable (and if conceived would have received another interpretation or none at all) until air was recognized as an elastic fluid to which all the elaborate concepts of hydrostatics could be applied" (p. 28).

## 7.2. Lattice Theory of Gases

Before going into the origins of the kinetic theory of gases, it is important to point out that the theory could not flourish until heat as a substance (caloric theory of heat) had been replaced by heat as atomic motion. Furthermore, Newton's theory, based on repulsive forces between gas atoms, had already been firmly established as the explanation of Boyle's law, both by the prestige of Newton and by its simplicity. 'Newton's hypothesis' of static repulsion between particles led to the formulation of the lattice theory of gases: "... atoms (or molecules) in gases were arranged in a regular lattice, rather as if gases were highly expanded solids – but, whereas the forces between atoms in solids were attractive, in gases they became repulsive and this gave rise to the pressure on the walls of a containing vessel" (Mendoza, 1990, p. 1040). Interestingly, the lattice theory of gases was accepted by most chemists between about 1770 and almost up to the Karlsruhe Conference of 1860, including Lavoisier, Dalton, Ampere, and Avogadro.

## 7.3. Origins of the Kinetic Theory of Gases

The origins of the kinetic theory of gases can be traced back to the work of various scientists, starting in the 18th century. Jacob Hermann (1678-1733) proposed in 1716 that other things being equal, heat is proportional both to the density of a hot body and to the square of the agitation of its particles. The agitation of the particles was the root mean square of the individual speeds with which the particles of a hot body were agitated. Next, Leonhard Euler in 1727 made an attempt to deduce the gas laws on a kinetic basis by the use of Cartesian vortices and 'subtle matter'. Daniel Bernoulli (1700-82) in 1738 presented a theory which is considered to be the first quantitative version of the modern kinetic theory. Bernoulli showed that the pressure of a gas should be proportional to the square of the molecular velocity. However, he was criticized for not explaining how heat increases the motion of particles. It is interesting to note that Bernoulli's contribution was forgotten until it was revived in the middle of the 19th century. Brush (1976) has attributed this to the fact that Newton's theory based on repulsive forces between gas atoms had already been firmly established as the explanation of Boyle's law.

John Herapath (1790-1868) postulated that the heat of a gas is proportional to the momentum of internal motions of its atoms, based on his theory of collisions which emphasized conservation of momentum in atomic collisions. According to Herapath a system is in thermal equilibrium when all its atoms have the same momentum. Herapath's main contribution was to have moved beyond the lattice theory of gases, which held a strong sway in academic circles at the beginning of the 19th century, and is considered to be one of the earliest dynamical theories of gases. It was worked out with mathematical details and published in a series of papers in 1821-22. Herapath's hypothesis, viz., pressure of a gas could be explained in terms of the rectilinear movement of its molecules, led him to derive an ideal gas law of the form PV proportional to $T^2$, instead of the later PV proportional to T. Herapath's work was the subject of considerable controversy when the Royal Society in England, due to the opposition of Humphry Davy and others, refused to publish his work. In Herapath's model, the particles were arranged on a more or less regular lattice but exerted forces on their neighbors, not through their atmospheres of caloric but by their motion. This aspect of 'Herapath's hypothesis' was adopted by Joule, and facilitated the abandonment of the idea that the molecules retained their mean positions fixed in space.

Waterston (1811-83) suggested that the increase of temperature in gases might correspond to increase of molecular kinetic energy and showed that the distance traveled by a molecule, after hitting one and before encountering another, is inversely as the density of the medium and also inversely as the square of the diameter of the molecules.

It is interesting to observe that many versions of the kinetic theory (based on movement of the molecules) were proposed during the 18th and the early part of the 19th century and yet most scientists continued to accept the lattice theory of gases until almost 1860. It appears that a critical source of support for the kinetic theory was provided by the experiments of Joule and Thomson. Writing at the turn of the century, Merz (1904) noted: "The real proof that the kinetic, in contradistinction to what we may call the Newtonian, view of the motion of the molecules of a gas is the correct one, and that Newtonian (attracting and repelling) forces play only a subordinate, if any, part in the observable phenomena of gaseous bodies, is based upon Joule and Thomson's experiments made in 1853" (p. 434).

## 7.4. MAXWELL'S KINETIC-MOLECULAR THEORY OF GASES

The starting point of Maxwell's work on the kinetic theory of gases was his reading in April 1859 of a translation in the *Philosophical Magazine* of a paper by Rudolf Clausius. Maxwell (1860) recognizes the work of early kinetic theorists in the following terms:

> Daniel Bernouilli, Herapath, Joule, Krönig, Clausius, &c. have shewn that the relations between pressure, temperature, and density in a perfect gas can be explained by supposing the particles to move with uniform velocity in straight lines, striking against the sides of the containing vessel and thus producing pressure. It is not necessary to suppose each particle to travel to any great distance in the same straight line; for the effect in producing pressure will be the same if the particles strike against each other; so that the straight line described may be very short. M. Clausius has determined the mean length of path in terms of the average distance of the particles, and the distance between the centres of two particles when collision takes place (p. 377).

Besides the influence of the early kinetic theorists, it seems that the work of greatest influence on Maxwell's development of the kinetic theory of gases may well have been the Essays by Adolphe Quetelet on the *Theory of Probabilities* in the early 19th century. Maxwell is supposed to have read, soon after its publication in July 1950, a review of the 'Essays' by John Herschel. What, however, is of interest for science educators is that Quetelet was a social scientist and his work dealt with the application of the theory of probabilities to the moral and political sciences. Porter (1981) has argued that since the inspiration for Maxwell's introduction of statistical methods into physics came from a review of Quetelet's work, one should associate Maxwell's early thinking about molecular velocity distributions with the kind of statistical reasoning used in the social sciences by Quetelet and others. Thagard (1992) has referred to such episodes in the history of science as, "... cross-domain analogies, as when Darwin used Malthus's notions of population increase in humans to help develop his theory of natural selection" (p. 538). Porter (1981) considers this episode to represent a 'creative synthesis' of a great range of knowledge. More recently, Porter (1994) has presented a detailed account of the transition from social statistics to statistical physics. Similarly, Niaz (1991a) has drawn an analogy (abduction) between Piaget's epistemic subject and the ideal gas law that derives its meaning from the theoretical formulation of the kinetic theory of Maxwell and Boltzmann. Nevertheless, it is important to note that 'statistical' for Maxwell in 1860 had the connotation of an emergence of regularity out of the apparently chaotic behavior of large numbers of molecules, which had little to do with its later recognition that the macroscopic gas laws are only probabilistic. Maxwell in his 1860 paper sets down the following basic assumptions of his theory:

1.  Gases are composed of minute particles in rapid motion.
2.  Particles are perfectly elastic spheres.
3.  Particles act on each other only during impact.
4.  Motion of the particles is subject to mechanical principles of Newtonian mechanics.
5.  Velocity of the particles increases with the temperature of the gas.
6.  Particles move with uniform velocity in straight lines striking against the sides of the container, producing pressure.
7.  Derivation of the distribution law assumes that he x-, y-, and z-components of velocity are independent.

Achinstein (1987) has raised an important issue with respect to Maxwell's assumptions: "How did Maxwell arrive at them [assumptions]? They are highly speculative, involving as they do the postulation of unobserved particles exhibiting unobserved motion" (p. 410). Did Maxwell have an independent warrant (i.e., plausibility of the hypotheses) for his basic assumptions? Based on the framework outlined in this book (chaps. 1, 2, & 3), Maxwell's basic assumptions are precisely the *ceteris paribus* clauses mentioned earlier, which helped him to progress from simple to complex models of the gases. Taking our cue from Galilean idealizations, it is plausible to interpret Maxwell's basic assumptions in the following terms:

> The move from the complexity of nature to the specially contrived order of the experiment is a form of idealization. The diversity of causes found in Nature is reduced and made manageable. The influence of impediments, i.e., causal factors which affect the process under study in ways not at present of interest, is eliminated or lessened sufficiently that it may be ignored (McMullin, 1985, p. 265).

Interestingly, Maxwell's research program is yet another example of a program progressing on inconsistent foundations (similar to Bohr, cf., Lakatos, 1970). Among other assumptions, Maxwell's 1860 paper was based on 'strict mechanical principles' derived from Newtonian mechanics and yet at least two of Maxwell's basic assumptions (referring to the movement of particles and the consequent generation of pressure) were in contradiction with Newton's hypothesis explaining the gas laws based on repulsive forces between particles. Apparently, due to Newton's vast authority, Maxwell even in his 1875 paper, 'On the dynamical evidence of the molecular constitution of bodies' reiterated that Newtonian principles were applicable to unobservable parts of bodies. Similarly, Brush (1976) has pointed out the contradiction: "... Newton's laws of mechanics were ultimately the basis of the kinetic theory of gases, though this theory had to compete with the repulsive theory attributed to Newton" (p. 14).

In the next three sections results obtained from three studies are reported in order to illustrate a reconstruction of students' understanding of the behavior of gases.

## 7.4. STUDY 1: FROM 'ALGORITHMIC MODE' TO 'CONCEPTUAL UNDERSTANDING'

The main objectives of this study were: a) to show that there are two distinct modes of understanding gas problems in the classroom, viz, the 'algorithmic mode' and the 'conceptual gestalt' or 'conceptual understanding'; and b) investigate the degree to which cognitive variables, such as developmental level, mental capacity, and disembedding ability explain performance on problems requiring either of the two modes.

Results reported here are adapted from Niaz and Robinson (1992a). 'Algorithmic mode' in the context of this study refers to solving gas problems that primarily require manipulation (enumerating particulars, cf. Hanson, 1958, p. 70) of different variables of the ideal gas equation based on the work of Boyle, Charles, and Gay-Lussac. On the other hand, 'conceptual understanding' (cf. Hanson, 1958, p. 90) refers to the recognition of observed phenomena within patterns that make data intelligible. More explicitly, Hanson (1970) elaborates in a lucid fashion:

> Consider Boyle's law as understood in 1662, then simply a stack of statistical correlations. Boyle did not extract that famous generalization himself; his followers did. That law, that correlation considered before the advent of kinetic theory and before classical statistical mechanics, resembles the dots without the pattern, the observations without the theory, the descriptions without the explanations. Boyle's law began life as the merest correlation. It explained nothing. Only when the general gas theory and the kinetic hypothesis caught up with it did Boyle's generalization come to function as laws of nature are reputed to do (p. 237).

Similarly, it is plausible to suggest that a knowledge of Maxwell's basic assumptions (presented above) would form part of the students' 'conceptual gestalt'.

The study is based on 82 students enrolled in one section of a preparatory chemistry course for prospective science and engineering students at Purdue University in the U.S. (Mean age = 19.1 years; SD = 1.8; females = 31; males = 51). All students were tested to determine the following cognitive variables: a) Developmental level: This variable was supposed to indicate the reasoning ability of the students and was evaluated by Group Assessment of Logical Thinking, GALT (Roadrangka et al., 1983); b) Mental capacity: This variable is based on the student ability to process information (Pascual-Leone, 1987) and was evaluated by the Figural Intersection Test, FIT (Pascual-Leone & Burtis, 1974); and c) Disembedding ability: This variable is based on student ability to separate relevant from irrelevant information and was evaluated by the Group Embedded Figures Test, GEFT (Witkin et al., 1971). All students were asked to solve the following items related to the behavior of gases, which formed part of their regular evaluation during the semester. Items 1, 2, 5, 6, and 7 formed part of an exam which was given during the 15th week of the semester, and Items 3, 4, and 8 formed part of the final exam during the 17th week. All items were scored on the basis of correct response (1 point) and incorrect response (0 point). Items are presented on the left side, whereas the column on the right side provides the mean score of the students and standard deviation (SD):

| Items | Mean Score (SD) |
|---|---|
| 1. How many moles of $CH_4$ are in a container, if the pressure of the gas is 0.75 atm, its volume is 0.75 L and its temperature is 75°C? a) 0.00019 moles; b) 0.020 moles; c) 0.091 moles; d) 0.75 moles; e) 9.1 moles | 0.84 (0.37) |
| 2. A gas has a pressure of 208 kPa and a volume of 3.32 L at 27°C. What is its volume when the pressure is 104 kPa at 27°C? a) 0.138 L; b) 1.66 L; c) 3.32 L; d) 6.64 L; e) Impossible to tell unless the temperature is in kelvin. | 0.74 (0.44) |
| 3. What is the pressure in atmospheres in a container with a volume of 3.00 L that contains 35 g of $CO_2$ at a temperature of 400 kelvin? a) 8.7 atm; b) 14 atm; c) 15 atm; d) 382 atm; e) 881 atm | 0.73 (0.44) |
| 4. A cylinder contains chlorine gas at a pressure of 4.0 atm and a temperature of 35°C. What is the pressure of chlorine gas at 130°C? a) 1.1 atm; b) 3.0 atm; c) 5.2 atm; d) 15 atm; e) The problem cannot be solved without the mass of chlorine or volume of the cylinder. | 0.46 (0.50) |
| 5. The ideal gas equation may be modified to calculate the density, D, of a gas. The modified equation is $D = PM/RT$, where M is the mole mass of the gas and the other letters have their usual meaning. In this equation D is: a) directly proportional to M and inversely proportional to T; b) inversely proportional to the product of P and M; c) directly proportional to R and inversely proportional to M; d) a constant; e) both (b) and (c) are correct. | 0.59 (0.49) |
| 6. Which of Fig. 1 (a)-(e) indicates the direct proportionality between the volume of a gas and its temperature? | 0.63 (0.48) |
| 7. Why does the pressure of a gas in a closed container increase when it is warmed? a) pressure is inversely proportional to the temperature; b) molecules of the gas move faster and hit the walls harder; c) molecules of the gas expand and these larger molecules hit the wall harder; d) molecules of the gas expand and press harder against the walls of the container; e) molecules of the gas expand and move faster. The combination of the faster speed and larger molecules makes them hit the walls of the container harder. | 0.46 (0.50) |
| 8. Figure 2 represents a steel tank holding hydrogen gas at 20°C and 3 atm pressure.(The dots represent hydrogen molecules). | 0.09 (0.29) |

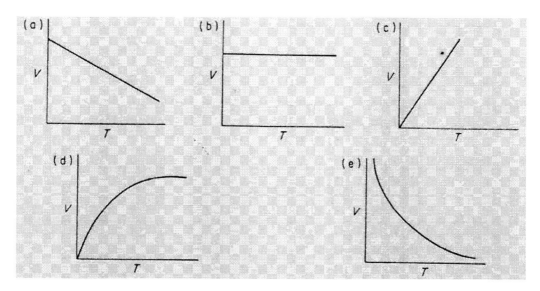

Figure 1.

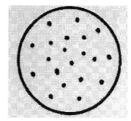

Figure 2.

Which of Figure 3 (a)-(d) represents the distribution of hydrogen molecules if the temperature is lowered to $-20^{\circ}C$?

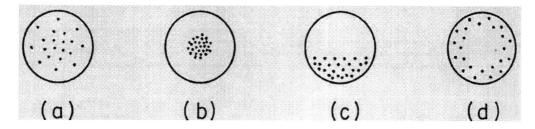

Figure 3.

Most science teachers would agree that Items 1-6 basically require the 'algorithmic mode', whereas Items 7 and 8 require 'conceptual understanding'. Students' performance (column on the right hand side) shows that except for Item 4, in all items requiring the 'algorithmic mode' the mean score of the students is fairly high. The poor performance on Item 4 could be attributed to the presence of alternative (e), which was selected by 37%. Interestingly, in Item 2, which is quite similar to Item 4, performance is fairly high. It can be further observed that performance on Items 7 and 8 requiring 'conceptual understanding' is quite poor. It is important to note that during the semester 13 items were used to evaluate understanding of the behavior of gases and of these only 2 (15%), i.e., Items 7 and 8 required 'conceptual understanding'. This finding coupled with De Berg's (1989) finding that text books do not emphasize conceptual understanding is a cause of concern. In Item 7, for example, 37% selected alternative (e), i.e., they conceptualize the increase in pressure of a gas as a product of both the expansion of the molecules and the faster speed. On the other hand, alternatives (c) and (d) were selected by only 1% and 5% of the students, respectively. These results indicate that students were not convinced that the expansion of the gas molecules could lead to an increase in the pressure of the gas. However, a combination of the faster speed and larger molecules did convince 37% of the students, i.e., alternative (e). This also coincides with previous findings (cf. Novick & Nussbaum, 1978; Ben-Zvi et al., 1986) that Ss hold macroscopic notions of the atom and assume that a single atom has the properties of the substance, i.e., expands, is malleable, etc. According to Herron (1990): "Students manipulate symbols according to memorized rules without connecting the symbols with the macroscopic events and the microscopic models that the symbols represent" (p. 31).

Results obtained from multiple regression analyses show that GALT (formal operational reasoning in the Piagetian sense) explained a significant amount of the variance in student performance on Item 2 ($F = 4.11$; $p < 0.05$) and Item 4 ($F = 4.53$; $p < 0.05$). Comparing Items 5 and 6, it can be observed that both involve the concept of proportionality, based on the algebraic and figural formats, respectively. In Item 5 none of the predictor variables explained a significant amount of the variance. However, in Item 6, based on the figural format students perceived the difficulty of the problem primarily due to the field effect (GEFT, disembedding ability), which explained 10% of the variance ($F = 8.93$; $p < 0.005$). In both items requiring 'conceptual understanding' the information processing demand (M-demand, cf. Niaz, 1988, 1989a) of the problems appear to be an important constraint as the FIT explained 7.6% ($F = 6.57$; $p < 0.05$) of the variance in Item 7 and 4.8% ($F = 4.11$; $p < 0.05$) in Item 8. A further regression analysis was conducted by including performance on Item 7 along with cognitive predictor variables (GALT, FIT, and GEFT) as an independent variable, whereas performance on Item 8 remained as the dependent variable. It was observed that performance on Item 7 entered first into the regression equation, explaining 10.8% of the variance ($F = 9.69$; $p < 0.01$), followed by FIT (2.3%), GEFT (0.5%), and GALT (0.3%). This is quite consistent, as it shows that those who perform well on one conceptual item (Item 7) also perform well on the other conceptual item (Item 8). Similarly, regression analyses were performed by including performance on Items 1, 2, and 5 as independent variables (along with the cognitive variables), whereas performance on Item 8 remained as the dependent variable. It was observed that in all three analyses, the FIT explained a significant amount of the variance (5.6%; $F = 4.71$; $p < 0.05$), whereas none of the items based on the 'algorithmic mode' (1, 2, and 5) explained a significant amount of the variance on the conceptual Item 8.

Results obtained in this study provide support for the two distinct approaches to solving problems based on the behavior of gases, viz., the 'algorithmic mode' and problems requiring 'conceptual understanding'. Similar results have also been reported in the literature. Furthermore, the finding that the ability to solve quantitative problems (manipulation of variables in the equation, $PV = nRT$) is not the major factor in predicting success in solving qualitative problems based on 'conceptual understanding', poses a major dilemma for science educators. For example, Sawrey (1990) considers that, this research issue, "... cuts to the core of our ideas about teaching freshman chemistry" (p. 253). What makes this problem more difficult is the fact that this has been an, "... unquestioned axiom of freshman chemistry teaching for the last 30 years" (Pickering, 1990, p. 254).

According to Gabel et al. (1984): "One way of helping students overcome this 'algorithmic mode' is to make certain that students understand the chemical concepts qualitatively before they are presented quantitatively" (p. 232). In the case of gases this strategy could represent considerable difficulty for the students. Furthermore, according to De Berg (1989), history of science receives only scant treatment in most text books and "Generally, the presentation of gas properties follows the sequence of qualitative to quantitative and verbal to algebraic mathematical" (p. 131). This sequence coincides with the strategy suggested by Gabel et al. (1984). More recently, De Berg (1992) has presented a historical profile of the pressure-volume law and its use in the classroom, which constitutes one way of introducing history of science.

## 7.6. STUDY 2: PROGRESSIVE TRANSITIONS FROM ALGORITHMIC TO CONCEPTUAL UNDERSTANDING

The main objective of this section is to construct models based on strategies students use to solve the gas problems and to show that these models form sequences of progressive transitions similar to what Lakatos (1970) in the history of science refers to as progressive 'problemshifts' (cf. GL1, chap. 3). Guideline GL1, suggests a rational reconstruction of students understanding of gases based on progressive transitions from the 'algorithmic mode' (work of Boyle and others in the 17th century) to 'conceptual understanding' (work of Maxwell and Boltzmann in the 19th century). Results reported here are adapted from Niaz (1995a).

Sixty freshman students enrolled in Chemistry I at the Universidad de Oriente, Venezuela were asked to solve the following problems, which formed part of a monthly exam. Students were encouraged and given credit for providing justification for their answers.

*Item A*

A certain amount of gas occupies a volume ($V_1$) at a pressure of 0.60 atm. If the temperature is maintained constant and the pressure is decreased to 0.20 atm, the new volume ($V_2$) of the gas would be:

a) $V_2 = V_1/6$     b) $V_2 = 0.33 \, V_1$
c) $V_2 = V_1/3$     d) $V_2 = 3 \, V_1$

*Item B*

An ideal gas at a pressure of 650 mmHg occupied a bulb of unknown volume. A certain amount of the gas was withdrawn and found to occupy 1.52 mL at 1 atm pressure. The pressure of the gas remaining in the bulb was 600 mmHg. Assuming that all measurements were made at the same temperature, calculate the volume of the bulb.

Item B was adapted from Mahan (1968) and requires conceptual understanding, whereas Item A was adapted from Niaz (1989b) and requires an algorithmic strategy. Results obtained show that 52 (87%) students solved the algorithmic Item A correctly, whereas only 4 (7%) solved the conceptual Item B correctly. All 4 students who solved the conceptual Item B correctly also solved the algorithmic Item A. The 13 students who got partial credit for Item B, correctly identified the final pressure (1 atm) and the final volume (1.52 mL). These students, however, could not conceptualize the initial pressure to be 50 mmHg, and instead used either 600 mmHg or 650 mmHg. This lack of conceptualization clearly shows, how Ss simply memorize the scientific laws (Boyle's law in this case) and the corresponding mathematical equation and look for values to plug in. This is particularly true of another group of 16 students who got no credit as they could correctly identify only the final volume (1.52 mL) and used 650 mmHg as the initial pressure and 600 mmHg as the final pressure. Apparently, these students had even more difficulty in conceptualizing that 650 mmHg was the initial pressure of the gas in the bulb but not the pressure of the gas that was withdrawn. Furthermore, these students could not conceptualize that 600 mmHg was the pressure of the gas that remained in the bulb, whereas the gas that was withdrawn had a pressure of 1 atm. Given the close relationship between the basic skills (Boyle's law) required to solve both Items A and B, it is surprising that out of the 52 Ss who solved the algorithmic Item A, only 4 could solve the conceptual Item B. This result coincides with that in Study 1 and provides an opportunity to reflect over the usefulness of spending much class time over such algorithmic problems. Based on strategies used in solving Items A and B it is plausible to suggest that students go through the following process of progressive transitions.

## Progressive Transitions (Models) Leading to Greater Conceptual Understanding of Gases

Model 1: Strategies used to solve Item A correctly, that is, ability to manipulate the three variables of the Boyle's law equation ($P_1V_1 = P_2V_2$) to calculate the fourth (N = 52).

Model 2: Strategies used to correctly identify the final volume in Item B, that is, partial conceptualization of the property of a gas when it is withdrawn from a vessel (N = 16).

Model 3: Strategies used to correctly identify and conceptualize two properties of a gas (final volume and pressure in Item B), when it is withdrawn from a vessel (N = 13).

Model 4: Strategies used to correctly identify and conceptualize all the variables of a gas (Item B) when it is withdrawn from a vessel (N = 4).

## 7.7. STUDY 3: GASES AS LATTICES: TAKING A CUE FROM THE HISTORY OF SCIENCE

The main objective of this study was to establish a relationship between students' understanding of gases and its parallels in the history of science (cf. GL6, chap. 3). Guideline GL6, suggests that students' alternative conceptions be considered not as mistakes but as alternative theories that compete with the scientific theories. Results reported here are adapted from Niaz (2000a). Fifty-nine freshman students enrolled in Chemistry I at the Universidad de Oriente, Venezuela were asked to solve Item 8 of Study 1 (reported above). In contrast to the previous study, Item 8 (as part of a monthly exam) was given to the students about a month after they had seen the kinetic theory of gases. Treatment of the kinetic theory involved simple mathematics as presented in Mahan and Myers (1990). However, conceptual problems of the sort represented by Item 8 (Study 1) were not treated during the course. Students were encouraged to explain and justify their answers in writing. It was explained to the students that hydrogen is still a gas at -20°C. Students' responses showed the following distribution: a = 10, b = 22, c = 11, d = 9, and those who did not respond = 7. It is important to mention that of the 10 students who selected the correct response (a) only three provided an adequate justification. Apparently, the most convincing answer was response (b). In what follows, some of the explanations (quite representative) of students who selected responses (b) and (c) are presented.

## Explanations of Students who Selected Response (b)

Student 1

"We know that V is proportional to T. If the temperature decreases the volume occupied by the hydrogen molecules would decrease, as the kinetic energy would decrease. Consequently, the gas would start to condense slowly, that is, the force of attraction between the molecules would increase, leading to a decrease in volume occupied. Although response (c) [cf. Figure 3] also shows a decrease in volume, there is no reason to believe that the molecules of the gas would deposit in the lower part of the vessel, as hydrogen is still a gas."

Student 2

"As the temperature decreases the volume occupied by the hydrogen molecules would also decrease. Molecules would have less movement and hence a greater force of attraction among themselves, which if increased sufficiently would characterize the gaseous phase."

Student 3

"At the lower temperature the molecules of hydrogen gas unite among themselves."

Student 4

"Gases tend to expand when the temperature increases. So the contrary should happen when the temperature decreases."

Student 5

"As the temperature decreases, molecules of hydrogen shrink."

Student 6

"As the temperature decreases, the pressure exerted by the gas decreases. Consequently, there is less movement among the molecules and the collisions decrease."

Student 7

"As the temperature decreases, the hydrogen molecules are found closer to one another, and hence occupy less volume."

# Explanations of Students who Selected Response (c)

Student 8
>  "A decrease in temperature leads to a decrease in the movement of the molecules, and hence they settle in the bottom of the vessel."

Student 9
>  "As the temperature decreases the molecules stop colliding with each other and come to rest in the bottom of the vessel."

Student 10
>  "On decreasing the temperature, the molecules tend to form groups in the bottom of the vessel."

Student 11
>  "A decrease in temperature leads to a decrease in pressure of the gas."

It is important to note that students were given explicit instructions to the fact that hydrogen at -20°C is still a gas. Interestingly, 56% selected responses (b) and (c). These results are all the more significant as these students had already been exposed to an elementary version of the kinetic theory of gases. A closer look at some of the explanations helps to unfold the complexity of the issues involved. Explanations of students who selected response (b) or (c) provide clues, which suggests the following sequence in conceptualization:

Step 1: decrease in temperature.
Step 2: less movement of the gas molecules.
Step 3: greater force of attraction among the gas molecules.
Step 4: less chaos and more order among the gas molecules.
Step 5: gas molecules occupy less volume.
Step 6: formation of lattices, reminiscent of a neglected episode in the history of chemistry (cf. Mendoza, 1990).

Step 3 is crucial, as students seem to be reasoning that a decrease in movement of the molecules leads to an increase in the force of attraction (students 1 and 2 refer to it explicitly), whereas the correct conclusion should have been a decrease in the kinetic energy of the gas molecules. It is plausible to suggest that students may be thinking (in spite of having seen the kinetic theory of gases in class) in terms of the Lattice theory of gases, which stated: "... whereas the forces between atoms in solids were attractive, in gases they became repulsive and this gave rise to the pressure on the walls of a containing vessel" (Mendoza, 1990, p. 1040). Furthermore, all students who selected responses (b) and (c) seem to be contributing to the idea that gas molecules do not occupy all the space available in a vessel. At this stage it is important to mention that the sequence of 6 steps presented above is a rational reconstruction of students conceptualization of the behavior of gases.

## 7.8. METHODOLOGY FOR TEACHING THE BEHAVIOR OF GASES IN THE CLASSROOM

Conceptual framework (as presented above) provided by the history and philosophy science suggests that it could be helpful for science teachers to take the following into consideration:

1. A good starting point can be the presentation of experimental results based on the variation of pressure and volume of a sample of air at constant temperature, quite similar to Boyle's 1662 data. Among other text books, Masterton et al. (1985) provide such data. A similar approach can be adopted for other gas laws. This suggestion is based partly on Matthews' (1987) recommendation: "... let children be good Aristotelians before trying to develop them as modern scientists" (p. 294). Exploration phase of the Karplus learning cycle will also endorse a similar strategy (Lawson, et al. 1989).

2. The presentation of quantitative data can be followed by verbal statements of the gas laws, which in turn can be followed by algebraic statements, such as PV = constant. Plotting of P against V or 1/V can be the next step. The important point is that manipulation of the variables is relatively easy, whereas the significance of PV = constant is fairly complex and abstract and even eluded Boyle.

3. Manipulation of the different variables of the ideal gas equation (PV = nRT) as presented in Items 1, 2, 3, 4, 5, and 6 of Study 1 (this chapter, presented above). The ability to manipulate observable variables is important, and most text books emphasize this aspect of the gases. Nevertheless, teachers must be aware that there is little correlation between the resolution of quantitative problems and conceptual understanding of gaseous behavior (cf. results presented in Study 1, this chapter).

4. History of science shows that starting from the early work of Boyle in 1660, it required the work of various scientists that finally led after almost 200 years towards a conceptual framework of the behavior of gases, based on the Maxwell-Boltzmann kinetic theory of gases (1860). Maxwell's basic assumptions (presented above) are a good introduction for the students to understand the complexity of gas behavior. According to Hanson (1970) before the kinetic theory of gases, all quantitative measurements represented, "... the dots without the pattern, the observations without the theory, the descriptions without the explanations" (p. 237).

5. Derivation of the ideal gas equation based on a simple mathematical treatment of the kinetic-molecular theory of gases (cf. Holtzclaw & Robinson, 1988) or a more rigorous treatment (Mahan & Myers, 1990), depending on the mathematical background of the students. At this stage, it is important that students be provided an insight into the rationale for the origin of the kinetic theory, through qualitative problems, such as Items 7 and 8 (Study 1, this chapter), and Item B (Study 2, this chapter).

6. Given the commonality between psychogenesis and the history of science (cf. chap. 2), and the evidence provided in this chapter, it is suggested that solving gas problems based on the 'algorithmic mode' before those based on 'conceptual gestalt' would be more conducive to understanding the behavior of gases, that is, quantitative precedes the qualitative (Niaz, 1994e). 'Conceptual understanding' in the educational context would refer primarily to Maxwell's assumptions, which are basically qualitative

(speculative if you prefer) and a simple derivation of the ideal gas equation based on the kinetic-molecular theory. On the other hand, the 'algorithmic mode' would refer to the quantitative manipulation of the variables in the ideal gas equation.

7. It is plausible to suggest that based on the students' alternative conceptions (Study 3, this chapter), they hold to a core belief, viz., gas in a vessel may not occupy all the space available to it.


## 7.9. CONCLUSION

This chapter shows how our present conceptualization of gases based on the kinetic theory has developed through a very slow and difficult process, that started almost three hundred years ago with the work of Boyle around 1660. The transition from the 'algorithmic mode' of solving quantitative gas problems to the qualitative mode of 'conceptual understanding' is a major obstacle for the students. Lack of 'conceptual understanding' represents a collection of a large number of experimental facts that resemble 'dots without the pattern' (Hanson, 1958). Students' understanding of gases is facilitated by the construction of models that represent progressive transitions, as they start to make sense of the 'dots.' During the construction of the new conceptualization students' previous ideas (alternative conceptions) compete with the scientific theories (kinetic theory) and some of the alternative conceptions referred to as 'core beliefs' are more resistant to change. An example of the core belief is the idea that gas in a vessel may not occupy all the space available to it.

# Chapter 8

# Understanding Heat Energy and Temperature: How Students Resist Conceptual Change from Caloric to Kinetic Theory?

Differentiation between heat energy and temperature has been the subject of considerable interest and a series of studies have shown that a majority of 4- to 18-year-olds do not understand the difference (Eylon & Linn, 1988). Many studies have shown that children aged 11 to 16 construed heat to be a substance which could be added to or removed from an object very similar to the caloric theory of heat held by scientists in the 18th and the 19th century. The caloric theory considered heat to be a substance that can be added to or subtracted and might have a mass. The history of the development of heat is intertwined with that of the kinetic theory: The proponents of the caloric theory of heat were also in many cases atomists, but they attributed the expansive force of a gas to the repulsion of its atoms rather than to their free motion.

Kesidou and Duit (1993) have reported a series of alternative conceptions in students understanding of heat energy and temperature. Cowan and Sutcliffe (1991) have reported that students' (9-12 year-olds) understanding of heat as a substance is not consistent over varying situations. Students found the task much easier when asked to predict the temperature if water is poured from a can into different glasses (division) as compared to the inverse procedure (combination). This finding raises important theoretical questions, as it is difficult to explain children's misconceptions of temperature in terms of underlying theories as has been done in other physical science domains.

The main objective of this chapter is to investigate whether students' understanding of heat energy and temperature forms part of a 'hard-core' (Lakatos, 1970; Chinn & Brewer, 1993) of epistemological beliefs and the degree to which it affects their ability to learn thermodynamics in the classroom. The hard-core of a research program, consists of basic assumptions considered 'irrefutable' by the methodological decision of its protagonists, and does not allow refutation to be directed at this hard-core.

# 8.1. STUDENTS' UNDERSTANDING
## OF HEAT ENERGY AND TEMPERATURE
.

In this section we report results (adapted from Niaz, 2000b) of the application of a pencil-and-paper test based on the following three items designed to evaluate freshmen students' understanding of heat energy and temperature (Test of Heat Energy and Temperature, THT).

*Item 1*
We have two glasses of exactly the same volume and full of water, and both are at a temperature of $40^{\circ}C$ (see Figure 4). The contents of both glasses are transferred to a vessel. It is assumed that the temperature of water in both glasses remained constant during the transfer. It can be concluded that the temperature of water in the vessel is:

a)  $80^{\circ}C$
b)  $40^{\circ}C$
c)  Between $40^{\circ}C - 80^{\circ}C$
d)  Less than $40^{\circ}C$
e)  Greater than $80^{\circ}C$

(Justify your response)

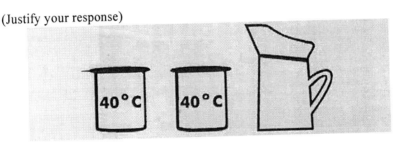

Figure 4.

*Item 2*
Two glasses full of water at a temperature of $20^{\circ}C$ are mixed in a vessel with another two glasses full of water at a temperature of $80^{\circ}C$. All four glasses had the same volume of water. After mixing the temperature of water in the vessel is $50^{\circ}C$. Now, instead if we had mixed one glass full of water at a temperature of $20^{\circ}C$ with another glass full of water at a temperature of $80^{\circ}C$, the temperature of water in the vessel would have been:

a)  Greater than $50^{\circ}C$
b)  Less than $50^{\circ}C$
c)  $50^{\circ}C$

See Figure 5 (Justify your response)

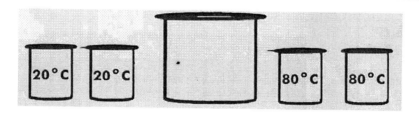

Figure 5.

*Item 3*

We have a vessel A with 2 liters of water and a vessel B with 1 liter of water. Both vessels are placed on exactly the same burners and the water in both vessels is heated till it starts boiling (100°C). It can be concluded that:

a) Water in both vessels received the same amount of heat.
b) Water in vessel A received more heat.
c) Water in vessel B received more heat.

See Figure 6 (Justify your response)

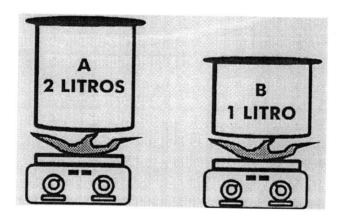

Figure 6.

All three items were adapted from Wiser (1988). Students were tested in groups of about 25 in intact classrooms and were encouraged to justify their answers. Given that enough exploratory work has been done on this topic we consider the use of a group-format paper-and-pencil test appropriate for this study (cf. Shayer & Wylam, 1981). The test was administered about a month before the topic of thermodynamics was taught. Before thermodynamics the course includes the following topics: electrochemistry, gas phase chemical equilibrium, and ionic equilibrium. Although instruction was imparted by the traditional expository method, all four teachers encouraged students to ask questions and were frequently called to the chalk-board to solve problems. The study is based on 99 science major students enrolled in four sections of Chemistry II at the Universidad de Oriente, Venezuela (mean age = 20.5 years; SD = 1.9; female = 44, male = 55). Students were also asked to indicate their career choice, which gave the following distribution: chemistry = 38, physics = 12, mathematics = 25, and engineering = 24.

## Results and Discussion Based on Item 1

Table 2 shows that 83% of the students selected the correct response (b) with an adequate justification. This shows that most of the students understood that the temperature of water (an intensive property) in the vessel is independent of the number of glasses used to transfer heat energy (an extensive property).

**Table 2. Students' responses on the Test of Heat Energy
and Temperature, THT (N = 99)**

| | Number of students with responses on Items | | |
|---|---|---|---|
| Response | 1 | 2 | 3 |
| a | 4 | 17 | 30 |
| b | 83[*] | 21 | 48[*] |
| c | 4[***] | - | 2[**] |
| c | - | 3[**] | - |
| c | - | 13[***] | - |
| d | 6 | - | - |
| e | - | - | - |

[*]Correct response with adequate justification.
[**]Correct response without justification.
[***]Correct response with incorrect justification (additive strategy).

Responses of those who selected response (a), that is, an increase in temperature was characterized by the following types of reasoning: i) "Temperature would increase as the volume of the vessel is greater. As we increase volume, temperature increases"; (ii) "As each glass has a temperature of 40°C, after transferring the contents of the two glasses into the vessel, the temperature would double, i.e., 80°C". Reasoning (i) perhaps represents the application of the kinetic theory of gases, which formed part of the Chemistry I program in the previous semester. Reasoning (ii) represents a thinking quite similar to the caloric theory of heat. Responses of those who selected the correct response (b) with an incorrect justification was characterized by the following type of reasoning: "It is an average of the two temperatures, i.e., 40°C + 40°C = 80°C/2 = 40°C (total temperature)". Although the numerical answer is correct the reasoning is based on an *additive strategy*, in the sense that temperature could be added like heat.

Interestingly, history of science shows that some scientists reasoned in a similar fashion during the 19th century. John Herapath (1790-1868), who is considered to be the first important kinetic theorist (see chap. 7) in the 19th century had an argument with conventional theorists who believed that: "If one mixes, for example, equal portions of water at 32° and 212° on the Fahrenheit scale ... the temperature of the mixture by conventional theory would be ½ (32 + 212) = 122°F" (Brush, 1976, pp. 111-112). According to thermodynamics, the temperature of the mixture will depend on the specific heats of the liquids, and the *additive strategy*, of course would work only if we mix the same quantities of the same liquid. Responses of those who selected response (c) were characterized by the following type of reasoning: "In the vessel water has the possibility of more movement, it absorbs heat, which leads to an increase in temperature." Once again it shows the incorrect analogy between the kinetic theory of gases and the present situation. Responses of those who selected response (d) was characterized by the following type of reasoning: "Volume available to water in the vessel is greater, hence the temperature must be less than 40°C." Interestingly, students could reason for an increase in temperature (responses a and c) or a decrease (response d) with considerable ease and apparently no cognitive conflict.

## Results and Discussion Based on Item 2

As compared to Item 1, performance of the students on Item 2 (correct response c, 45%) decreases considerably (see Table 2). It is important to note that the 83 students who responded correctly on Item 1 had the following response distribution on Item 2: response a = 15, b = 16, $c^*$ (correct) = 42, $c^{***}$ (additive strategy) = 8, and $c^{**}$ (without justification) = 2. How do we explain the finding that 41(49%) students did understand in Item 1 that the temperature in the vessel did not depend on the number of glasses of water poured into it and still responded incorrectly on Item 2? What is even more significant is the fact that 8 of these students explicitly used the *additive strategy* mentioned above, quite similar to the caloric theory of heat. One of these 8 students used the following additive strategy:

"First case:   T1 = 20°C, T2 = 20°C, Total = 40°C, Mean1 = 20°C
               T3 = 80°C, T4 = 80°C, Total = 160°C, Mean2 = 80°C
               Total mean = 20 + 80/2 = 50°C.
Second case: Total mean = 20 + 80/2 = 50°C."

This shows the attractiveness and the latent power of the additive strategy and shows once again the importance of the ontogeny/phylogeny hypothesis (see chap. 2. Also Niaz, 1995b; Strauss, 1988; Vosniadou & Brewer, 1987). Furthermore, it is important to note that these were college students on the threshold of their careers and considered the test seriously and took lot of pains to justify their responses. Consistency of the results can be observed from the fact that out of the 45 students who responded to Item 2 correctly, 42 had previously responded correctly to Item 1.

Following are two examples of the reasoning used by those who responded correctly to Item 2: i) "You may add n number of glasses at 20°C and the same number at 80°C, the final temperature will always be the same. The number of glasses will have no effect on the final temperature." ii) "As we are mixing water at two different temperatures in the same proportion, the final temperature will be the same". Responses of those (n=17) who selected response (a) on Item 2 was characterized by the following types of reasoning: i) "In the first case there are more liters of water and for this reason the temperature decreases more. In comparison, in the second case there are less liters of water." ii) "As the volume of water is lesser, the temperature would be greater." Responses of those (n=21) who selected response (b) on Item 2 was characterized by the following types of reasoning: i) "First we mixed two glasses of water for each of the two temperatures and the final temperature was 50°C. Now if we mix one glass for each of the two temperatures, the final temperature would be 25°C." ii) "The final temperature would decrease because we are adding half of the initial temperatures." These two types of reasoning clearly show a conceptualization quite similar to that of the caloric theory of heat in the 18th and 19th centuries, according to which heat is a substance that can be added or subtracted.

## Results and Discussion Based on Item 3

Once again performance on Item 3 (correct response b, 48%) decreases considerably as compared to Item 1 and is quite similar to that of Item 2 (see Table 2). Interestingly, out of the 83 who responded correctly on Item 1, 42 (51%) responded correctly on Item 2 and these 42 had the following response distribution on Item 3: response a = 10, b[*] (correct) = 24, and c = 8. How do we explain the finding that even after having responded correctly on Items 1 and 2, 43% (18 out of 42) of the students still responded incorrectly on Item 3? What is even more significant is the fact that the incorrect responses (a and c) show a lack of differentiation between heat and temperature that approximates the caloric theory of heat. For example, those who selected response (a) reasoned: "As both vessels reached 100°C, they must have received the same amount of heat" and those who selected response (c) reasoned: "This vessel contains a lesser volume of water, boils sooner and hence received more heat." Table 1 also shows that for the total sample of students, response (a) was selected by 30% and response (c) by 19%, which shows the degree to which these propositions were plausible for the students.

## 8.2. ABILITY TO DIFFERENTIATE BETWEEN HEAT ENERGY AND TEMPERATURE AND ITS RELATIONSHIP TO PROBLEM SOLVING ABILITY IN THERMODYNAMICS

In this section we explore the relationship between ability to differentiate between heat energy and temperature (reported in the previous section) and its relationship to student performance on a problem drawn from thermodynamics, which formed part of a semester exam of the Chemistry II program. Results reported in this section (n = 31) are based on two (selected randomly) of the four sections of Chemistry II students that responded to the test of heat energy and temperature (THT). Thermodynamics is the last topic of the program and many of the students at this stage of the semester withdraw due to poor performance, which explains the smaller number of as compared to those who presented the THT. However, it is important to point out that these represented better than average students.

Given the importance of domain-specific restructuring (see chap. 2) it is plausible to hypothesize that those who differentiate between heat energy and temperature should have a better chance of solving problems of thermodynamics. However, it is difficult to select a problem from the instructional context that would correspond closely to the differentiation between heat energy and temperature. Furthermore, we wanted to evaluate students in an intact classroom, on a problem that forms part of their course content. The following problem (adapted from Oxtoby, Nachtrieb & Freeman, 1990) was considered to require an understanding of the difference between heat energy and temperature to a fair extent and was accepted by the teachers of the two sections as such:

## Thermodynamics (Thermochemistry) Problem (TP)

A piece of metal having a mass of 61 g and at a temperature of 120°C was introduced in 100 g of water at a temperature of 20°C. The metal cools and the water warms up till both have a common temperature of 26°C, assuming no heat loss to the surroundings. If the specific heat capacity of water is 4.18 J/g K calculate the specific heat capacity of the metal.

## Dimensional Analysis

In order to understand the conceptual and epistemological basis of performance, a dimensional analysis (a type of task analysis) based on student responses was conducted according to Pascual-Leone's theory of constructive operators (Pascual-Leone, 1978, 1987). According to Pascual-Leone, informational dimensions appear in the subject's more or less conscious mental examination of the problem and anticipation of its solution. In this examination subjects often begin by recalling the idealized objects or scientific general facts that inform the problem in question, inform in the sense that the problem is a particular case or concretization of the idealized objects or principles. This is what Pascual-Leone calls a *general figurative model*. The second step of the subject's dimensional analysis often involves concretization or specification, that is, adaptation of the general figurative model so that it more closely reflects the concrete solution of the actual problem. This is what Pascual-Leone calls a *specific figurative model*. The remaining steps of the subject's execution of the problem represent an application to the specific figurative model of 'operative transformations', that is, operations needed to obtain the results and prescribed by the subject's *general and specific operative models*, according to the problem domain in question. Dimensional analyses based on the epistemological principles outlined above have been conducted in science education and complete details are available in the literature (Niaz, 1987, 1988, 1989b; Niaz & Robinson, 1992b, Tsaparlis, 1998).

## Dimensional Analysis of the Thermodynamics Problem (TP)

Based on the methodology outlined above, it is postulated that students who solved this problem went through the process of building the following models:

1.  General Figurative model (GFM)
    Hypothesize: $q(H_2O) + q(metal) = 0$, where
    $q(H_2O) =$ Heat gained by water, $q(metal) =$ heat lost by metal.
2.  Specific Figurative Models (SFM)
    $q(H_2O) = g\ C_p(H_2O)\ (T_f - T_i)$ and
    $q(metal) = g\ C_p(metal)\ (T_f - T_i)$ where
    $g =$ grams, $C_p =$ specific heat capacity, $T_f =$ final temperature, $T_i =$ initial temperature.
3.  General operative models (GOM)
    a)  Identification of the common temperature as the final temperature for both the water and metal.
    b)  Identification of the initial temperature of water.

    c) Identification of the initial temperature of metal.

4. Specific operative models (SOM)

Calculation of the specific heat capacity of metal, by using the GFM and SFM, given all the necessary data.

Following scoring procedure was used to evaluate responses on a scale of 0-10: GFM = 4 points, SFM = 2 points, GOM = 3 points and SOM = 1 point. Based on this scoring procedure only a score of 5 or more would indicate conceptual understanding.


## Results and Discussion

Table 3 shows the relationship between performance on the test of heat energy and temperature (THT) and score on the thermodynamics problem (TP). It can be observed that of the 6 students who responded correctly on Items 1, 2 & 3 of THT, 2 obtained the maximum score of 10 on the TP. In contrast, of the 10 students who responded correctly on Item 1 of THT, 3 obtained the maximum score on the TP. Similarly, of the 4 students who responded correctly on Item 3 of THT, 2 obtained the maximum score of 10 on the TP.

Results become even clearer if we divide the students into two groups on the basis of their performance on the THT. Those who solved at least two or more items correctly on THT were classified as above average and those who responded correctly to only one or none of the items on the THT were classified as below average. Mean scores of the above and below average students were computed for the thermodynamics problem (TP), and found to be 3.27 (SD = 2.86) and 5.06 (SD = 4.25), respectively. Although the below average students scored higher on the thermodynamics (TP) problem the difference was statistically not significant (t = 1.32, ns). How do we interpret these results? It appears that students who have a fairly good understanding of the difference between heat energy and temperature do not necessarily perform better on a problem of thermodynamics which formed part of their instructional context. On the contrary, students who had a poor understanding of the difference between heat energy and temperature did fairly well on the TP.

These results show that there is very little relationship between the ability to differentiate between heat energy and temperature and performance on a problem of thermodynamics. Actually, performance in the science classroom is complex and nobody would expect a simple relationship between domain-specific knowledge and performance. Nevertheless, a study helps to explicate issues. Based on a teaching strategy that articulated both the caloric and the kinetic theories during class (as alternative viewpoints of heat), Rogan (1988) found that students (15 year olds) with higher formal reasoning ability (Inhelder & Piaget, 1958) were more adept at making the conceptual shift from the caloric to the kinetic theory of heat. The crux of the issue can be summarized in the following terms: "Switching to the kinetic theory would undoubtedly involve a complete conceptual reorganization" (Wiser, 1988, p. 48). It appears that even those students who performed above average on the test of heat energy and temperature, perhaps have not made a conceptual shift in their 'core epistemological beliefs' (cf. 'hard-core' of beliefs, Lakatos, 1970). In this context Ausubel's advice (as advocated by Novak, 1977), 'Find out what they know and teach them accordingly' is of little help to the science teacher.

**Table 3. Relationship between students' performance on the Test of Heat Energy and Temperature (THT) and their score on the Thermodynamics Problem, TP (N = 31)**

| Performance on THT | Number of students with score[*] on TP | | | | | | |
|---|---|---|---|---|---|---|---|
| | 0 | 2 | 3 | 4 | 7 | 8 | 10 |
| Items 1, 2 & 3 correct (N=6) | 1 | 2 | 1 | - | - | - | 2 |
| Items 1 & 2 correct (N=6) | 1 | 3 | 1 | 1 | - | - | - |
| Items 1 & 3 correct (N=3) | - | 1 | 1 | 1 | - | - | - |
| Items 2 & 3 correct (N=0) | - | - | - | - | - | - | - |
| Item 1 correct (N=10) | 2 | 1 | 1 | - | 1 | 2 | 3 |
| Item 2 correct (N=0) | - | - | - | - | - | - | - |
| Item 3 correct (N=4) | 1 | - | 1 | - | - | - | 2 |
| None correct | 2 | - | - | - | - | - | - |

[*]Performance was evaluated by dimensional analysis (see text) on a scale of 0-10 points.

An observation by Carey and Smith (1993) provides food for thought and is more sobering: "Although many have speculated that students' epistemological beliefs interfere with successful learning of science and mathematics, there is little empirical evidence on this point. We know of no studies, for example, that show that changes in students' epistemological views affect their success in learning content" (p. 247).

## Can the Study of Thermochemistry Facilitate Students' Differentiation between Heat Energy and Temperature?

At this stage readers must be wondering as to the possibility of evaluating students' understanding of heat energy and temperature after having studied thermodynamics (especially the topic of thermochemistry). In order to pursue this question, a follow-up study (similar to the one reported earlier in this chapter), was designed. This study is based on 76 students who had registered for Chemistry II, at the same university as the previous study and with similar academic and socio-economic background. The Test of Heat Energy and Temperature (THT) and the Thermodynamics Problem (TP), same as in the previous study, were applied after the students had finished the topic of thermochemistry. Results obtained (adapted from Niaz, 2006) show that even after having studied thermochemistry, students have considerable difficulty in differentiating between heat energy and temperature. In the follow-up study, student performance decreased (84% to 72%) on Item 1 of THT. On Item 2, there was an increase (45% to 64%) and similarly on Item 3 there was an increase (48% to 51%). Furthermore, it was found that students who had a good conceptual understanding on the Thermodynamics Problem (TP) did not perform significantly better on the THT, as compared to those who did not have conceptual understanding of TP. Overall, the results of the two studies are quite similar and hence a cause for concern. It appears, that teaching of thermochemistry also requires rethinking in order to facilitate conceptual understanding and not simple manipulation of algorithms.

## 8.3. CONCLUSIONS: HOW STUDENTS RESIST CONCEPTUAL CHANGE FROM CALORIC TO KINETIC THEORY

Students' understanding of heat energy and temperature varies considerably from one context to another. Even after having responded correctly in a context that approximates the kinetic view of heat energy students fall back on the caloric theory in a different context. For example, in the first study 83 of the 99 students responded correctly on Item 1 (see above) which requires an understanding of the kinetic view of heat energy. However, on Item 2, of the 83 students who responded correctly on Item 1, 41 responded incorrectly and at least 8 switched to the caloric theory. Results from Item 3 are even more revealing. Of the 42 students who had responded correctly on both Items 1 and 2, 18 responded incorrectly with a reasoning quite similar to that of the caloric theory. For the total sample, the number of responses based on the caloric theory increased from 8 on Item 1 to 21 on Item 2 and 49 on Item 3. Results from the follow-up study are quite similar. These results raise fundamental theoretical issues with respect to consistency of the underlying epistemological beliefs that students bring to the classroom. According to Wiser (1988): "There is no reason for students who are taught the kinetic theory to ever develop the caloric theory" (p. 47). In the light of this observation results here are even more problematic. Students in this study had been exposed to the kinetic theory in the previous semester, and yet some of them had no problem in consistently using the caloric theory, while others switched between the two conceptualizations.

This shows that students resist the conceptual shift beyond the caloric theory, which perhaps forms part of the 'hard-core' (Lakatos, 1970; also GL4, chap. 3) of students' epistemological beliefs. Guideline GL4, suggests that just as the scientists resist changes in their hard core of beliefs, similarly students offer more resistance to changes in their core beliefs. Taking a cue from the history of science it is interesting to reflect on Einstein's observation: "The most fundamental concepts in the description of heat phenomena are *temperature* and *heat*. It took an unbelievably long time in the history of science for these two to be distinguished, but once this distinction was made rapid progress resulted" (Einstein & Infeld, 1971, p. 36). Similarly, Brush (1976) has emphasized that, " The kinetic theory could not flourish until heat as a substance had been replaced by heat as atomic motion" (p. 8). A study by Lewis and Linn (1994) shows that even some of the experts (Ph.D. in physics/chemistry) had difficulty in explaining the difference between heat energy and temperature, as one of the experts stated: "... although he uses a kinetic model in class, he now realizes that he has simply been 'parroting ideas' he was taught and he doesn't think about these phenomena [cooling of silver and pottery platters] in terms of kinetic theory" (p. 668). The rivalry between the caloric and the kinetic theory has played an important part in the history of science (cf. Psillos, 1994, for a recent appraisal) and a detailed account goes beyond the scope of this article.

Based on the results obtained in this study and a review of the literature, it is plausible to suggest that an epistemological belief in the caloric theory of heat forms part of the hard-core of students' framework and that the conceptual shift to the kinetic theory requires radical restructuring. Just as the hard-core of a research program is 'irrefutable' by the methodological decision of its protagonists, the hard-core of students' beliefs also resists changes. Nevertheless, according to Lakatos (1970) when a program ceases to anticipate novel facts it will have to be abandoned and, "... may crumble under certain conditions" (p. 134). Consequently, the question teachers need to ask is not only what are the students' prior epistemological beliefs, but as to what are the 'conditions' under which the hard-core could 'crumble'. Chinn and Brewer (1993) have presented a detailed analysis and shown that a change in hard-core (conceptual shift) may be preceded by a series of strategies in which students treat anomalous data by: ignoring, rejecting, excluding, holding it in abeyance, reinterpreting, peripheral change, and finally theory change.

More recently, Niaz (1995a) has shown that the difference between student performance on algorithmic and conceptual problems can be interpreted as a process of progressive transitions (models) that facilitate different degrees of explanatory/heuristic power to student conceptual shifts. Although hard-core beliefs are resistant to change, they develop slowly by a long preliminary and any change perhaps will also follow a similar process.

This chapter illustrates that although students may have a series of alternative conceptions of heat energy and temperature, it is useful to differentiate between 'hard core' and 'soft core' of students' beliefs. This opens the possibility that all alternative conceptions may not be an obstacle to the same degree (cf. 'anchoring conceptions' of Clement, Brown, & Zietsman, 1989). In the case of heat energy and temperature it is interesting to observe how students fall back on the caloric theory (hard core of beliefs) even after having responded correctly in a context that approximates the kinetic view. Study of the rivalry between the caloric and the kinetic theories in the history of science can provide the science teacher a greater insight for designing teaching strategies.

# Chapter 9

# UNDERSTANDING CHEMICAL EQUILIBRIUM: FACILITATING CONCEPTUAL CHANGE

Chemical equilibrium is considered to be one of the most difficult topics in the general chemistry program (Piquette & Heikkinen, 2005; Quílez-Pardo & Solaz-Portolés, 1995). Various studies have investigated student difficulties in chemical equilibrium, and Camacho and Good (1989) have shown that chemical equilibrium is a "... well-structured, semantically rich, and formal domain for observing problem-solving behaviors" (p. 268). It appears that the nature of 'balanced dynamic equilibrium' requires a clear understanding of how chemical reactions proceed through molecular collisions (Maskill & Cachapuz, 1989). According to Hackling and Garnett (1985) one of the most significant alternative conception students hold is that, "The rate of the forward reaction increases with time from the mixing of the reactants until equilibrium is established" (p. 213), which could perhaps be attributed to the fact that many students fail to discriminate clearly between the characteristics of completion and reversible reactions.

One of the findings of these studies is the clear advantage of successful subjects in having an adequate 'conceptual framework' to guide the solution process and to justify their answers and reasons. Recent research indicates that many students solve chemistry problems using only algorithmic strategies and do not understand the underlying chemical concepts. It appears that for most teachers solving numerical problems, that require algorithmic solution strategies in contrast to conceptual understanding, is a major behavioral objective of freshman chemistry. According to Nurrenbern and Pickering (1987) chemistry teachers have assumed implicitly that the ability to solve quantitative numerical problems is equivalent to conceptual understanding of molecular concepts. Camacho and Good (1989) have found that most textbooks emphasize, "... quantitative aspects of learning at the expense of qualitative reasoning" (p. 269). Niaz (1989a) has emphasized that the use of algorithms may decrease the M-demand (amount of information processing required) of a problem, but it does not necessarily facilitate conceptual understanding. From an epistemological perspective it is important to note that according to Hanson (1958) a physical theory is not pieced together from observed phenomena (empirical data), but rather provides patterns within which data appear intelligible, that is a sort of 'conceptual gestalt' (p. 90), which provides an explanation of the data. It is suggested that successful subjects are not only capable of manipulating the data (i.e., computational problems that require algorithms) but also have a 'conceptual framework' or 'conceptual gestalt' (Hanson, 1958). It is plausible to hypothesize that students who have a 'conceptual framework' and perform better on problems requiring conceptual understanding, should also perform better on problems requiring algorithmic strategies.

The main objectives of this chapter are:

1. Compare the performance of students on problems requiring conceptual understanding or the use of algorithmic solution strategies, that is computational problems. It is predicted that students who perform better on problems requiring conceptual understanding, should also perform better on problems requiring algorithmic solution strategies.
2. To show that students conceptualize the rates of the forward and reverse reactions in chemical equilibrium as forces, perhaps in the same sense as used in the historical evolution of the concept of chemical equilibrium and student alternative conceptions about Newton's third law of motion.
3. Construct a teaching strategy that can facilitate conceptual change in students' understanding of chemical equilibrium.

## 9.1. STUDY 1: FROM ALGORITHMIC TO CONCEPTUAL UNDERSTANDING – QUANTITATIVE PRECEDES THE QUALITATIVE

Seventy eight freshman students enrolled in two sections of Chemistry II for science majors at the Universidad de Oriente (Venezuela) were selected for the study (mean age = 19.5 years; SD = 1.3 years). Results reported here are adapted from Niaz (1995d). All students were administered the following 11 items based on different aspects of chemical equilibrium (Items are presented on the left hand side and the percentage of students with correct response on the right hand side):

| Items | Percentage students with correct response |
|---|---|
| 1. A certain amount of NO(g) and $Cl_2$(g) are introduced in a vessel, whose temperature is maintained constant. After the reaction has started and before the equilibrium is reached, it can be concluded that: | |
| $2NO(g) + Cl_2(g) \leftrightarrow 2NOCl(g)\ (\Delta H < 0)$ | |
| *Item 1a*: Forward reaction rate increases as the reaction gets going. | 22 |
| *Item 1b*: Reverse reaction rate increases as the concentration of the products increases. | 49 |
| *Item 1c*: In the beginning the reverse reaction rate is zero. | 49 |
| *Item 1d*: Reverse reaction rate is the same as the forward reaction rate. | 62 |
| 2. A certain amount of NO(g) and $Cl_2$(g) are introduced in a vessel and the temperature is maintained constant. After the equilibrium is reached, a certain amount of NO(g) is introduced into the vessel. As a consequence it can be concluded that: | |
| $2NO(g) + Cl_2(g) \leftrightarrow 2NOCL(g)\ (\Delta H < 0)$ | |
| *Item 2a:* Reverse reaction rate decreases. | 15 |

| Items | Percentage students with correct response |
|---|---|
| *Item 2b:* Forward reaction rate increases instantaneously. | 60 |
| *Item 2c:* Initially the reverse reaction rate remains constant. | 30 |
| *Item 2d:* Reverse reaction rate increases gradually. | 31 |
| 3. Ammonium carbamate dissociates completely as shown by the reaction: $NH_4CO_2NH_2$ (s) $\leftrightarrow$ $2NH_3(g) + CO_2(g)$ | |
| *Item 3a:* At 25°C the total pressure of the gases in equilibrium with the solid is 0.116 atm. Calculate $K_p$ of the reaction. If 0.1 atm of $CO_2(g)$ is introduced after equilibrium is reached, as a consequence it can be concluded that: | 49 |
| *Item 3b:* Final pressure of $CO_2(g)$ is greater than 0.1 atm. | 5 |
| *Item 3c:* Final pressure of $NH_3(g)$ increases. | 39 |
| 4. A certain amount of NO(g) and $Cl_2(g)$ are introduced in a vessel at a certain temperature: $2NO(g) + Cl_2(g) \leftrightarrow 2NOCl(g)$ ($\Delta H < 0$) After the equilibrium is reached the temperature is increased and as a consequence it can be concluded that: | |
| *Item 4a:* Forward reaction rate decreases. | 3 |
| *Item 4b:* Reverse reaction rate increases. | 63 |
| *Item 4c:* Forward reaction rate increases gradually. | 27 |
| *Item 4d:* When the equilibrium is re-established, the equilibrium constant remains the same. | 27 |
| *Item 4e:* Reverse reaction rate would be greater than the forward reaction rate. | 49 |
| *Item 4f:* When the equilibrium is re-established the equilibrium constant decreases. | 41 |
| 5. Nitrosyl bromide decomposes according to the following reaction: $NOBr(g) \leftrightarrow NO(g) + 1/2Br_2(g)$ At 77° C, $K_p$ of the reaction is 0.15. If 0.50 atm of NOBr(g), 0.20 atm of NO(g), and 0.40 atm of $Br_2(g)$ are introduced in a vessel at 77° C, it can be concluded that in the state of equilibrium: | |
| *Item 5a:* $P_{NO}$ is greater than 0.20 atm. | 22 |
| *Item 5b:* $P_{Br}$ is greater than 0.40 atm. | 22 |
| *Item 5c:* $P_{NOBr}$ is less than 0.50 atm. | 22 |
| *Item 5d:* $P_{Br}$ is less than 0.30 atm. | - |
| *Item 5e:* $P_{NOBr}$ is greater than 0.70 atm. | - |
| 6. Consider the following reaction in equilibrium: $2Cl_2(g) + 2H_2O(g) \leftrightarrow 4HCl(g) + O_2(g)$ ($\Delta H > 0$) Describe the effect of the following on the position of the equilibrium: | |
| *Item 6a:* Addition of $O_2(g)$. | 72 |
| *Item 6b:* Addition of $Cl_2(g)$. | 69 |
| *Item 6c:* Decrease in the volume of the vessel. | 31 |
| *Item 6d:* Increase in the temperature of the vessel. | 39 |

| Items | Percentage students with correct response |
|---|---|
| 7. In which of the following solutions would $CaF_2$ be the least soluble? a) 0.1M NaCl, b) 0.1M KCl, c) 0.1M $Ca(NO_3)_2$, d) 0.02M NaF | 23 |
| 8. A saturated solution of lanthanum iodate, $La(IO_3)_3$ in water has an iodate ion concentration of $2.07 \times 10^{-3}$ mol/L. Calculate $K_{sp}$ of the salt. | 28 |
| 9. Calculate pH of a solution obtained by mixing 0.6 moles of $H_3CCOOH$ ($K_a = 1.8 \times 10^{-5}$) and 0.5 moles of sodium acetate $Na^+H_3C_2O_2^-$ in 200 ml of water. | 37 |
| 10. One liter of a solution contains 0.5 moles of $H_3CCOOH$ ($K_a = 1.8 \times 10^{-5}$). In order to prepare a buffer solution which of the following should be added: a) 0.5 moles of NaOH; b) 0.2 moles of NaOH; c) 15 moles of $Na^+H_3C_2O_2^-$; d) 0.04 moles of $Na^+H_3C_2O_2^-$. | 6 |
| 11. Calculate the solubility (in moles/L) of $Mg(OH)_2$ in water, knowing that its $K_{sp} = 1.8 \times 10^{-11}$. | 78 |

All items formed part of the regular evaluation of the students and they were asked to respond and justify all answers in writing and were encouraged to give detailed explanations and credit was given only if an answer was accompanied by an adequate reasoning. All items were scored: 0 point for an incorrect response and 1 point for a correct response. Items 1, 2, and 3 formed part of Exam 1, which was given during the 6th week of the semester. Items 10 and 11 formed part of Exam 2, which was given during the 8th week. Items 4, 5, 6, 7, 8, and 9 formed part of Exam 3, which was given during the 10th week.

Items for this study were selected on the basis of the alternative conceptions found by Hackling and Garnett (1985) and can be grouped into three categories: a) Approach to equilibrium (Items 1 and 5); b) Changing equilibrium conditions (Items 2, 3b, 3c, 4, and 6); c) Characteristic of chemical equilibrium (Items 3a, 7, 8, 9, 10, and 11). Items 3, 5, 7, 8, and 11 were adapted from Mahan and Myers (1990). Items 1, 2, 3b, 3c, 4, 5, 6, 7, and 10 were classified as conceptual. Items 3a, 8, 9, and 11 were classified as computational.

A conceptual item in this study generally represents considerable difficulty for the students, as it cannot be solved by memorized algorithms or formulae, and students were generally not exposed to such items during class. This is particularly true of Items 1, 2, and 4. Furthermore, most of the conceptual items in this study consisted of a series of related and probing questions that help to construct student understanding of chemical equilibrium. A computational item in this study requires mathematical transformations that are well rehearsed in class, and in most cases can be solved by memorized algorithms. Students felt very comfortable with the sort of computational problems used in this study, as most of the class time was spent in solving similar problems. It is argued that the degree to which a problem is classified as conceptual or computational is a function of the students' background and the sort of problems they are exposed to in class. It is possible that students with a different background may not consider items used in this study as requiring conceptual or computational reasoning. Finally, although a computational item in this study primarily requires memorized algorithms and a conceptual item departs considerably from routine algorithms, the relationship between the two is by no means dichotomous.

## Results and Discussion

### Items 1a, 1b, 1c, and 1d

It was found that 22% of the students responded to Item 1a correctly, that is, 78% held the alternative conception that the forward reaction rate increases as the reaction gets going. Many of the students reasoned: "As the reaction has to reach equilibrium its forward rate must increase". 49% of the students responded to Items 1b and 1c correctly, which shows that in spite of the alternative conception in Item 1a, about half do understand that to begin with the rate of the reverse reaction is zero and increases progressively as the concentration of the products increases. Many of the students who did not respond correctly to Item 1c, reasoned: "The rate of the reverse reaction is zero, as this reaction proceeds from left to right", which indicates the lack of a distinction between completion and reversible reactions. It was found that 14 (18%) students responded to all four (1a, 1b, 1c, 1d) items correctly. It was further observed that out of the 17 who responded to Item 1a correctly, 15 (88%) responded to Item 1b correctly, 16 (94%) responded to Item 1c correctly, and all 17 (100%) responded to Item 1d correctly. These results indicate that those who understand correctly that the rate of the forward reaction decreases as the reaction gets going, also understand better other aspects of chemical equilibrium.

### Items 2a, 2b, 2c, and 2d

It was found that 15% of the students responded to Item 2a correctly, that is, 85% held the alternative conception that the reverse reaction rate decreases. Many of the students in this study invoked LeChatelier's principle to explain that the rate of the forward reaction is favored, but seem to ignore that an increase in the concentration of $NOCl(g)$ will lead to an increase in the rate of the reverse reaction. Many of the students reasoned: "The rate of the forward reaction has to increase in order to eliminate the excess of $NO(g)$ in the reactants, and the rate of reverse reaction must decrease as it produces $NO(g)$, which is already in excess". 60% of the students responded to Item 2b correctly. In spite of the alternative conception observed (85%) in Item 2a, it is interesting to observe that 30% understood that initially the reverse reaction rate remains constant (Item 2c) and 31% understood that the reverse reaction would increase gradually (Item 2d). It is suggested that the closely related probing questions utilized in this study may have helped the students to understand (perhaps on second thought) the underlying concepts better. It was found that 7 (9%) students responded to all four (2a, 2b, 2c, 2d) items correctly. Of the 12 students who responded to Item 2a correctly, 11 (92%) responded to Item 2b correctly, 10 (83%) responded to Item 2c correctly, and 9 (75%) responded to Item 2d correctly. These results indicate that those who understand correctly that the rate of the reverse reaction also increases, also have a better understanding of other aspects of chemical equilibrium.

### Items 3a, 3b, and 3c

It was found that 49% of the students solved the computational Item 3a correctly, and only 5% responded to the conceptual Item 3b correctly. This indicates that success in manipulation of the data, basically requires an algorithmic solution strategy, which does not help the students to understand the conceptual question that the final pressure of $CO_2(g)$ has to be greater than (0.1 atm) the amount of $CO_2(g)$ added after the equilibrium is reached. Many of the students responded: "In order to reach equilibrium again, the reverse reaction must increase, and consequently the final pressure of $CO_2(g)$ is less than 0.1 atm". It appears that most students do not realize the implications of decreasing the final pressure of $CO_2(g)$ less than 0.1 atm, and what they really understand is that the pressure of $CO_2(g)$ must decrease (LeChatelier's principle). This is corroborated from the fact that performance of the students in Item 3c (39%) increases considerably in comparison to that of 5% in Item 3b. This indicates that conceptual problems can vary in depth and success on a conceptual item like 3c does not ensure the same on items of the type 3b.

### Items 4a, 4b, 4c, 4d, 4e, and 4f

It was found that 3% of the students responded to Item 4a correctly. In spite of the alternative conception in Item 4a, 27% of the students responded to Item 4c correctly, that is, forward reaction rate increases gradually. This indicates once again that students can perhaps (on second thought) give up a certain mode of thinking, provided they are given an opportunity to do so. It was observed that 19 (24%) students did not respond to any of the items (4a-4f) correctly.

### Items 5a, 5b, 5c, 5d, and 5e

It was found that the same 17 (22%) students responded to Items 5a, 5b, and 5c correctly. However, none responded to Items 5d and 5e correctly, which shows that students had considerable difficulty in understanding this particular 'approach to equilibrium'. Even the 4 students who had previously solved Item 3b correctly (a similar item) could not solve Items 5d and 5e. Many of the students who did not respond correctly to Items 5a, 5b, and 5c, reasoned: "As the reaction has to proceed from left to right, $P_{NO}$ and $P_{Br}$ increase, whereas $P_{NOBr}$ would decrease". Apparently, this insistence on the reaction always proceeding from left to right, irrespective of the experimental conditions is a serious obstacle in understanding the dynamic nature of equilibrium. Gorodetsky and Gussarsky (1987) have referred to this as the 'feature of sidedness', which "... reflects the inability of treating the system as a whole – as unity, but rather splicing it into constituents such as 'reactants' and 'products' or 'left' and 'right' sides" (p. 191). These results indicate once again different levels of performance on items requiring conceptual understanding. In this particular case two levels are clearly discerned: a) the ability to solve items of the type 5a, 5b, and 5c, which is based on a comparison of the theoretical value of $K_p$ to that obtained from experimental values in a particular situation; and b) the ability to solve items of the type 5d and 5e, which requires the understanding that although LeChatelier's principle helps to predict the favored reaction, the degree to which it is favored depends on other constraints, such as stoichiometry of the reaction.

### Items 6a, 6b, 6c, and 6d

It was found that performance on Items 6a (72%) and 6b (69%) is fairly high, which requires the prediction of the direction of the favored reaction, and not the understanding of the degree to which the reaction is favored. On the other hand, performance on Items 6c (31%) and 6d (39%) is considerably lower. Many of the students who did not respond to Item 6c correctly, reasoned: "On decreasing the volume the pressure increases and the greater number of molecular collisions leads to a greater production of HCl(g) and $O_2$(g), that is, the reaction proceeds from left to right". Once again it can be observed that the 'feature of sidedness' persists. It was also found that 14 (18%) students responded to all four (6a, 6b, 6c, and 6d) items correctly.

### Items 7, 8, and 11

All three items are based on the solubility product constant. Results obtained show a considerable difference in performance on computational Items 8 (28%) and 11 (78%). On the other hand, the difference in performance between the conceptual Item 7 (23%) and the computational Item 8, is small. It can be observed that Items 7, 8, and 11 are based on ionic equilibrium, in contrast to Items 1-6, which are based on gas phase equilibrium. Camacho and Good (1989) have reported a decrease in performance on items based on ionic equilibrium, as compared to those based on gas phase equilibrium, which they have attributed to greater, "... conceptual knowledge involved in ionic equilibrium as compared to gas-phase equilibrium" (p. 255). Results obtained in this study, however, did not manifest this trend.

### Items 9 and 10

Both items are based on ionic equilibrium and require knowledge of buffer solutions. It was found that performance on the computational Item 9 (37%) is much better than the conceptual Item 10 (6%). Once again the difficulty of the students can perhaps be attributed to the reasoning demand of the item, rather than the involvement of ionic equilibrium.

## Relationship between Performance on Conceptual and Computational Items

In this section performance on conceptual (qualitative) Items 1, 2, 4, and 6 is compared to that of computational (quantitative) Items 3a and 8. The criteria for selecting these items was that student performance should not be either too high or too low.

Of the 14 students who solved all 4 conceptual items (1a, 1b, 1c, 1d) correctly, 9 (64%) also solved Item 3a and 7 (50%) solved Item 8, both of the latter being computational items. On the other hand, of the 38 students who solved Item 3a correctly, only 9 (25%) solved all 4 conceptual items (1a, 1b, 1c, 1d) correctly. Similarly, of the 22 students who solved Item 8 correctly, only 7 (32%) solved all 4 conceptual items correctly. These results indicate that success on conceptual items is more conducive to resolution of computational items, than vice versa.

Furthermore, of the 7 students who solved all 4 conceptual items (2a, 2b, 2c, 2d) correctly, 5 (71%) also solved computational Items 3a and 8. On the other hand, of the 38 students who solved Item 3a correctly, only 5 (13%) solved all 4 conceptual items. Similarly, of the 22 students who solved Item 8 correctly, only 5 (23%) solved all 4 conceptual items correctly. These results indicate that those who are consistently good at solving conceptual items have a considerably greater chance of solving computational items, rather than the other way round.

Of the 20 students who solved 4 or more parts of Item 4 (4a-4f), 15 (75%) also solved Item 3a and 7 (35%) Item 8. Again, of the 38 students who solved Item 3a, 15 (40%) solved 4 or more parts of conceptual Item 4. Of the 22 students who solved Item 8 correctly, 7 (32%) solved 4 or more parts of conceptual Item 4.

Of the 14 students who solved all 4 conceptual items (6a, 6b, 6c, 6d), 9 (64%) also solved Item 3a and 6 (43%) Item 8. Again, of the 38 students who solved Item 3a correctly, only 9 (25%) solved all 4 conceptual items. Similarly, of the 22 students who solved Item 8, 6 (27%) solved all conceptual items. Application of the McNemar test (Guilford & Fruchter, 1978) for significant differences between the performance on conceptual and computational items gave the following results:

1. Comparison of conceptual Item 1 and computational Item 3a: $\chi^2 = 15.56$ (p = 0.001).
2. Comparison of conceptual Item 1 and computational Item 8: $\chi^2 = 2.23$ (ns).
3. Comparison of conceptual Item 2 and computational Item 3a: $\chi^2 = 25.71$ (p = 0.001).
4. Comparison of conceptual Item 2 and computational Item 8: $\chi^2 = 10.32$ (p = 0.01).
5. Comparison of conceptual Item 4 and computational Item 3a: $\chi^2 = 30.25$ (p = 0.001).
6. Comparison of conceptual Item 4 and computational Item 8: $\chi^2 = 16.06$ (p = 0.001).
7. Comparison of conceptual Item 6 and computational Item 3a: $\chi^2 = 15.56$ (p 0.001).
8. Comparison of conceptual Item 6 and computational Item 8: $\chi^2 = 2.04$ (ns).

It can be observed that except for comparisons 2 and 8, those students who performed well on conceptual items also obtained significantly better performance on computational items. These results suggest that by solving computational problems only, students may not achieve an understanding of chemical equilibrium that leads to a 'conceptual framework' (Camacho & Good, 1989), or 'conceptual gestalt' (Hanson, 1958).

## Conclusions and Educational Implications

This study provides evidence against the widely prevalent idea that the ability to solve computational (numerical) problems leads to conceptual understanding, which according to Pickering (1990) has been the unquestioned axiom of freshman chemistry for the last 30 years. It is suggested that solving computational problems before solving problems that require conceptual understanding, would be more conducive to learning, that is, quantitative precedes the qualitative. At first sight this may appear counter intuitive. Generally, students find conceptual problems much more difficult than computational problems. Thus solving computational problems first provides the basic background (prior) knowledge necessary for understanding conceptual problems.

The major difference between our approach and that presented in most text books is that very little effort is devoted to facilitate the transition from the quantitative (algorithmic) to the qualitative (conceptual) mode. Most text books emphasize only quantitative problems (cf. Items 3a, 8, 9, and 11 of the present study). For example, conceptual problems of the type used in this study (cf. Items 1, 2, 3b, 3c, and 4) are not found in textbooks. It is interesting to observe that even one of the reviewers of our article (Niaz, 1995e) found such problems confusing. This shows, once again the popularity and the belief that experience with solving quantitative problems would help conceptual understanding. Niaz and Robinson (1992a) have reported similar results for gas problems (cf. chap. 7, Study 1). Furthermore, this coincides with the epistemological perspective of Hanson (1958), who has suggested that in order to achieve 'conceptual gestalt', which provides an explanation of the data, scientists previously do 'enumerate particulars', observe phenomena and manipulate data.

This study also provided evidence to the effect that those students who have a conceptual understanding of the underlying principles (cf. Item 1, Rate of the forward reaction decreases as the reaction gets going), subsequently perform extremely well on other related aspects of chemical equilibrium. This suggests that by emphasizing certain key aspects of a topic we may start a 'chain reaction' that may help facilitate conceptual understanding. Another important finding of this study is that given an opportunity, and after having been exposed to closely related, alternative probing questions, students give up a certain mode of thinking, at least partially. Furthermore, students adopt an alternative view that apparently contradicts their previous thinking.

## 9.2. STUDY 2: CHEMICAL EQUILIBRIUM AND NEWTON'S THIRD LAW OF MOTION: ONTOGENY/PHYLOGENY REVISITED

Results reported in Study 1 show that students have the following difficulties (alternative conceptions) in understanding chemical equilibrium: a) After the reaction has started, the rate of the forward reaction increases with time, until equilibrium is reached; b) When a system is at equilibrium and a change is made in the conditions, the rate of the favored reaction increases but that of the other reaction decreases; c) When a system is at equilibrium and a change is made in the conditions, students can predict the direction of the favored reaction, however, they have serious difficulties in taking into consideration other constraints, that determine the degree to which the reaction is favored; and d) Lack of a distinction between completion and reversible reactions. At this stage it is important to point out that the presentation of this topic (chemical equilibrium) in the textbooks itself may have influenced student understanding.

### Historical Evolution of the Concept of Chemical Equilibrium

According to Lindauer (1962): "Although chemical equilibrium is no longer looked upon as a *revelation of the forces* which control chemical change, much of its development arose out of just such an expectation" (p. 384, emphasis added). Similarly, Gorodetsky and Gussarsky (1987) have pointed out that the concept "equilibrium" acquired from physical or everyday experience, "... represents a system that is composed of two or more forces reaching a situation of balance" (p. 189).

Although Berthollet (1809) is given credit for his emphasis on the influence of the quantity of reactants (as compared to affinity) upon the course of chemical reactions, as late as 1809 he still emphasized the role of contending forces. Berthollet wrote: "... until equilibrium of the *contending forces* ends the operation, and limits the effect" (emphasis added, reproduced in

Lindauer, 1962). According to Lindauer (1962), Berthollet used the term equilibrium, "... to denote a balance of chemical forces, exactly as the term is used in mechanics" (p. 386). Even Guldberg and Waage who presented their law of mass action in 1864, initially viewed the state of equilibrium as resulting from an equality of the chemical forces exerted by the forward and reverse reactions. Commenting on the work of Guldberg and Waage, Lindauer (1962) wrote: "The influence of Newtonian mechanics appears throughout this early work on chemical equilibrium, and the idea that chemical combinations are the result of mutual attractive forces acting between the reactants is implicit in the term affinity" (p. 387).

## Dynamic Nature of Chemical Equilibrium

It was in 1884 that Van't Hoff (1896) finally presented the law of mass action on the basis of reaction velocities and the dynamic nature of chemical equilibrium was recognized as a consequence of the velocities of the forward and reverse reactions being equal at equilibrium.

When a student is first introduced to the concept of "chemical equilibrium" she/he already has a concept of "equilibrium" based on macrophenomena, that is physical and everyday experience (e.g., see-saw, bicycling, balance, etc.). According to Gorodetsky and Gussarsky (1987): "The attribution of dynamism to chemical equilibrium cannot be abstracted directly from macrophenomena, rather it is part of the model concerning the structure of matter" (p. 189). The concept of "equilibrium" based on macrophenomena, involves features of rest, staticity, and sidedness, whereas "chemical equilibrium" involves a system that stresses the conception of dynamism and reversibility.

## Newton's Third Law of motion and Chemical Equilibrium

In this section we report results of a study conducted to replicate the Study 1(Niaz, 1995d). The research design is the same as that of the previous study and is based on twenty-seven freshman students enrolled in one section of Chemistry II for science majors at the Universidad de Oriente (Venezuela). Results obtained were very similar to the previous study and in general the students were found to have the same difficulties (summarized above) in understanding chemical equilibrium. The main objective of this section is to analyze the reasons given by three of the students in order to justify their answers in Item 6 (Study 1). All three responded to Item 6b in the following terms:

> "The addition of $Cl_2(g)$ would lead to a *greater production of products* and in order to counteract the equilibrium the reaction would proceed from right to left so that the previous equilibrium is restored" (emphasis added).

The underlined part of the answer shows that the students started correctly by reasoning that the addition of $Cl_2(g)$ would lead to a greater formation of the products, and that is how according to LeChatelier's principle the external effect would be neutralized. It is, however, the second part of the answer that is problematic as it suggests that in order to counteract the increase in the concentration of the products, the reaction would proceed from right to left, which indicates that the students may be using Newton's third law of motion in its algorithmic version, "for every action there is an equal and opposite reaction" (Brown & Clement, 1987). On the other hand, a correct understanding of LeChatelier's principle would lead to the following reasoning: "... the system adjusts to reestablish equilibrium in such a way as to partially *counteract the imposed change*" (Hackling & Garnett, 1985, emphasis added). Thus according to LeChatelier's principle the imposed change is the addition of $Cl_2(g)$ and as a consequence the system counteracts by increasing the rate of the forward reaction. It is quite clear that the students consider the increase in the rate of the forward reaction as the imposed change and that the system counteracts by increasing the rate of the reverse reaction. Apparently, this reasoning is in accord with alternative conceptions about forces in general and the third law in particular (Brown & Clement, 1987). It is important to note that in Item 6b, after an increase in the rate of the forward reaction the rate of the reverse reaction also increases gradually, until equilibrium is established. Viewed from this perspective it can be argued that in a sense the students are saying the same, that is, "... the reaction would proceed from right to left so that the previous equilibrium is restored". Empirical evidence against this interpretation is provided by the fact that all three students responded incorrectly to Items 2a, 2c, and 2d (see Study 1), which are based on the understanding that if the concentration of a reactant increases after equilibrium is established, it leads to an increase in the rates of both the forward and the reverse reactions.

The same three students responded to Item 6d (Study 1) in the following terms:

As the reaction is endothermic, on increasing the temperature much more heat would be absorbed, which leads to the *production of more products* and in order to counteract the effect, the reaction would proceed inversely, that is, from right to left (emphasis added).

Once again the students start off correctly by reasoning that on increasing the temperature the forward reaction is favored. Later, however, the students suggest that in order to counteract the increase in the concentration of the products, the inverse reaction is favored. It appears that the students consider the rates of the forward and reverse reactions as forces, perhaps in the same sense as used in the evolution of the concept of chemical equilibrium (Lindauer, 1962) and alternative conceptions about the third law of motion (Brown & Clement, 1987). Furthermore, it is quite clear that the students consider the increase in the rate of the forward reaction as the imposed change and that the system counteracts by increasing the rate of the reverse reaction. Students do not interpret the increase in the rate of the reverse reaction as resulting from the dynamic nature of chemical equilibrium, and this is substantiated by the fact that all three students responded incorrectly to Items 4a and 4c (see Study 1).

It is interesting to note that two of the students responded to Item 3c correctly and although none of the three responded to Item 3a correctly, the reasoning employed does not reflect the alternative conception about Newton's third law of motion. It appears that the students perhaps invoke the third law, that is, for every action (forward reaction) there is an equal and opposite reaction (reverse reaction), only when the forward reaction takes place from left to right.

These results indicate that at least some students conceptualize chemical equilibrium as a product of opposing forces ("Force" interpretation), rather than a dynamic equilibrium based on the rates of the forward and reverse reactions. In order to test student ability to select the "force" interpretation in the presence of the correct response, seventy-seven freshman students enrolled in two sections of Chemistry II (science majors) at the Universidad de Oriente (Venezuela) were given the following item, as part of a monthly exam:

Consider the following reaction in equilibrium:

$$2Cl_2(g) + 2H_2O(g) \leftrightarrow 4HCl(g) + O_2(g) \; (\Delta H > 0)$$

Describe the effect of the following on the position of the equilibrium:

*Item a*: Addition of $Cl_2(g)$.
   Select one of the following responses and justify

   $a1^{\#}$ On addition of $Cl_2(g)$ more products will be produced and in order to counteract the effect, the reaction would proceed from right to left.
   $a2^{*}$ On adding $Cl_2(g)$ the system must counteract and consequently the rate of the forward reaction would increase.
   $a3$ None of the previous.

*Item b*: Increase in the temperature of the vessel.
   Select one of the following responses and justify

   $b1^{*}$ *As the reaction is endothermic, an increase in temperature would lead to the absorption of heat and the system must counteract, leading to an increase in the rate of the forward reaction.*
   $b2^{\#}$ *As the reaction is endothermic, an increase in temperature would lead to the absorption of heat, producing more product and in order to counteract the effect the reaction would proceed from right to left.*
   $b3$ *None of the previous.*

[#] 'Force' response.
[*] Correct response.

Results obtained (adapted from Niaz, 1995b) show that 23%, 56%, and 21% of the students responded correctly to Items a1, a2, and a3 respectively. Similarly, on Items b1, b2, and b3, percentages of the correct responses were 57%, 32%, and 10% respectively. It can be observed that responses a1 and b2 represent the "force" interpretation as utilized by the students in the replication study discussed above. Almost one-fourth of the students accepted the "force" interpretation (response a1) on Item a and about one-third of the Ss accepted the "force" interpretation (response b2) on Item b. Although a little over half of the students selected the correct responses on Items a and b (i.e., a2 and b1), only 29 (38%) selected the correct response in both Items a and b. Similarly, students using the "force" interpretation seem to shift strategies, as only 9 (12%) selected the "force" interpretation in both Items a and b. Again, only 5 (7%) selected the response, 'None of the previous' (a3 and b3) in both Items a and b. It is interesting to analyze the justification given by those who selected response a3. Some of them reasoned in the following terms:

In order to increase the concentration of the products, the concentration of the reactants must decrease. Nevertheless, this does not imply that the rate of the forward reaction must increase.

It seems that these students do understand that in order to decrease the concentration of the reactants (effect of adding $Cl_2$, g), the concentration of the products must increase. However, this expectation is not associated with the correct response a2, apparently because they do not have a conception of the dynamic nature of chemical equilibrium, based on the rates of the forward and reverse reactions. Some students even added:

The rate of the forward reaction does not increase because $Cl_2(g)$ is not a catalyst.

These responses lead us to conclude that those who selected response a3, have a conception closer to that of the "force" interpretation (response a1), than that of the correct response a2. Similar cases were found in Item b.

## Conclusions and Educational Implications

This study has attempted to show that at least some students consider the forward and reverse reactions as a sort of chemical analogue of Newton's third law of motion. Student difficulty is compounded further, by the fact that they adopt a concept of force as an innate or acquired property of objects, rather than as arising from an interaction between two objects, which leads to an epigrammatic version of the third law, "... for every action there is an equal and opposite reaction (Brown & Clement, 1987). If we accept this interpretation then it is plausible to hypothesize that student conceptualization of the forward and reverse reactions as forces is ontogenetically a step towards the deeper understanding of a dynamic chemical equilibrium. This interpretation is reinforced by the fact that as late as 1864, chemical equilibrium was conceived of as resulting from an equality of the chemical forces exerted by the forward and reverse reactions and the influence of Newtonian mechanics on the evolution of chemical equilibrium has been recognized in the literature (Lindauer, 1962). It is important to point out that ontogenesis is not an exact and detailed recapitulation of phylogenesis (Piaget & Garcia, 1989. Also see chap. 2).

Results obtained can also be interpreted within a Lakatosian framework It is plausible to hypothesize that as scientists build models of increasing complexity, which lead to epistemic transitions (i.e., increase heuristic/explanatory power, cf. Lakatos, 1970), similarly, students build a series of evolving models (progressive transitions), leading to greater conceptual understanding. In the present case there is a progressive "problemshift" (cf. GL2, chap. 3). Guideline GL2, suggests a progressive transition in students' thinking, between the model which represents chemical equilibrium as resulting from an equality of the chemical forces and the model that represents the dynamic nature of chemical equilibrium.

Results obtained in this study and their interpretation is important, as they help us to anticipate student utilization of Newton's third law in understanding chemical equilibrium, before the dynamic nature of equilibrium is understood.

## 9.3. STUDY 3: CONCEPTUAL CHANGE TEACHING STRATEGY BASED ON STUDENT ABILITY TO BUILD MODELS WITH VARYING DEGREES OF CONCEPTUAL UNDERSTANDING

According to Hackling and Garnett (1985) one of the most significant alternative conception (misconception) students hold is that, "The rate of the forward reaction increases with time from the mixing of the reactants until equilibrium is established" (p. 213). Niaz (1995d) found that those students who understood that the "... rate of the forward reaction decreases as the reaction gets going ..., subsequently perform extremely well on other related aspects of chemical equilibrium" (p. 352). For example (see Study 1), it was found that in spite of the misconceptions with respect to the rate of the forward reaction (only 22% of the students responded correctly on Item 1a): 1) 49% of the students do understand that to begin with the rate of the reverse reaction is zero and increases progressively as the concentration of the products increases (cf. Items 1b and 1c); 2) 62% of the students understand that the rates of the forward and reverse reactions are equal only at equilibrium; 3) of the students who correctly (22%) predicted that the rate of the forward reaction decreases, 88% understood that the rate of the reverse reaction increases as the concentration of the products increases, 94% understood that in the beginning the rate of the reverse reaction is zero, and 100% understood that the rates of forward and reverse reactions are equal only at equilibrium. Similar results were obtained in other items (cf. Niaz, 1995d). Furthermore, support was found for the hypothesis that students who perform better on problems requiring conceptual understanding also perform significantly better on computational problems requiring algorithms. These results indicate that student conceptualization of the rate of the forward reaction is more resilient to instruction in the traditional classroom, and thus can be considered as a major theoretical framework (core belief, see chap. 2) of student misconceptions. On the other hand, students who responded correctly to Item 1a, performed extremely well on Items 1b, 1c, and 1d (Study 1). It is plausible to suggest that student misconception of the rate of forward reaction represents the hard core (negative heuristic) of their framework in the Lakatosian (cf. GL4, chap. 3). Guideline GL4, suggests that just as scientists resist changes in the hard core of their theories, similarly students offer more resistance to changes in their core beliefs. Again, student understanding of Items 1b, 1c, and 1d would represent the soft core (positive heuristic) of their framework, which offers relatively less resistance to conceptual change. Chinn and Brewer (1993), taking their cue from Lakatos have emphasized that students resist changes in their major theoretical frameworks (e.g., Item 1a), by accepting 'auxiliary hypotheses.' Niaz (1995e) found that many students who held the misconception regarding the rate of the forward reaction (Item 1a) reasoned by postulating an 'auxiliary hypothesis' in the following terms: "As the reaction has to reach equilibrium its forward rate must increase" (p. 346). Taking our cue from the philosophy of science (see chap. 2) in the present context student understanding of Item 1a would require 'radical restructuring' and Items 1b, 1c, and 1d would require 'weak restructuring'. Given the parallel between the process of theory development by scientists and an individual's acquisition of knowledge (Piaget & Garcia, 1989), it is not surprising that students resist changes in their major theoretical frameworks. According to Lakatos (1970), scientists do not abandon a theory on the basis of contradictory evidence alone and, "There is no falsification before the emergence of a better theory" (p. 119).

Let us now try to understand the classification of Items 1a, 1b, 1c, and 1d (see Study 1) according to the criteria for the classification of students' responses as part of a Lakatosian core belief (presented in chap. 3). As suggested previously, Item 1a can be considered as a 'core belief' of student understanding, whereas Items 1b, 1c, and 1d would represent the dispensable part (soft core / positive heuristic). Results obtained in a previous study (Niaz, 1995d) with similar students have shown that most of those who responded correctly to Item 1a also responded correctly to Items 1b, 1c, and 1d. A careful look at Items 1b, 1c, and 1d would show them to be partial constituents of Item 1a, viz., a correct understanding of Item 1a (forward reaction rate decreases with time), leads to the following conceptualizations:

- reverse reaction rate increases because the forward reaction rate provides the product (Item 1b).
- when the reaction has just started and the product is absent, the reverse reaction rate is zero (Item 1c).
- as the reaction progresses, the forward and reverse reaction rates would be equal only in the state of equilibrium (Item 1d).

This shows quite clearly how Item 1a affects understanding of Items 1b, 1c, and 1d. Deletion of Items 1b / 1c / 1d would perhaps partially affect understanding on Item 1a. However, deletion of Item 1a would perhaps lead to a 'scrapping' of the entire framework of students' understanding. Deletion in this context would amount to solving this problem without the understanding provided by Item 1a, viz., forward reaction rate decreases with time.

Summarizing: application of Beilin's 'deletion criterion' (criterion 1, chap. 3) shows that deletion of student understanding of Item 1a (core belief) would lead to a 'scrapping' of the entire framework of student understanding (criterion 2) and hence they use 'auxiliary hypotheses' precisely to protect their core belief (criterion 3).

The main objective of this study is to construct a teaching strategy that could facilitate conceptual change in students' understanding of chemical equilibrium. A major hypothesis of this study is that students' participation in 'teaching experiments' (strategies) facilitates their conceptual understanding. Besides the Guidelines presented in Chapter 3 the teaching strategy is based on the following fundamental assumptions:

1. By emphasizing certain key aspects of chemical equilibrium (cf. Lakatos's, 1970, hard core) we may start a 'chain reaction' that may facilitate conceptual understanding.
2. After being exposed to closely related, alternative probing questions students may give up a certain mode of thinking, at least partially. This was observed in a previous study (Niaz, 1995d) based on student understanding of chemical equilibrium. According to Duschl and Gitomer (1991): "Careful evaluation of student knowledge claims can help teachers design instructional experiences that will force a grappling with those beliefs, and thereby encourage conceptual restructuring" (p. 840).

This study is based on two intact sections of freshman students who had registered for Chemistry II at the Universidad de Oriente, Venezuela, and the results reported here are adapted from Niaz (1998b). One of the sections (N = 32) was randomly designated as the control group and the other section (N = 36) as the experimental group. Students' assignment to a section is not based on any particular variable related to their academic / cognitive ability. Furthermore, author's previous experience shows that students in different sections perform at about the same level. Both sections were taught by the author. Mean age of the students in the control and experimental groups was 18.9 years (SD = 1.2) and 19.1 years (SD = 1.3), respectively. All students had one or more of the following textbooks: Mahan (1968); Mahan and Myers (1990); Masterton, Slowinski, and Stanitski (1985); and Whitten, Gailey and Davis (1992). Besides the textbooks students were given handouts with problems quite similar to Posttests 3 and 4.

## Teaching Experiments

In order to implement the teaching strategy the experimental group was exposed to two 'teaching experiments' based on the Guidelines (chap. 3) and fundamental assumptions mentioned earlier. The idea of a 'teaching experiment' was adapted from Cobb and Steffe (1983) and D'Ambrosio and Campos (1992). Details are presented in Chapter 5 in the context of a strategy based on cognitive conflict. The two experiments were conducted during the fourth and fifth week of the semester and dealt with the topic of chemical equilibrium. Besides the two problems included in the two teaching experiments, both the experimental and control groups solved the same set of 8 other problems of chemical equilibrium. In order to compensate for the two teaching experiments, the control group solved two similar problems with a traditional format. Both the control and the experimental groups used an interactive participatory approach to problem solving. In both groups the students were encouraged to discuss the problems, express their opinions and often called to the chalkboard to solve problems. Except for the two teaching experiments, every effort was made to provide similar experiences to the two groups. It is important to note that both groups had very similar opportunities to ask questions, propose solutions, generate discussions and encouraged to use the chalkboard to express their points of view.

## Teaching Experiment 1

During the fourth week of the semester students in the experimental group were presented the following problem:

A certain amount of NO(g) and Cl$_2$(g) are introduced in a vessel, whose temperature is maintained constant. After the reaction has started and before the equilibrium is reached, it can be concluded that:

$$2NO(g) + Cl_2(g) \leftrightarrow 2NOCl(g) \ (\Delta H < 0)$$

*Item 1a*: Forward reaction rate increases as the reaction gets going.
*Item 1b*: Reverse reaction rate increases as the concentration of the products increases.
*Item 1c*: In the beginning the reverse reaction rate is zero.

*Item 1d*: Reverse reaction rate is the same as the forward reaction rate.

This item was adapted with some changes from Hackling and Garnett (1985), and formed part of Niaz (1995d) discussed previously in Study 1. Students were first given about 10 minutes to read the problem and familiarize with the problem situation. One of the students then was asked to read the problem loud to the rest of the class. Another student was asked to suggest a solution to Item 1a. In an attempt to provide a conflicting situation students were asked to consider the consequences of the statement in Item 1a, whether correct or incorrect. They were asked to consider the following possibilities: a) As the reaction gets going, concentration of the reactants would decrease. How would that effect the rate of the forward reaction?; b) If the forward reaction rate increases, would that mean more of the reactants are available. Students were encouraged to express their opinions and discuss with their neighbors. After some discussion some of the students grasped the contradiction between the two possibilities mentioned earlier. When the correct response sort of emerged from the discussion it was quite clear that not all them were equally convinced. Items 1b, 1c, and 1d were dealt with in a similar manner. The whole experiment lasted about 40 minutes. Some of the salient points regarding the teaching experiment were:

a) Students were sort of surprised to be solving a problem that involved so much reasoning and discussion; b) The fact that no quantitative calculations were required, was another novel feature; c) Item 1a was clearly the most difficult; and d) Some of the students were clearly not satisfied with various aspects of the discussion and the correct responses.

## Teaching Experiment 2

During the fifth week of the semester, students in the experimental group were presented the following problem:

A certain amount of $NO(g)$ and $Cl_2(g)$ are introduced in a vessel at a certain temperature:

$$2NO(g) + Cl_2(g) \leftrightarrow 2NOCl(g) \ (\Delta H < 0)$$

After the equilibrium is reached the temperature is increased and as a consequence it can be concluded that:

*Item 2a*:  Forward reaction rate decreases.
*Item 2b*:  Reverse reaction rate increases.
*Item 2c*:  Forward reaction rate increases gradually.
*Item 2d*:  When the equilibrium is re-established, the equilibrium constant remains the same.
*Item 2e*:  Reverse reaction rate would be greater than the forward reaction rate.
*Item 2f*:  When the equilibrium is re-established the equilibrium constant decreases.

This problem was adapted with some changes from Hackling and Garnett (1985) and formed part of Niaz (1995d) discussed previously in Study 1. Procedure for presentation and discussion by the students was the same as in Teaching Experiment 1, and is not reported here. Total time required for the experiment was about 45 minutes.

.

## Evaluation of the Teaching Experiments

In order to evaluate the effectiveness of the teaching experiments, both the experimental and the control groups were tested on five different problems at different intervals of time, referred to as posttests, according to the following schedule: Posttests 1, 2 and 3 (8 week, monthly exam); Posttests 4 and 5 (13 week, semester exam). All 5 posttests formed part of the regular evaluation of the Ss. Posttest 1 was adapted with some changes from Hackling and Garnett (1985). Posttest 2 was adapted from Mahan (1968). Posttests 3 and 4 were adapted from Masterton, Slowinski and Stanitski (1985). Posttest 5 was adapted from Niaz (1995b). Posttests 1, 2 and 3 also formed part of the study by Niaz (1995d), and were designed as immediate posttests. Posttests 4 and 5 were considered to be delayed posttests. Posttest 1 was quite similar to the problems used in the two teaching experiments. The other posttests were different and designed to evaluate transfer of problem solving strategies. Students were encouraged to explain and justify all responses. Posttests 2, 3 and 4 are generally found in textbooks. On the other hand, formats of posttests 1 and 5 are fairly novel (based on statements rather than formal questions, with no calculations) requiring greater conceptual understanding and effort on the part of the students. A major objective of this format is that we wanted the students to interpret the underlying concept in their own words and not just use calculations based on memorized rules and formulae. Recent literature in chemistry education has been particularly critical of the algorithmic (plug-and-chug) approach to freshman chemistry. Before starting to respond the posttests students were specifically asked to: a) read the items carefully; and b) note that except for Posttest 5, these were not multiple-choice items and hence they were supposed to respond to all parts of an item and justify every part in order to get full credit. Students at this university are fairly accustomed to justifying their responses in writing and exams are not corrected by the computer. Even on Posttest 5 they were asked to justify the selected response.

### Posttest 1 (8 Week)

A certain amount of NO(g) and $Cl_2$(g) are introduced in a vessel and the temperature is maintained constant. After the equilibrium is reached a certain amount of NO(g) is introduced into the vessel. As a consequence it can be concluded that:

$$2NO(g) + Cl_2(g) \leftrightarrow 2NOCl(g) \ (\Delta H < 0)$$

*Item a*: Reverse reaction rate decreases.
*Item b*: Forward reaction rate increases instantaneously.
*Item c*: Initially the reverse reaction rate remains constant.
*Item d*: Reverse reaction rate increases gradually.

### Posttest 2 (8 Week)

Nitrosyl bromide decomposes according to the following reaction:

NOBr(g) $\leftrightarrow$ NO(g) + 1/2Br$_2$(g)

At 77° C, K$_p$ of the reaction is 0.15. If 0.50 atm of NOBr(g), 0.20 atm of NO(g), and 0.40 atm of Br$_2$(g) are introduced in a vessel at 77° C, it can be concluded that in the state of equilibrium:

*Item a:* P$_{NO}$ is greater than 0.20 atm.
*Item b:* P$_{Br}$ is greater than 0.40 atm.
*Item c:* P$_{NOBr}$ is less than 0.50 atm.
*Item d:* P$_{Br}$ is less than 0.30 atm.
*Item e:* P$_{NOBr}$ is greater than 0.70 atm.

## Posttest 3 (8 Week)

Consider the following reaction in equilibrium:
2Cl$_2$(g) + 2H$_2$O(g) $\leftrightarrow$ 4HCl(g) + O$_2$(g) ($\Delta$H > 0)

Describe the effect of the following on the position of the equilibrium:

*Item a:* Addition of O$_2$(g).
*Item b:* Addition of Cl$_2$(g).
*Item c:* Decrease in the volume of the vessel.
*Item d:* Increase in the temperature of the vessel.

## Posttest 4 (13 Week)

Consider the following reaction in equilibrium:

2NO(g) + O$_2$(g) $\leftrightarrow$ 2NO$_2$(g) ($\Delta$H > 0)

In order to increase the concentration of O$_2$(g) in the vessel should we (justify each response):

*Item a:* Increase the pressure of the vessel.
*Item b:* Add a certain amount of NO$_2$(g).
*Item c:* Extract a certain amount of NO(g).
*Item d:* Increase the temperature.

## Posttest 5 (13 Week)

Consider the following reaction in equilibrium:

2 Cl$_2$ (g) + 2 H$_2$O (g) $\leftrightarrow$ 4 HCl (g) + O$_2$ (g) ($\Delta$H > 0)

Describe the effect of the following on the position of the equilibrium:

*Item a:* Addition of Cl$_2$ (g).
    Select one of the following responses and justify:

$a1^{\#}$ On addition of $Cl_2$ (g) more products will be produced and in order to counteract the effect, the reaction would proceed from right to left.

$a2^{*}$ On adding $Cl_2$ (g) the system must counteract and consequently the rate of the forward reaction would increase.

$a3$ None of the previous.

*Item b*: Increase in the temperature of the vessel.
Select one of the following responses and justify:

$b1^{*}$ As the reaction is endothermic, an increase in temperature would lead to the absorption of heat and the system must counteract, leading to an increase in the rate of the forward reaction.

$b2^{\#}$ As the reaction is endothermic, an increase in temperature would lead to the absorption of heat, producing more products and in order to counteract the effect the reaction would proceed from right to left.

$b3$ None of the previous

[#] 'Force' response.
[*] Correct response.

This item was also used in Study 2, to test student ability to select the correct response in the presence of the 'force' interpretation, and was adapted from Niaz (1995b).

## Results and Discussion

### Posttest 1

Results obtained show the advantage of students in the experimental group in all four items (see Table 4). The difference, however, is significant only in Item d. In spite of the close relationship between the problems used in Teaching Experiment 1 and Posttest 1, very few in the experimental group responded correctly to Item a. It is important to note that the problem in Posttest 1 deals with a situation conceptually more difficult (i.e., a change in experimental conditions) as to the one presented in Teaching Experiment 1 (approaching equilibrium). Interestingly, only 11% of the students in the experimental group understood that the rate of the reverse reaction cannot decrease (Item a) and yet 39% responded correctly to Item d, that is, reverse reaction rate increases gradually. This once again shows the contradiction in student responses and perhaps a propensity to change. It is plausible to suggest that Item a represents the core belief of the students. Some of the students in the experimental group reasoned along the following lines:

- "As the forward reaction rate increases, the reverse reaction rate must decrease gradually, in order to establish equilibrium once again". Apparently, the Ss are not aware of the contradiction involved in this response. One could ask: If the forward reaction rate increases and the reverse reaction rate decreases gradually, how would the two reach equilibrium once again.

- "Forward reaction rate is favored in order to consume the excess of NO, and at the same time the production of NOCl is limited". Again it is interesting to ask: How can we increase the forward reaction rate and not increase the production of NOCl.
- Reverse reaction rate is proportional to $[NOCl]^2$. Consequently, the rate of the reverse reaction must decrease".

These three types of responses show the contradictory nature of student understanding and it is plausible to suggest that such reasoning is invoked in order to protect the hard core of student beliefs and can be considered as 'auxiliary hypotheses' within the Lakatosian framework (cf. GL8, chap. 3). Guideline GL8, suggests that just as scientists, students also use strategies to protect the hard core of their beliefs and such strategies can be considered as 'auxiliary hypotheses.'

### Posttest 2

Results obtained once again show the advantage of students in the experimental group (see Table 4). The same 8 students in the experimental group responded correctly to Items a, b, and c. Items d and e were not solved correctly by any of the students in the experimental and control groups.

### Posttest 3

Results obtained show the advantage of students in the experimental group (see Table 4), especially on Items a and b. The difference, however, is significant only in Item a. It is plausible to suggest that the problem situation in Posttest 3 requires considerably less conceptual understanding as compared to the problems in posttests 1 and 2 and also the teaching experiments. It is interesting to observe that even on a fairly traditional question (Posttest 3, found in textbooks) performance of the experimental group is generally better than that of the control group.

### Posttest 4

This being a delayed posttest, it can be observed that the difference in the performance of the two groups (except for Item b) is considerably less (see Table 4). Comparing the performance of the two groups on Posttests 3 and 4, it can be observed that even a small change in the problem format, affects student performance considerably. Both problems being quite similar, it was expected that a training effect could have improved performance on Posttest 4 as compared to Posttest 3.

**Table 4. Comparison of performance of the experimental and control groups on different posttests**

| Posttest | Number of students with correct response | | |
| --- | --- | --- | --- |
| | Experimental Group (N=36) | Control Group (N=32) | $\chi^2$ (Sig.) |
| 1 | | | |
| Item a | 4 (11)* | - | |
| Item b | 12 (33) | 6 (19) | 1.18 (ns) |
| Item c | 7 (19) | 1 ( 3) | 2.92 (ns) |
| Item d | 14 (39) | 4 (13) | 4.78 (p<.05) |
| 2 | | | |
| Item a | 8 (22) | 3 ( 9) | 1.22 (ns) |
| Item b | 8 (22) | 3 ( 9) | 1.22 (ns) |
| Item c | 8 (22) | 2 ( 6) | 2.29 (ns) |
| Item d | - | - | |
| Item e | - | - | |
| 3 | | | |
| Item a | 25 (69) | 13 (41) | 4.59 (p<.05) |
| Item b | 25 (69) | 14 (44) | 3.58 (ns) |
| Item c | 10 (28) | 8 (25) | |
| Item d | 12 (33) | 5 (16) | 1.97 (ns) |
| 4 | | | |
| Item a | 6 (17) | 5 (16) | |
| Item b | 19 (53) | 11 (34) | 1.64 (ns) |
| Item c | 11 (31) | 8 (25) | |
| Item d | 11 (31) | 9 (28) | |
| 5 | | | |
| Item a | 21 (58) | 15 (47) | 0.49 (ns) |
| Item b | 16 (44) | 13 (41) | |

*Figures in parentheses represent percentages.

### *Posttest 5*

The objective of this posttest was to evaluate the teaching strategy developed in this study with respect to the utilization of a 'force' interpretation. Niaz (1995b) has shown that students tend to conceptualize the rates of the forward and reverse reactions in chemical equilibrium as forces, perhaps in the same sense as used in the evolution of the concept of chemical equilibrium and student misconceptions about Newton's third law of motion (see Study 2). Results obtained (see Table 4) show that students in the experimental group have a better understanding of the forward and reverse reactions as velocities. Nevertheless, it appears that as compared to the previous results (Niaz, 1995b) the teaching experiments in this study did not improve student understanding of the dynamic nature of chemical equilibrium. The following are some examples of the force responses given by the experimental group:

- "On increasing the concentration of the reactants, that of the products decreases, and in order to counteract this, the rate of the forward reaction is favored. Now in order to counteract the increase in [$Cl_2$], the rate of the reverse reaction increases" (Item a). It appears that in order to respond, the student has first cast the problem within his/her own framework. For example, it helps the student to invoke the force response (based on an epigrammatic version of Newton's third law, viz., for every action there is an equal and opposite reaction, cf., Brown & Clement, 1987) by hypothesizing that when the concentration of the reactants increase that of the products would decrease.

- "As the concentration of the reactants increase that of products would decrease. The relation between the concentration of the products and reactants decreases, and consequently the rate of the reverse reaction would also decrease. This leads to an increase in the rate of the forward reaction" (Item a).
- "If the concentration of the products increases, *logically* the rate of the reverse reaction would increase" (Item b, emphasis added). Once again the student has hypothesized on his own account that the concentration of the products was also altered as an external effect.

## Conclusions and Educational Implications

Results obtained show that performance of the experimental group was generally better than that of the control group. Nevertheless, it is important to point out that on an item related to a core belief of the students (posttest 1, Item a) the gain of the experimental group is fairly modest. It was also observed that results of the immediate posttests (3 weeks after intervention) were better than those of the delayed posttests (8 weeks after intervention). In general student performance on traditional and familiar items generally found in textbooks (e.g., posttests 3 and 4) was better than on novel problems requiring greater conceptual understanding (e.g., posttest 1). It is concluded that even relatively short periods of appropriate experiences can facilitate student understanding of chemical equilibrium. Further research could show the advantage of extended periods of intervention.

It is plausible to suggest that results obtained in this study reflect, primarily a change/shift in the soft core of students' beliefs. This raises an important issue: In order to be accepted as valid, should teaching strategies necessarily produce changes in the hard core of students' beliefs? A study by Dagher (1994) provides a possible answer:

Restricting worthwhile conceptual change to the radical type is equivalent to restricting worthwhile science to revolutionary science – at a time when, if one accepts Kuhn's theory of scientific activity, it is during the normal and ordinary tinkering within a given paradigm that crises arise and eventual dissatisfaction ensues. The small changes in conception are worth tracking because their significance to the intellectual life of individuals is far beyond our ability to ascertain at this stage of our understanding (p. 609).

## 9.4. STUDY 4: RESPONSE TO CONTRADICTION:
## CONFLICT RESOLUTION STRATEGIES USED BY STUDENTS IN
## SOLVING PROBLEMS OF CHEMICAL EQUILIBRIUM

One of the most significant alternative conception students hold about chemical equilibrium is that, "After the reaction has started, the rate of the forward reaction increases with time and that of the reverse reaction decreases, until equilibrium is reached". Study 3 in this chapter has shown that this alternative conception offers considerable resistance to change and hence can be considered as part of students' 'hard core' of beliefs. Epistemologically, this study considers students' alternative conceptions not as mere mistakes but as conceptions that compete with scientific theories (cf. Strike & Posner, 1992). Burbules and Linn (1988) have emphasized how students' alternative conceptions if contradicted can produce cognitive conflict and hence be the source of conceptual change. In Chapter 5 we have already dealt with the role of cognitive conflict in understanding stoichiometry. One of the items used by Niaz (1995d, Item 2, Study 1 in this chapter) to evaluate student understanding of chemical equilibrium is given below:

Item 1    A certain amount of $NO(g)$ and $Cl_2(g)$ are introduced in a vessel and the temperature is maintained constant. After the equilibrium is reached a certain amount of $NO(g)$ is introduced into the vessel. As a consequence it can be concluded that:

$$2NO(g) + Cl_2(g) \leftrightarrow 2NOCl(g) \ (\Delta H < 0)$$

Item 1a:  Reverse reaction rate decreases.
Item 1b:  Forward reaction rate increases instantaneously.
Item 1c:  Initially the reverse reaction rate remains constant.
Item 1d:  Reverse reaction rate increases gradually.

It is important to note that this was not a multiple choice question. Students were asked to respond to each of the four items and provide justifications. It was found that 15% of the students responded correctly by disagreeing with Item 1a. This shows that 85% (those who agreed) of the students held the alternative conception that the reverse reaction rate decreases. Furthermore, it was found that of the 12 students who responded to Item 1a correctly, 11 (92%) responded to Item 1b correctly, 10 (83%) responded to Item 1c correctly, and 9 (75%) responded to Item 1d correctly. These results show that those students who understand correctly that the rate of the reverse reaction also increases, have a better understanding of other aspects of chemical equilibrium. In a subsequent study (Niaz, 1998b, Study 3 in this chapter), it was found that some of the students responded to Item 1d correctly without having answered to Item 1a correctly. In order to pursue further, this apparently contradictory result, three new studies were conducted, whose results are presented in this article.

The main objective of this study is to analyze strategies used by students in solving a novel item (Items 1a, 1b, 1c, and 1d, presented above), that can facilitate conceptual change. In Study A the sequence of items were presented in the following order: 1a, 1b, 1c, 1d. In

Study B the order was inverted, i.e., 1d, 1c, 1b, 1a. In Study C only Item 1d was presented. The rationale for the differences in the three studies is presented in the Method section.

## Method

Study A is based on 151 freshman students, Study B on 30 students and Study C on 27 (adapted from Niaz, 2001). Students in all three studies were enrolled in Chemistry II for science majors at the Universidad de Oriente (Venezuela). All students were familiarized with the format of Item 1 (presented in the Introduction section), by solving 2 similar problems during class. Item 1 formed part of the regular evaluation (monthly exam) of the students and they were encouraged to explain all answers in writing. Students were given explicit instructions with respect to the fact that Item 1 was not a multiple-choice question and that they were supposed to respond to each part of the item and justify it. Students in Study A were evaluated on Item 1 with the sequence 1a, 1b, 1c, and 1d. Students in Study B were evaluated on Item 1 with the sequence 1d, 1c, 1b, and 1a. Students in Study C were evaluated only on Item 1d. Comparison of the performance on the three studies is crucial for obtaining evidence in support of strategies that lead to conceptual change. If the order in which the items are presented facilitates conceptual change, students in Studies 1 and 2 should differ in their responses to Item 1d. Those who do 1d last are more capable of undergoing conceptual change, whereas those who do 1d first may not experience conceptual change. This of course is based on the assumption that most students do not go back and check their response on the previous items in the sequence. Comparison of performance in Study 3, with Studies 1 and 2 will show that if there is no difference across the three studies on Item 1d, then it could provide evidence that conceptual change is not occurring. Results obtained are summarized in Table 5.

## Results and Discussion

Table 5 shows that in Study A, 21% (31 out of 151) of the Ss responded incorrectly to Item 1a (i.e., students consider the reverse reaction rate to decrease – a major alternative conception) and yet responded correctly to Item 1d (i.e., reverse reaction rate increases gradually). How do we explain this contradictory response pattern? A major thesis of this study is to suggest that as these students solve the closely related sequence of Items 1a, 1b, 1c and 1d, they go through the process of: generation and resolution of a cognitive conflict (Burbules & Linn, 1988). Before we analyze this hypothesis any further it would be interesting to present some of the problem solving strategies used by the students. The following 5 strategies were considered to be representative of the 31 students who responded with this response pattern in Study A. Each strategy is reproduced verbatim from students' answer sheets, with only small grammatical corrections to facilitate understanding.

## Strategy 1: Increase in the Concentration of Products Makes its Dissociation more Difficult (n=8)

*Item 1a*

"Yes. Concentration of NO(g) increases, which increases the rate of the forward reaction, leading to the production of more NOCl(g), which makes its dissociation more difficult."

*Item 1b*

"Yes. Addition of NO(g) increases its concentration, which leads to an increase in the forward reaction rate".

*Item 1c*

"No. While the forward reaction rate starts decreasing the reverse reaction rate starts increasing."

*Item 1d*

"Yes. As the forward reaction rate starts decreasing gradually, the reverse reaction rate starts increasing gradually".

**Table 5. Response patterns used by students in Study A (N=151), Study B (N=30) and Study C (N=27)**

| No. | Response patterns | Number of students | | |
|---|---|---|---|---|
| | Items 1a, 1b, 1c & 1d | Study A | Study B | Study C |
| 1. | All 4 correct | 9 ( 6)* | 2 ( 7) | - |
| 2. | Conflict resolution strategy (1a = incorrect, 1d = correct) | 31 (21) | - | - |
| 3. | Only 1b correct | 33 (22) | 7 (23) | - |
| | Only 1c correct | - | 3 (10) | - |
| | Only 1d correct | - | - | 2 (7) |
| 4. | Ambiguous | 13 ( 9) | 2 ( 7) | - |
| 5. | All 4 incorrect | 65 (43) | 16 (53) | - |

*Figures in parentheses represent percentages.

Note: In Study A, the sequence of items were presented in the following order: 1a, 1b, 1c, 1d; in Study B, the sequence of items were presented in the following order: 1d, 1c, 1b, 1a; in Study C, only Item 1d was presented.

## Discussion

This strategy shows a progressive change in students' understanding, which can be summarized as follows: Increase in the concentration of NO (Item 1a) → Increase in the concentration of products (Item 1b) → On Item 1c, instead of accepting the plausibility of the reverse reaction rate being constant initially, these students asserted that the reverse reaction rate starts increasing, which contradicts their response on Item 1a. Finally, on Item 1d the reverse reaction rate is considered to increase. It is plausible to suggest, that these students did not go back and revise their response to Item 1a.

## Strategy 2: As Additional Reactants are Added, only the Rate of the Reaction that Consumes it will be Favored (n=6)

*Item 1a*

"Yes. On adding more $NO(g)$, the reaction that consumes it will be favored. This can be achieved by increasing the rate of the forward reaction, which automatically reduces the rate of reverse reaction."

*Item 1b*

"Yes. The moment additional $NO(g)$ appears, it progressively increases the rate of the forward reaction until equilibrium is established once again."

*Item 1c*

"Yes. Forward reaction rate will be favored until the additional amount of $NO(g)$ has been consumed. It is only then that the forward and reverse reactions will be equal. In the meantime the reverse reaction rate remains constant."

*Item 1d*

"Yes. After the additional amount of $NO(g)$ has been consumed, the system will be in equilibrium, and then the rates of the forward and reverse reactions will be the same. Hence the rate of the reverse reaction will have to increase progressively in order to be equal to that of the forward reaction."

## Discussion

This strategy considered that on Item 1a, an increase in the rate of the forward reaction automatically leads to a decrease in rate of the reverse reaction. This seems to be a memorized algorithm and may even reflect the application of an epigrammatic version of Newton's third law of motion, viz., for every action there is an equal and opposite reaction (cf. Brown & Clement, 1987). Responses to Items 1b and 1c indicate that students recalled that even after having additional reactant, equilibrium will be established once again. Finally, on Item 1d this is stated clearly and leads to the correct response.

## Strategy 3: An Increase in the Rate of the Forward Reaction Leads to a Decrease in the Rate of the Reverse Reaction (n=6)

*Item 1a*

"Yes. As can be observed from the equation, rate of the forward reaction is favored, which leads to a decrease in the rate of the reverse reaction."

*Item 1b*

"Yes. Until the equilibrium is established once again."

*Item 1c*

"Yes. In the initial phase only the reactants participate, leading to the increase in the rate of the forward reaction. Thus the rate of the reverse reaction remains constant."

*Item 1d*

"When the reaction reaches total equilibrium, the rates of the forward and reverse reactions are equal – thus the rate of the reverse reaction must increase gradually."

## Discussion

This strategy is quite similar to Strategy 2. The essential difference being that in Strategy 3 the decrease in the rate of reverse reaction (Item 1a) is attributed more directly to an increase in the rate of the forward reaction. Furthermore, the reference to "equilibrium being established once again" (Item 1b) and "initial phase" (Item 1c) shows that the students differentiate between the original state of equilibrium and the one that will be established after the changes due to the external effect.

## Strategy 4: As the Rate of the Forward Reaction Increases that of the Reverse Reaction Decreases (n=6)

*Item 1a*

"Yes. As the rate of the forward reaction increases that of the reverse reaction decreases"

*Item 1b*

"Yes. Due to an increase in the concentration of $NO(g)$, the rate of the forward reaction increases instantaneously, thus producing a disequilibrium."

*Item 1c*

"No. Due to the addition of $NO(g)$, the rate of the forward reaction increases, which leads to a change in the rate of the reverse reaction."

*Item 1d*

"Yes. If the system has to achieve the state of equilibrium again, it must counteract the increase in the rate of the forward reaction, which means that the rate of the reverse reaction must increase-"

## Discussion

The essential feature of this strategy is that it points out to a "disequilibrium" (Item 1b) in the rates of the forward and reverse reactions. Thus an increase in the rate of the reverse reaction is accepted in order to "counteract" (Item 1d) the increase in the rate of the forward reaction.

## Strategy 5: Displacement of the Reaction toward the Products Leads to a Decrease in the Rate of the Reverse Reaction (n=5)

*Item 1a*

"Yes. Concentration of one of the reactants is being increased. As a consequence the reaction displaces towards the products and the rate of the reverse reaction decreases."

*Item 1b*

"Yes. On adding NO(g) the rate of the forward reaction increases, leading to the production of more NOCl(g), and the establishment of the equilibrium".

*Item 1c*

"No. As the rate of the forward reaction increases, that of the reverse reaction decreases automatically".

*Item 1d*

"Yes. When the rate of the forward reaction increases that of the reverse reaction decreases. But in order to establish equilibrium again, the rate of forward reaction must be equal to that of the reverse reaction. Consequently, the rate of the reverse reaction will increase gradually".

## Discussion

The essential difference between this strategy and the previous ones is that even in Item 1c it maintains that the rate of the reverse decreases. Thus the change in understanding from Item 1c to 1d is more problematic. Even then it is interesting to observe that students apparently did not go back and check the response to Item 1a.

## General Discussion

All five Conflict Resolution Strategies presented above (Study A) show that these students while solving Item 1a, explicitly manifest / hold a major alternative conception, viz., rate of the reverse reaction decreases, which supports previous findings in the literature. While solving Item 1b, students in all five strategies reason more or less correctly, that the rate of the forward reaction would increase. Strategies used to solve Item 1c indicate that at least some of the students have a better understanding of the problem situation. Except for students using Strategy 5 (who still maintain that "reverse reaction decreases automatically"), other Strategies (1-4) do manifest a change / transition in students' thinking. These students now maintain (in contrast to their position in Item 1a) that the rate of the reverse reaction either remains constant (Strategies 2 and 3) or starts increasing / changes (Strategies 1 and 4). Finally, in Item 1d all five strategies respond correctly that the rate of the reverse reaction increases. Interestingly, students using Strategies 2-5, explicitly refer to the fact that as the system has to attain the state of equilibrium again, the rate of the reverse reaction must increase in order to counteract the increase in the rate of the forward reaction. It can be argued that students using Conflict Resolution Strategies do not experience a conceptual change /

transition but rather invoke a memorized algorithm, viz., 'in the state of equilibrium the rates of the forward and reverse reactions are equal'. This line of argument can be countered on the grounds that why did the students not use the memorized algorithm while solving Item 1a. Interestingly, none of the students responded with a response pattern in which only Item 1a would have been correct. These results raise an important issue: Did the students become aware of the contradiction, and if they did why they did not revise their responses to Item 1a? It is plausible to suggest that all or at least some of the 9 students who responded with response pattern 1 (all four correct, Study A) might have gone back and corrected their answer to Item 1a. Such students would have become aware of the contradiction. Thus, apparently it is the sequence of closely related probing items that force the students to grapple with their alternative conceptions. This shows that given the opportunity (solving the novel Item 1) students can alter their alternative conceptions. On the other hand, traditional text-book problems generally fail to provide such opportunities for conceptual change.

Results obtained in Study B (see Table 5) corroborate those obtained in Study A. In Study B the sequence of Items was inverted (1d, 1c, 1b, 1a) and hence the students did not have the opportunity of experiencing a conflict. Interestingly, none of the students responded with Response Pattern 2 (Conflict Resolution Strategy) or Response pattern 3 (Only 1d correct).

Results obtained in Study C (see Table 5) show that 2 (7%) of the students responded correctly (Response Pattern 3, Only 1d correct). It is important to note that in Study C, 1d was the only item presented. It is plausible to suggest these students used the experience gained in class when 2 problems with a format similar to that of Item 1 were discussed. At this stage it is important to observe that the percentage of students who responded with Response Pattern 1 (Studies A & B) and Response Pattern 3 (Only 1d correct, Study C) is about the same (6-7%). This shows that in all three studies, some students either went back to check their answers in response to the contradiction or gained sufficient experience to solve the problem correctly.

## Conclusions and Educational Implications

It is argued that the sequence of problems (1a, 1b, 1c, and 1d) used in this study facilitated, at least one group of students, to generate and resolve a cognitive conflict. The experience gained in solving the sequence of items and the knowledge that the system attains equilibrium again, conduces the students to the conclusion that the forward and reverse reaction rates must be equal, which contradicts a major belief (alternative conception) of the students that the rate of the reverse reaction decreases. As compared to most of the other studies, results reported here are fairly different and novel as the cognitive conflict was not induced from outside but instead generated by the students themselves. A review of the literature also provides support for conceptual change not driven by externally provided data (cf. Levin & Druyan, 1993; Levin, Siegler & Druyan, 1990; Levin, Siegler, Druyan & Gardosh, 1990). In spite of the promise such strategies may hold for introducing conceptual change in the classroom, we want to voice a word of caution as, "The course of conceptual change is anything but smooth" (Burbules & Linn, 1988, p. 75). Furthermore, we do not rule out alternative interpretations of the data. Taking our cue from the history of science, we suggest that students using Conflict Resolution Strategies in this study do accept and explain the anomalous data but still may have preserved the central hypothesis (hard core) of their alternative conceptions. This coincides with what Chinn and Brewer (1993) have referred to as Peripheral Theory Change: "... another response to anomalous data is for the individual to make a relatively minor modification in his or her current theory. An individual who responds in this way clearly accepts the data but is unwilling to give up theory A and accept theory B" (pp. 10-11). The idea of Peripheral Theory Change in the context of this study is particularly useful. Just as scientists, students may not accept contradictory evidence in order to produce radical changes in their alternative conceptions. Nevertheless, they may be more receptive to minor (progressive) changes. It is plausible to suggest that the novel item used in this study facilitates the transfer of knowledge gained in one item to the other (progressive transitions). Progressive transitions in the context of this study refer to models constructed by students that facilitate different degrees of explanatory power to their conceptual understanding (Niaz, 1995c).

Results obtained in this study have educational implications in the sense that problems generally found in textbooks do not assess the potential to which students are capable of making a conceptual change / progressive transition. These findings highlight the importance of including novel problems of the type presented in this study (Item 1), that make the possibility of conceptual change as part of normal classroom practice.

Studies reported in this chapter facilitate our understanding of the relationship between conceptual (qualitative) and computational (quantitative) problems in chemical equilibrium. It is concluded that solving computational problems before solving problems that require conceptual understanding would be more conducive to learning, that is quantitative precedes the qualitative (Study 1). Given the importance of Newtonian mechanics to the historical evolution of chemical equilibrium, Study 2 explored students' conceptualization of the forward and reverse reactions as forces. It is concluded that construction of a series of evolving models (progressive transitions) can facilitate conceptual understanding. In the present case there is a transition between the model which represents chemical equilibrium as resulting from an equality of chemical forces and the model that represents the dynamic nature of chemical equilibrium. Study 3 shows that a teaching strategy based on a series of related and probing questions can 'break' the cognitive complexity of the core belief (rate of forward reaction increases after mixing the reactants) of the students to a certain degree, and thus facilitate conceptual understanding. Finally, Study 4 shows that conceptual change can be facilitated by cognitive conflicts generated by students· themselves and hence the importance of class room practice.

# Chapter 10

# EPISTEMOLOGICAL BELIEFS OF STUDENTS AND TEACHERS ABOUT THE NATURE OF SCIENCE

The issues raised by the new philosophy of science (see chap. 1) has led educational researchers to examine the philosophical and epistemological underpinnings of their work (Phillips, 1983, 1987). Science educators have also shown a keen interest in philosophical and epistemological issues (Burbules & Linn, 1991; Matthews, 1994). This interest has led to the investigation of how students' and teachers' beliefs about the nature of science can influence their understanding of science (Abd-El-Khalick & Lederman, 2000).

At this stage it is important to point out that science educators' interest in the nature of science (NOS) dates back to at least the early 1960s (Conant, 1947; 1957; Cooley & Klopfer, 1961; Robinson, 1969a, 1969b). Lederman (1992) and Matthews (1990, 1994) provide a detailed review of the literature. In contrast, to these early attempts, the present approach to NOS is "... richer because we have access to the work of historians and philosophers of science, which has helped to develop the position that the growth of knowledge in science is best understood as a series of changes in scientists' fundamental explanations of how and why things work" (Duschl, 1990, p. 5).

Among the various issues debated by the new philosophers of science the following two have been of considerable interest to science educators due to their educational implications: a) The scientific method; and b) Theory ladenness of observations. Millar and Driver (1987) have expressed this concern very cogently: "... there is almost no support from historians, philosophers or sociologists of science that any such *method* exists, or can be described (p. 39, original italics). Furthermore, after considering Feyerabend's (1975) position on the subject as too extreme to command general agreement, Millar and Driver (1987) recommend: "... the substance of the disagreement between Lakatos and Kuhn ... shows that there is no agreed set of methodological rules for deciding which of two (or more) competing scientific theories is the better" (p. 41). Interestingly, this remains a controversial issue and science educators are far from reaching a consensus (for a critical appraisal, see Burbules & Linn, 1991; & Niaz, 1994a).

## RATIONALE OF THE STUDY

Lederman and O'Malley (1990) consider students' understanding of the nature of science as closely related to the understanding of the tentativeness and revisionary aspects of scientific knowledge: "... understanding of the tentativeness of science is viewed as a combination of one's views with respect to several historically recognized dichotomies (i.e., realist / instrumentalist, conclusive/tentative, subjectivist/objectivist, induction/invention)" (p. 226). For example, for the conclusive/tentative dichotomy Lederman and O'Malley (1990) asked high school students to respond to the following question in writing:

> After scientists have developed a theory (e.g., atomic theory), does the theory ever change? If you believe that theories do change, explain why we bother to learn about theories. Defend your answer with examples (p. 227).

In order to evaluate students' responses, Lederman and O'Malley (1990) used the following criteria: "... if the student stated that he/she believed that theories do change, the response was considered to be indicative of a tentative view of scientific knowledge. Alternatively, if the student did not believe that theories change, it was taken as evidence for an absolutist viewpoint" (p. 229). In our opinion it is difficult to capture the wide variety of students' beliefs by using a dichotomous (conclusive/tentative) criterion.

The main objectives of this study (based on Blanco & Niaz, 1997) are to:

a)  Investigate students' and their teachers' beliefs about the nature of science.
b)  Explore the relationship among the students' and teachers' beliefs.
c)  A rational reconstruction of students' and teachers' beliefs based on a Lakatosian perspective of the history and philosophy of science (Lakatos, 1970).

A major premise of this study is that students' and teachers' beliefs would show progressive transitions (based on the Lakatosian idea of progressive 'problemshifts'), from a positivist view to a more developed view of the nature of science. Niaz (1995a) has shown such a transition from algorithmic to conceptual understanding in student ability to solve chemistry problems. Lakatos' methodology of competing research programs has been applied previously to interpret research in science education (Chinn & Brewer, 1993; Niaz, 1994a, 1994b). It is suggested that the following aspects of the Lakatosian methodology would be helpful in a rational reconstruction of students' and teachers' beliefs of the nature of science:

1.  History of science can be conceived as that of competing rival research programs (Lakatos, 1971, p. 103).
2.  Scientists do not abandon a theory on the basis of contradictory evidence alone, and "There is no falsification before the emergence of a better theory" (Lakatos, 1970, p. 119).
3.  Some of the greatest scientific research programs progressed on inconsistent foundations (Lakatos, 1971, p. 113).
4.  Progress in science can be conceptualized within a pluralistic model, in which, "... the clash is not 'between theories and facts' but between two high-level theories:

between an *interpretative theory* to provide the facts and an *explanatory theory* to explain them" (Lakatos, 1970, p. 129, original italics).

## Method

This study is based on 89 freshman students enrolled in General Chemistry I at the Instituto Universitario de Tecnología, El Tigre, Venezuela and 7 chemistry teachers at the same institution. The teachers were either giving the course in the same semester or had given it previously. All 7 teachers had the equivalent of a 'Licenciatura' degree, which requires 5 years of academic work including a thesis, after high school. One of the teachers had a teaching experience of 16 years, five teachers from 8-14 years and one teacher of 2 years. All the students and teachers were asked to respond to a 4-item questionnaire and encouraged to explain their responses in writing. The questionnaire was adapted (with a small modification in Item 4) from Lederman and O'Malley (1990) and consisted of the following 4 items:

*Item 1*

After scientists have developed a theory (e.g., atomic theory) does the theory ever change? If you believe that theories do change, explain why we bother to learn about theories. Defend your answer with examples.

*Item 2*

What does an atom look like? How do scientists know that an atom looks like what you have described or drawn?

*Item 3*

Is there a difference between a scientific theory and a scientific law? Give an example to illustrate your answer.

*Item 4*

Some astrophysicists believe that the universe is expanding while others believe that the universe is in a static state without any expansion or shrinkage. How are these different conclusions possible if all of these scientists are looking at the same experiments and data?

## Criteria for Classification of Students' and Teachers' Responses

The criteria presented here are the same as used in Chapter 6.

a) *Positivist*: Responses included in this category emphasized experimental observation, demonstration and description of an absolute reality that has little to do with the hypotheses and theoretical framework of the scientist. According to Lakatos (1971) for an inductivist/positivist: "... only those propositions can be accepted into the body of science which either describe hard facts or are infallible inductive generalizations from them" (p. 92).

b) *Transitional*: These responses indicated a partial understanding with respect to the existence of alternative/competing models for explaining the experimental observations and that no knowledge is ever absolutely established (cf. Phillips, 1994).

c) *Lakatosian:* These responses indicated that scientific progress is subsumed by a process involving conflicting frameworks, based on processes that require the elaboration of rival hypotheses and their evaluation in the light of new evidence.

In order to facilitate the application of the above criteria, responses of 10 students (selected randomly) were classified into the three categories mentioned above, separately by the two authors. Almost 70% of the responses were classified as positivist, transitional or Lakatosian with no difficulty. All differences were resolved by discussion. Based on this experience, both authors classified separately responses of rest of the students and teachers, and there was consensus on almost 80% of the responses. All differences were resolved once again by discussion. Classification of the positivist, transitional and Lakatosian responses within subcategories was relatively more difficult. For example, in the case of positivist responses to Item 1, both authors looked together for conceptual themes referred to by the students and teachers in order to explain why theories change. We came up with the following tentative list for theory change: methods used by scientists for the resolution of a problem, presence of new scientists who introduce new experiments, presence of uncertain suppositions that lead to new experiments, need to clarify what was the true atomic theory, need for refuting existing theories, and a theory is not a law and hence could change. Similarly, we looked for responses that argued that theories do not change, and left open the possibility of finding other response patterns. With this tentative list as a guide, both authors classified separately all responses into these subcategories. Almost 70% of the responses were classified into the subcategories with relatively little difficulty. All differences were once again resolved by discussion. A similar procedure was followed in the other items.

## Results and Discussion

### *Tentative Nature of Scientific Theories (Based on Students' Responses on Item 1)*

*Positivist Responses*

a1  Science evolves with time. At times the discoveries of the scientists are innovative. Nevertheless, in some cases these discoveries change, when the methods for the resolution of a problem change. (N=12).

a2  Theories always change due to the presence of new scientists, who do new experiments and formulate new theories. (N=11).

a3  The theory changes if there is an uncertain supposition that cannot be verified through experiments. (N=5).

a4  Atomic theory has changed because as time went by the scientists investigated in order to clarify what was truly the atomic theory. Various scientists worked on the theory and Bohr's theory happened to be the correct one. (N=3).

a5  When the scientists have elaborated a theory it does not change. A theory once established is always a theory. Nevertheless, scientists keep developing it through the years by doing experiments that revolve around the theory. (N=6).

a6   Yes, the theory changes because some scientists say one thing and others say something else – this at times confuses us. Although the theory really does not change altogether, because in spite of the differences, scientists always try to reach the same law or theory. (N=3).

a7   The new discoveries help refute the existing theories. For example, according to Dalton's theory the atom was indivisible. Today we know that it is divisible. (N=2).

a8   A theory should not change as it is based on many observations and experiments. Nevertheless, due to the subjectivity of the scientist who formulates a theory, certain corrections are always required for its perfection but not its total elimination. (N=3).

a9   A scientist while formulating his theory could have made a mistake and this can be corrected in the future by another scientist. (N=3).

a10  A theory is not a law, which is always in force unless the contrary is demonstrated. (N=2).

a11  It is bothersome to learn about a theory that is subject to change. As the new knowledge contradicts our existing knowledge, we have to learn the same things all over again by using different methods. (N=15).

a12  It is bothersome to learn so many theories. Furthermore, it is confusing as they hardly coincide. (N=4).

## Transitional Responses

b1   The theory does not change, but rather is completed or in other words more information is provided about a subject. (N=1).

b2   It is possible that on developing a theory we may find new elements or components that may provide new insights. (N=3).

b3   A theory is something that has not been proved 100%. Nevertheless, it is important to point out that although a theory may not be accepted in totality, it serves as a guide for other scientists to develop their theories. (N=2).

## Lakatosian Responses

c1   Comparing Rutherford's theory to Thomson's, it can be observed that the two contradict each other. Although both of them presented their own point of view, they helped us to further our knowledge. (N=1).

Most of the responses to Item 1 were characterized by a positivist approach (see Table 6). It can be observed that the following responses accepted that theories change: a1, a2, a3, a4, a7, and a10; in contrast to the responses that held that theories do not change, viz., a5, a8, and a9. However, what is important is not the classification of the response as change/no change (cf. Lederman & O'Malley (1990), but rather the reasoning employed. It is interesting to observe that students use a series of different reasoning patterns to justify as to why theories change. For example:

**Table 6. Distribution of students' responses on all items (N=89)**

| Item | Positivist | Transitional | Lakatosian | Ambig | No |
|------|-----------|--------------|------------|-------|-----|
| 1 | 69 (78)* | 6 ( 7) | 1 ( 1) | 10 (11) | 3 ( 3) |
| 2 | 57 (64) | 5 ( 6) | 2 ( 2) | 17 (19) | 8 ( 9) |
| 3 | 58 (65) | 8 ( 9) | 1 ( 1) | 13 (15) | 9 (10) |
| 4 | 36 (40) | 34 (38) | - | 11 (12) | 8 ( 9) |

*Figures in parentheses represent percentages. Ambig = Ambiguous responses, No = No response.

- Response a1, attribute the change to the methods used for the resolution of a problem.
- Response a2, attribute the change to the presence of new scientists.
- Response a3, attribute the change to an uncertain supposition.
- Response a4, attribute the change to the scientists' need to clarify the true theory, clearly a thinking based on absoluteness of theories.
- Response a7, attribute the change to the need for refuting existing theories.
- Response a10, attribute the change to the fact that a theory is not a law, and hence could change.

Except for the reasoning employed in response a7, which would perhaps represent a Popperian approach, most of the other responses represent a positivist understanding. These results show that although the students did recognize the possibility of change in theories, it lacks the appreciation that scientific theories are tentative. Among the responses that did not admit the possibility of change in theories, Response a8 is fairly representative of a positivist approach, by emphasizing the primacy of observations and experiments and any change is attributed to the corrections required due to the 'subjectivity' of the scientists. Similarly, Response a9 considers that changes are necessary in order to correct the mistakes made by the scientists. Finally, Responses a6 and a11 showed students' 'uneasiness' regarding changes in theories.

Transitional responses to Item 1 showed a better understanding of tentativeness in science by attributing the changes to the need for completion (Response b1), new insights (Response b2) and as a guide for other scientists (Response b3). The only Lakatosian (c1) response to Item 1 shows how contradictions help to further our knowledge (cf. Rationale section and Lakatos, 1971, p. 113).

These results coincide with those obtained by Lederman and O'Malley (1990) through a follow-up interview. Nevertheless, our findings go beyond by not only showing that students may accept that theories change and yet it may not be indicative of a more developed epistemological belief (tentativeness) of the nature of science, but also as to the reasoning patterns used by students to protect their beliefs.

# What does an Atom Look Like? (Based on Students' Responses on Item 2)

## *Positivist Responses*

a1  The atoms look like our solar system, the nucleus being the sun and the electrons circle around it in orbitals like the planets. (N=20).

a2  An atom is a small particle like a sphere, that has positive and negative charges. (N=11).

a3  An atom has electrons, protons and neutrons, with a nucleus in the center and a series of shells in which the electrons are found. (N=6).

a4  As we all know the atom is the smallest particle and hence we cannot see it with the naked eye. It can only be seen by a special apparatus. (N=4).

a5  An atom is like a star, with a small nucleus in the center and the electrons circling around it. The scientists have observed this through a microscope. (N=5).

a6  An atom is a very small particle that cannot be seen by the naked eye and hence it is very difficult to describe it. However, as I have seen it drawn in books it looks like a series of oval shaped circles, with the nucleus in the center. (N=7).

a7  It has the form of gelatin with tufts of cotton inside. In order to describe it, I would follow the descriptions of the scientists as found in the text-books. (N=2).

a8  An atom is a very small particle, almost indivisible. The scientists can tell, what the atom looks like but I have never seen one. (N=1).

a9  An atom looks like a honeycomb with bees circling around it, just like the electrons around the nucleus. (N=1).

## *Transitional Responses*

b1  The scientists know what an atom looks like, as they have compared it to the models of the previous scientists – who elaborated models in order to have an idea about the atoms. (N=1).

b2  An atom can be considered as a fundamental part of all matter. We, like the scientists can imagine many things. It is something so complex that it would be impossible to describe it in a clear and precise manner. (N=1).

b3  The scientists do not know how an atom looks like – but they try to imagine it, as nobody has seen it. (N=2).

b4  An atom is a field of energy with positive and negative charges. (N=1).

## *Lakatosian Responses*

c1  According to the wave model of the atom, it is similar to the solar system. The knowledge about the atom was acquired progressively, step by step. In other words, one theory tried to improve upon the previous. (N=2).

Most of the responses to Item 2 were once again characterized by the positivist approach (see Table 6). One of the responses (a8) even had a Daltonian conception of the atom. It is important to note that all of the positivist responses have a very absolutist (in contrast to tentative) conception of our knowledge of the atom. It is interesting to observe that some of the positivist responses (a1 - a6) of our students (a small provincial town in Venezuela) are very similar to those of students (a small rural high school in Oregon, U.S.A.) in the previous study (Lederman & O'Malley, 1990). Transitional responses to Item 2 were clearly marked by a tentative view of scientific knowledge. For example, b1 'models of the previous scientists', and b2 'scientists can imagine many things'. Response c1 came quite close to a Lakatosian conception of the progress of science by emphasizing its 'progressive' nature. It, nevertheless, lacks the conceptualization of 'conflicting frameworks'.

## Is there a Difference between a Scientific Theory and a Scientific Law? (Based on Students' Responses on Item 3)

### Positivist Responses

a1   Yes. A scientific law has been proved by various scientists, who after having done the same experiments have arrived at the same conclusions, whereas a scientific theory is in a process of being proved (N=17).

a2   Yes. A theory is something that changes, whereas a law is something that has been established – based on a theory. (N=12).

a3   Yes. A theory is something that has not been proved in its totality, whereas a law has not only been proved but also universal. For example, the law of conservation of mass, that we can prove by an experiment, without any inconvenience. (N=7).

a4   Yes. A scientific theory is like a supposition that has not been proved by data, whereas a scientific law is that theory which has been proved by different means: objective, verifiable, clear and experimental data. (N=10).

a5   Yes. A theory is investigated until it is concretized, whereas a law is something constant – it always imposes. (N=5).

a6   Yes. A scientific theory studies in depth all that occurs around it and investigates in order to achieve deeper knowledge. On the other hand, a law is based on proving the scientific world, mathematically through formulas and experiments. (N=2).

a7   Yes. A law refers to something that has been proved, whereas a scientific theory refers to the theoretical aspects – the definition of something. For studying a law we need the scientific method, whereas for a theory we look for a book. (N=1).

a8   Yes. A theory tells us about more complex and explicit things. On the other hand, a law is based on concepts that must be complied with. (N=3).

a9   Yes. A law is formulated by a person who discovers something. On the other hand, theories are what the other scientists propound according to their studies. (N=1).

### Transitional Responses

b1   No. A scientific theory is based on investigation and it provides the basis of the law. (N=5).

b2   No. A scientific law originates from a scientific theory that has been corroborated. For example, Newton's theory provided the framework for Newton's laws. (N=3).

### Lakatosian Responses

c1   No. If a theory has been corroborated sufficiently and an experiment is performed, then it provides evidence in support of both the theory and the law. (N=1).

Responses to Item 3 were characterized primarily by the positivist approach (see Table 6). Most of the responses made a clear demarcation between a scientific theory and a law by emphasizing that the former is in the process of elaboration, whereas the latter has already been established. The transitional responses considered the difference between a scientific theory and a law, as much less dichotomous, and recognized how the two influence each other. The only Lakatosian response (c1) emphasized the importance of experimental evidence for both the theory and the law, and hence the difference more tenuous. Lederman and O'Malley (1990) considered the following response to this item as quite representative: "A scientific theory hasn't been proven yet. Laws have been proven to be true" (p. 230). It is interesting to observe once again, the degree to which this response resembles the following positivist responses in the present study: a1, a3, and a4. According to Lederman and O'Malley (1990) many students responded: "A theory is an explanation of how things work or about things that we can't see. Laws describe the things we can see" (p. 230), which they consider to be accurate. This conceptualization of the difference between a scientific theory and a law is quite similar to what Lakatos (1970, p. 147) has referred as a 'Baconian inductive ascent'.

Let us consider the gas laws in order to understand the issue: According to Lakatos the experimental work of Boyle with gases led to an empirical law (PV = nRT), which finally led Maxwell and Boltzmann to present kinetic-molecular theory of gases in order to explain the properties of gases (e.g., the law PV = nRT). It is important to understand that within the Lakatosian framework the development of a theoretical explanation is foremost, whereas the scientific laws based on experimental details are at best, secondary. In this respect, Lakatos (1970) goes so far as to suggest that, "... Boyle's and his successors' labours to establish PV = RT was irrelevant for the later theoretical development (except for developing some experimental techniques), as Kepler's three laws may have been superfluous for the Newtonian theory of gravitation" (p. 147).

## Controversial Nature of Experimental Data (Based on Students' Responses on Item 4)

### Positivist Responses

a1   Possibly some of the experiments were done many years ago, whereas others may have been conducted more recently, and perhaps there may be experimental errors as well. (N=9).

a2   They may have used the same data and studied the same experiments, but may have used different techniques and methods. (N=9).

a3   The universe is static. There is no expansion or reduction because it is of the same size as created by God at its origin. (N=4).

a4   Their conclusions are pure theory, with no probability of proving one way or the other. (N=4).

a5    The conclusions are different, as the astrophysicists analyze their experimental findings differently. (N=4).

a6    In order to reach a satisfactory conclusion one has to go to the universe, be in it and prove that it is real. Obviously, none of the astrophysicists has done this, as they base their conclusions only on observations and experiments. (N=2).

a7    They may have used different conclusions, because of the shape of the earth. Some of them may have obtained their data during the day, whereas others during the night. (N=1).

a8    The presentation of two different positions makes the scientific method and the study of science a fascinating enterprise with no limits. The two theories are looking for the same truth. (N=1).

a9    It cannot be concluded that the universe is expanding or is in a static state, as there exists a contradiction among these scientists. (N=1).

a10   The universe is static as each planet is in its place. However, from the scientist's point of view, the universe is expanding due to our interaction with science. (N=1).

### Transitional Responses

b1    It depends on the point of view of each investigator. Although, they observed the same data and experiments, their intentions were different; in other words a person describes and analyzes what he observes. (N=15).

b2    It is probable that this may happen, as all the scientists do not think the same way. (N=6).

b3    It may or may not be so. The universe is immense and new galaxies have been discovered, which does not allow a clear definition. (N=4).

b4    This is possible as the scientists have different points of view, due to objective or subjective reasons. (N=3).

b5    This is possible as each scientist has a different capacity to analyze, interpret and discuss data. (N=3).

b6    This is due to the fact that a scientist is subject to his beliefs and hence cannot achieve maximum objectivity. (N=1).

b7    This is possible as scientists have different emotional states, which leads to different perspectives. (N=1).

b8    The scientists do not stagnate with the same theory and nor do they stop investigating. If this were not so, we would not have all the progress in science. (N=1).

In comparison to other items, Item 4 presented a fairly different response pattern (see Table 6). Positivist responses decreased considerably, the transitional responses increased sharply and there was no Lakatosian response. Lederman and O'Malley (1990) found Item 4 to be the most difficult and had the highest frequency of 'No response'. Positivist responses were characterized by an attempt to attribute the differences in opinion of the scientists to: experimental errors (a1), different techniques and methods (a2), created by God (a3), pure theory (a4), and so on. Transitional responses attributed the differences to: different intentions (b1), ways of thinking (b2), no clear definition (b3), different points of view (b4), and beliefs of the scientists (b6).

**Table 7. Comparison of teachers' and students' responses on all items**

| Teacher | Item | | | |
|---|---|---|---|---|
| | 1 | 2 | 3 | 4 |
| 1 | st | b1 | a1 | st |
| | (P) | (T) | (P) | (P) |
| 2 | st | st | a8 | st |
| | (T) | (T) | (P) | (P) |
| 3 | st | a3 | a6 | st |
| | (P) | (P) | (P) | (P) |
| 4 | st | st | a3 | st |
| | (P) | (T) | (P) | (T) |
| 5 | a8 | a3 | a4 | a2 |
| | (P) | (P) | (P) | (P) |
| 6 | a11 | a1 | a1 | b4 |
| | (P) | (P) | (P) | (T) |
| 7 | a2 | a1 | st | st |
| | (P) | (P) | (P) | (T) |

P = Positivist, T = Transitional, L = Lakatosian, st = see text. Numbers such as, a1, b1, c1 ... refer to the students' responses (see text) and the teachers' responses were considered to be similar to these.

### Teachers' Responses

Table 7 presents a comparison of the teachers' responses with respect to that of the students' and their classification as positivist (P), transitional (T), or Lakatosian (L). Each of the teachers' response was compared to that of the students and assigned the same number (e.g., a1, b1, c1, etc.) as the students' responses. Below this number appears the classification: P, T, or L. When a teachers' response does not coincide with any of the students' responses, it is indicated by st (see text) with the respective classification below.

### Item 1

Six of the teachers responded with a positivist approach, one transitional and none Lakatosian (see Table 7). The following response by teacher 1 is fairly representative of a 'Baconian inductive ascent': "Theories are the result of systematic observation of phenomena that we try to explain. When some of these theories cannot be proved, they are subject to changes or modifications – which, permits the constant evolution of science."

The following response from teacher 2 is illustrative of a conflicting approach: "Rapid progress in chemistry during the present century is well illustrated by our increasing knowledge of the atom, which creates uncertainty as to where are we heading in our pursuit of the reality. *We only know, what we consider to be 'our truth' of the reality.* Atomic theory has been of incalculable value to the chemists. Nevertheless, the history of science shows that on more than one occasion, a hypothesis after having shown its utility for discovery and the coordination of knowledge has been abandoned for another more in harmony with later discoveries. Some distinguished scientists consider that the atomic theory awaits the same fate. At present we have a precise knowledge of many properties of the atoms and molecules, and hence *they cannot be considered as 'imaginary'.* New theories should be welcome as *they help us to get closer to the truth"* (emphasis added). This response was classified as transitional as it helps to highlight (consider the parts in italics) the contradiction in the teacher's thinking. To begin with the teacher accepts the tentative nature of science by considering the reality to be 'our truth', but later she/he considers that the atomic theories can no longer be considered as 'imaginary' and finally considers the new theories to be an attempt 'to get closer to the truth'. The latter part of the response clearly shows positivist thinking.

Teacher 3 responded by a positivist approach by attributing the changes in scientific theories to valid investigations that can provide proof: "Progress in science is characterized by a change in the postulates of a theory. In medicine, for example constant changes in the theories (*attributable to proofs provided by valid investigations*) have helped us to achieve a better quality of life" (emphasis added). Teacher 4 used a similar reasoning by pointing out: "A change in theories shows that we are careful enough to *demonstrate* each one of the postulates that form a theory."

### Item 2

Four of the teachers responded with a positivist approach, three transitional and none Lakatosian (see Table 7). The following response by teacher 2 was classified as transitional as it showed a contradiction: "The experimental work of the following scientists has helped to describe the atom: Stoney (particle nature of electricity), Thomson (existence of the electron), and Millikan (value of the charge of the electron). Each one of them proposed a model of the atom – although all the models are different, it is possible to use the important elements in each model, in order *to create a model that adapts more to the reality*" (emphasis added). Except for some experimental details this response starts well but the latter part (underlined) is problematical. On the one hand it lacks the appreciation that the different models are based on rival hypotheses that conflict with each other (Lakatos, 1970) and besides it conceptualizes the scientists' models as an adaptation of the reality. Teacher 4 also used a similar approach in the following terms: "I accept the model that *truly* represents the information provided by investigation, viz., the vector model of the atom" (emphasis added).

### Item 3

All seven teachers responded with a positivist approach and six of them coincided with at least one of the students' responses (see Table 7). Teacher 7 responded in the following positivist terms: "A scientific law summarizes a large number of facts in an abbreviated fashion, and can be generalized to other analogous phenomena. On the other hand, a scientific theory explains and interprets the observed facts and the established laws. Examples: Laws of conservation of matter and energy and Einstein's theory in which he expressed that energy and matter are different forms of the same substance." It is interesting to observe the degree to which this teachers' response is similar to what Lederman and O'Malley (1990) consider to be a definition of a theory and a law as presented by the teacher (p. 231).

Furthermore, the similarity between this teachers' response and the following textbook description of the scientific method is striking: "The results are examined for general relationships that will unify the observations. Sometimes a wide variety of observations can be summarized in a general verbal statement or mathematical equation known as a *law*. One example is the law of conservation of matter ..., which summarizes the results of thousands of experimental observations. More often, however, a tentative explanation is suggested. Such a proposal is called a *hypothesis*.... A hypothesis is tested by further experiments, and, if it is capable of explaining the large body of experimental data, it is dignified by the name *theory*" (Holtzclaw & Robinson, 1988, pp. 10-11, original italics). It is interesting to observe that the authors have used the word 'dignified' in this context, perhaps in order to emphasize the difference between laws and theories.

*Item 4*

Four of the teachers responded with a positivist approach, three transitional and none Lakatosian (see Table 7). Teacher 1 responded with the following positivist approach: "I consider the beliefs of the astrophysicists to be based on the invention of new technologies, which helps them to explore the universe and discover new stars. And if there are some who have the contrary opinion, it indicates that they recognize *His existence in all its dimensions*" (emphasis added). Teacher 2 responded in the following terms: "If we accept that the universe is expanding, it implies that we are creating matter, which contradicts the laws of conservation of matter and energy". This teacher apparently considers any alternative interpretation of nature as a refutation of the existing laws, perhaps in a Popperian sense. Teacher 3 reacted strongly against the possibility of any alternative interpretation: "Human ability to think rationally has permitted us to develop science to its present stage. If the proposition in this item is logical then in the field of chemistry we would still be following the criteria of the Greeks of year 400 B.C."

The following response by teacher 4 was classified as transitional: "Each one of the scientists has an established conception of what scientific rigor is all about and hence discrepancies must appear." This response falls short of a Lakatosian interpretation as it does not explicitly postulate the possibility of rival hypotheses. Teacher 7 gave the following transitional response: "This is due to the creative impulse of these scientists, which led their imagination to interpret the experimental findings differently."

# CONCLUSION: FROM 'BACONIAN INDUCTIVE ASCENT' TO THE 'IRRELEVANCE' OF SCIENTIFIC LAWS

Most of the students and teachers responded to all four items with a positivist approach and what is more important is the fact that both use the same sort of reasoning. Epistemological beliefs of students and teachers in this study can be summarized in the following terms: A scientific theory has not been proved in its totality, whereas a scientific law has not only been proved but is also universal, and furthermore, a theory tells us about more complex and explicit things. Apparently, the widespread belief in this conceptualization of the difference between theories and laws by both teachers and students, is a stumbling block towards a deeper understanding of the scientific endeavor.

In order to clarify the issue and explore possible educational implications, let us consider Newton's law of gravitation, discussed previously in chapter 2. According to Lakatos (1970), it is one of the, "... best-corroborated scientific theory of all times ...." (p. 92). Note that Lakatos refers to it as a theory. Feynman (1967) endorses the view that it is, "... the greatest generalization achieved by the human mind" (p. 14). In spite of such impressive credentials, Cartwright (1983) asks: "Does this law (gravitation) truly describe how bodies behave?" (p.57) and responds laconically: "Assuredly not" (p. 57). Cartwright (1983) explains further: "*These two laws are not true: worse they are not even approximately true*" (p. 57, emphasis added). It is plausible to suggest that Newton was not aware hence did not entertain the idea that charge on a body could influence the force exerted between two bodies. Consequently, his quantitative data could not be predicted by the law of gravitation. Thus, in order to formulate his law, Newton inevitably resorted to idealization based on a hypothesis (despite claims to the contrary), that is an interaction between the quantitative data and the imperative of presuppositions (cf. Niaz, 2005).

The crux of the issue is that following Galileo's method of idealization (considered to be at the heart of all modern physics, by Cartwright, 1989, p. 188), scientific laws, being epistemological constructions, do not describe the behavior of actual bodies (for further discussion see chap. 2 and 10). Newton's laws, gas laws, Piaget's epistemic subject – they all describe the behavior of ideal bodies that are abstractions from the evidence of experience and the laws are true only when a considerable number of disturbing factors, itemized in the *ceteris paribus* clauses, are eliminated (cf. Ellis, 1991; Garrison, 1986; Kitchener, 1993; Lewin, 1935; Matthews, 1987; McMullin, 1985; Niaz, 1991a).

At this stage it is important to point out that Cartwright's (1983) thesis about the nature of physical laws has not gone unchallenged and is the subject of considerable debate in the philosophy of science literature (cf. Cartwright, 1989, 1991; Needham, 1991; Nugayev, 1991; Papineau, 1991).

More recently, Christie (1994) has shown that how even one of the most cherished laws of most chemistry textbooks, viz., the law of multiple proportions is not even a precise proposition and concluded: " ... on a more revolutionary note, .... many quite respectable laws of science are non-universal, and even that there are a few that cannot be formulated as precise propositions" (p. 613).

With this background, it is essential that science teachers reconsider the dichotomous presentation found in most textbooks of scientific progress in terms of theories and laws. As an example, a reconstruction of students' responses on Item 3 shows that the following responses constitute a progressive transition: a3 → b2 → c1, in students' thinking, similar to a Lakatosian progressive 'problemshift' (Lakatos, 1970). Responses similar to a3 would conceptualize progress in science in the positivist sense, with a clear demarcation between laws and theories, referred to as 'Baconian inductive ascent' by Lakatos (1970, p. 147). Responses, similar to b2 consider the law to originate from a theoretical framework and finally response c1 considers the experiments to provide corroboration for both theories and laws – thus making the difference between the two almost superfluous.

Lakatos (1970), for example, has clearly pointed out the 'irrelevance' of Boyle's gas law for the later development of the kinetic theory of gases by Maxwell and Boltzmann (p. 147). Similarly, Niaz (1995a) has shown that the mere ability to manipulate the different variables of the ideal gas law (PV = nRT) does not facilitate conceptual understanding of the kinetic theory of gases. The above reconstruction of students' and teachers' responses is important as it provides: 1) a rationale for considering the difference between theories and laws as superfluous and hence 'irrelevant'. According to Lakatos (1970, p. 129) the conflict is not between theories and laws but rather between an interpretative and an explanatory theory; and 2) a plausible blueprint for alternatives to the traditional textbook treatment of progress in science.

At this stage it is important to explain how this chapter is relevant with regards to chapters 4-9 of this book. These chapters described the application of history and philosophy of science in domain-specific content areas, such as the mole (chap. 4), stoichiometry (chap. 5), atomic structure (chap. 6), gases (chap. 7), heat energy and temperature (chap. 8), and chemical equilibrium (chap. 9). In contrast, chapter 10 provides a rationale for the integration of the domain-specific studies by facilitating a common denominator. Items 1 and 3 of the study reported in chapter 10 are particularly relevant for establishing the relationship between the domain-specific studies and students' understanding of scientific theories and laws in general. Two examples taken from chapters 5 and 6 will be discussed to illustrate this relationship.

Chapter 5, had concluded that students' difficulty in stoichiometry could be attributed to a hard/soft core of beliefs and furthermore these beliefs were strengthened by epigrammatic versions of the Law of Definite Proportions and the Law of Conservation of Mass, as found in most textbooks. Let us now see how students responded to Item 3 (Is there a difference between a scientific theory and a scientific law? Give an example to illustrate your answer) in this study (chap. 10). Most of the students with a positivist response clearly differentiated between a scientific theory and law. The following response (a3) is particularly relevant: "Yes. A theory is something that has not been proved in its totality, whereas a law has not only been proved but is also universal. For example, the Law of Conservation of Mass, that we can prove by an experiment without any inconvenience." This finding provides support for considering the Law of Conservation of Mass as one of the sources of students' hard/soft core of beliefs.

In chapter 6, Item 4 had asked the students: "How would you have interpreted, if on using different gases in the cathode-ray tube, the relation (e/m) would have resulted different?" Although most of the positivist responses considered this to be not possible, the following response (a7) is quite revealing: "That is a poor interpretation, as we *already know* that the relation (e/m) is independent of the gas" (emphasis added). This response clearly shows that students consider Thomson's experimental finding that the charge-to-mass (e/m) ratio of all gases was constant, as 'predetermined' or even perhaps a well established law, and hence not subject to change. Many responses on Items 1 and 3 of chapter 10, reflected a similar thinking.

Finally, a major contribution of chapter 10 is that it corroborates students' thinking in domain-specific content areas, as reported in chapters 4-9.

# Chapter 11

# CONCLUSION

A major contribution of the history and philosophy of science to science teaching is to facilitate the transition from our present textbook presentation of scientific laws as inductive generalizations to a more complex and intricate understanding. In the new conceptualization of science, scientific progress is subsumed by a process involving conflicting frameworks based on processes that require the elaboration of rival hypotheses and their evaluation in the light of new evidence (Lakatos, 1970). It provides a rationale for understanding the difference between scientific theories and laws, by pointing out that the conflict is rather between an interpretative and an explanatory theory, and hence the 'irrelevance' of scientific laws. According to Machamer, Pera and Baltas (2000), although most achievements in scientific progress have involved controversies, it is paradoxical that there is a dissociation between science as actually practiced and science as perceived by both scientists and philosophers:

> While nobody would deny that science in the making has been replete with controversies the same people often depict its essence or end product as free from disputes, as the uncontroversial rational human endeavor par excellence (p. 3).

Once again textbooks will have to abandon the 'post-Whewellian' tradition, in which authors first state the principles, definitions, and laws and then ask the students to work out exercises as illustrations of the laws (Stinner, 1992). Whewell (1856) emphasized the importance of learning the concepts outside the grip of a mathematical formulation and that we do not start with the right concepts at the beginning of an inquiry, but rather we arrive at them as a result of the inquiry. According to Brown (1990): "Whewell and Lakatos are equally and vehemently opposed to that spirit of inquiry that says define your terms before you start" (p. 127). Given the widespread use and popularity of behavioral objectives (Mager, 1962) most science teachers will find the new approach if not counter intuitive, quite novel. The following comment in the science education literature shows that teachers are becoming more aware of such problems: "It is also in the nature of chemistry that the appropriate meaning for a term develops as the student passes from school to college to university" (Taber, 1995, p. 56).

The methodology of rational reconstruction of students' and teachers' understanding of the nature of science by using a domain-specific topic (atomic structure) is an important application of the history and philosophy of science to science teaching (see chap. 6). In comparison to previous work in the literature (cf. Lederman, 1992 for a review) the rationale of this study is based explicitly on an historical development of the subject and its treatment by philosophers of science. The methodology developed explores students' and teachers' understanding through a series of probing questions. The main objective is not to emphasize experimental details but to reconstruct the 'heuristic principle' required to 'structure inquiry' (Schwab, 1974).

For example, in the case of J.J. Thomson's work besides the experimental details of cathode ray particles (emphasized by most textbooks), the 'heuristic principle' involved the testing of rival hypotheses, viz., a determination of the charge-to-mass ratio for the cathode ray particles would help to identify it as an ion or some other charged particle (Niaz, 1994a, 1994b). Item 1, helped students to recall that Thomson's work dealt with the determination of the charge-to-mass (e/m) relation. Item 2 was designed to make students reflect as to why Thomson determined the charge-to-mass relation (e/m) relation. Item 3 was more specific, as it provided a clue by pointing out that the relation (e/m) remained constant on using different gases. Finally, Item 4 provided a challenge by providing a hypothetical experimental finding: How would you have interpreted, if on using different gases in the cathode-ray tube, the relation (e/m) would have resulted different? Not surprisingly, Item 4 was perhaps not only difficult for the students but also disconcerting as 40% of the students did not respond to it. It is plausible to suggest that this reconstruction of students' and teachers' understanding of structure of the atom can facilitate more meaningful learning.

Progressive transitions referred to in this book (see chapters 4, 6, and 7) require an explanation. For example, on comparing Strategy A and B in Item 1B about the mole (Study 2, chap. 4), it is pertinent to ask: Is the use of strategies indicative of greater conceptual understanding or the ability to 'chunk' more variables without losing sight of the main solution plan? From a neo-Piagetian perspective, it is the dynamic interaction between various organismic factors (constructive operators, such as mental capacity, field factor, content and logical learning; cf. Niaz, 1991b) that lead to conceptual understanding and not chunking alone. According to Pascual-Leone (1987), this is based on the:

> ... dialectical-constructivist idea that quantitative limitations and/or increments in mental processing capacity are, in dynamic interaction with other organismic factors, the efficient causes of qualitative stages" (p. 535).

## 11.1. PROLIFERATION OF MODELS OF CONCEPTUAL CHANGE

A review of the literature shows that theories in science and philosophy of science are generally overthrown (discarded or progressive changes) by the competition between rival theories (cf. Hunt, 1994, p. 138). Given this insight from the history and philosophy of science, it is plausible to suggest a similar process of confrontation between rival conceptualizations (models of conceptual change) in science education (cf. Niaz, 1993b; Power, 1976). A detailed account of the different models of conceptual change is beyond the scope of this essay. Nevertheless, a brief review of the literature shows that we are heading towards a proliferation of models of conceptual change, which is a positive development.

The increase in literature on conceptual change is indeed impressive (see references section). Although different models have drawn inspiration from various philosophical sources, and a detailed analysis of the subject being beyond the scope of this essay, it is observed that the following models have been more explicit in pointing out some of the major sources of philosophical inspiration:

Models based on the philosophy of Kuhn: Posner, Strike, Hewson, and Gertzog (1982); Strike and Posner (1992).

Models based on the philosophy of Laudan: Duschl (1990); Villani (1992).

Models based on the philosophy of Toulmin: Nussbaum (1989); Mortimer (1995).

Models based on the philosophy of Lakatos: Chinn and Brewer (1993); Niaz (1995a, 1998b, & Guidelines in chapter 3).

Models based on Worldview theory: Cobern (1996).

## 11.2. THE ROLE OF IDEALIZATION IN THE BUILDING OF MODELS

Importance of the research methodology of idealization (building of models, based on simplifying assumptions) in the history and philosophy of science was shown in Chapter 2 and 10. This section provides an illustration of how scientists and philosophers of science differ sharply on the role of idealization, which shows the complexity of the underlying issues and hence the difficulties faced by the students. The following dialogue took place at a Conference held in Jerusalem (January, 1971). Besides the participants mentioned below, J. Agassi, I.B. Cohen, Y. Elkana, E. Hiebert, G. Holton, M. Jammer, I. Lakatos, S. Sambursky, and S. Toulmin, were also present.

"Bechler: The historical fact is that Newton writes that he derived it [his laws] and shows the derivation, but the derivation is false – completely false, ... The crucial fact is that he assumes the trajectories of the planets to be firstly circular, which is false, and secondly concentric, which is also false. And from these two assumptions, plus Kepler's third law, .... plus Huygens' law of centripetal force – he derives the inverse square law. So the whole thing, the whole derivation is valid, but baseless. That is to say: if you assume concentric and circular trajectories the conclusion follows validly, but these assumptions simply happen not to be true of the planetary motions.

Rosenfeld: I think you put the thing too sharply... you say that Newton's derivation is false – you used that word – because he assumed a circular orbit.

Bechler: He made false assumptions.

Rosenfeld: Well, you must be careful in calling the assumption of circular orbits false – it is not what a physicist would call a false assumption. He would say it is an approximation with a high degree of validity.

Bechler: No! It has not even a high degree of validity.

Rosenfeld: But of course it has – I mean the moon's orbit is almost circular.

Bechler: The moon's yes, but not the planets. The planets are off-circle.

Rosenfeld: Most of the planets are not. The physicist never bothers with inessential complications when he tries to find something. One first tries to simplify the problem as much as possible. Now that is a dangerous step, of course, because one may throw away something which one thinks is unimportant and which then turns out to be important – well, one has to learn" (Elkana, 1974, pp. 280-281).

This dialogue among some of the leading philosophers of science, could very well have taken place at a science teachers' conference as well. Annual conferences of the National Association for Research in Science Teaching (NARST), held in Atlanta (1990) and Lake Geneva, WI (1991) bear witness to this. Issues raised at the two conferences highlight cogently the conceptual complexity of idealization and are available in the literature (cf. Kitchener, 1993; Lawson, 1991; 1993; Niaz, 1991a, 1993c, 1995e; Shayer, 1993). For example, Lawson (1991) while discussing the case of Galileo and falling bodies concludes:

> How can Galileo's theory be correct when its predictions are false? The *answer is simple. We need not even concern ourselves with experiments with inclined planes.* All that need be done is to add an additional assumption to Galileo's theory that bodies must fall in a vacuum so that they are not hindered by *collisions with invisible gas molecules.* When this assumption is added, the theory's predictions become in complete agreement with empirical data (p. 583, emphasis added).

Thus in one stroke, Lawson not only simplifies issues but also dismisses Galileo's research methodology of idealization. Lawson's lack of a historical perspective becomes even more evident when he asks: "Are you willing to grant Galileo this additional assumption? Most people are; therefore Galileo' view has triumphed" (p. 583). Interestingly, Lawson ignores the fact that Galileo had to convince his contemporaries and not present day scientists, regarding the very existence of a vacuum, which was then considered to be a sensitive hypothesis, and the first vacuum pump itself was built around 1658 (cf. Agassi, 1977, p. 204) after Galileo's death in 1650.

Again, as late as 1860 scientists did not conceptualize 'collisions with invisible gas molecules' (cf. Mendoza, 1990), as Lawson seems to be suggesting. Similarly, referring to Galileo's discovery of the isochronic movement of the pendulum, Matthews (1994, p. 111) points out that, "... the most widely used high school physics text in the world – the Physical Science Study Committee's *Physics* (PSSC, 1960)" misinterprets the Galilean methodology. According to the textbook, Galileo's observation of the chandelier in the church at Pisa led to the discovery of the Law of Isochrony. This poses a dilemma: If the textbook account is to be believed then why was the isochronism of the pendulum only seen in the sixteenth century, when thousands of people of genius with acute powers of observation had seen swinging lamps and weights for years. Lawson (1991) has suggested that Galileo's view would triumph if he was granted additional assumptions. History of science, however, shows that Galileo was not granted such assumptions (ceteris paribus clauses).

As early as 1636 the notable physicist Mersenne reproduced Galileo's experiments and not only agreed with del Monte (Galileo's patron and adversary) but doubted whether Galileo had ever conducted the experiments (cf, Koyré, 1968, pp. 113-117). Del Monte and other critics pointed out that actual pendulums, do not behave as described by Galileo. Matthews (1994, p. 117) has pointed out that even modern researchers have duplicated the experimental conditions described by Galileo and have found that they do not give the results that Galileo claimed. According to Matthews (1994): "No amount of looking [observations] will reveal isochronic motion [of the pendulum]; looking is important, but something else is required: a better appreciation of what science is and what it is aiming to do; an epistemology of science" (pp. 117-118).

We should not lose sight of the fact that starting from the work of Galileo, building of models based on simplifying assumptions (idealization) is considered to be an important characteristic of modern non-Aristotelian science (see chap. 2 for details). Lakatos (1970) specifically used this methodology to study Newton's and Bohr's research programs. Kuhn (1977) in his 'A function for thought experiments' (first published 1964) pointed out that thought experiments assist scientists in arriving at laws and theories different from the ones they had held before and that the new understanding, "... is not an understanding of *nature* but rather of the scientist's *conceptual apparatus* (p. 242, original emphasis). According to McMullin (1985):

> The move from the complexity of nature to the specially contrived order of the experiment is a form of idealization. The diversity of causes found in Nature is reduced and made manageable. The influence of impediments, i.e., causal factors which affect the process under study in ways not at present of interest, is eliminated or lessened sufficiently that it may be ignored (p. 265).

More significantly, Papineau (1976) has interpreted the process of idealization within the Lakatosian framework by pointing out that:

> ... the ideal type generalisation itself is the 'negative heuristic', a basic principle which is itself unfalsifiable, but which together with the 'positive heuristic' generates a series of empirical generalisations. The 'positive heuristic' would be some 'partially articulated suggestions' of the following kind: suggestions about the limits within which situations approximating to the ideal type situation will approximately satisfy the consequent term of the ideal type generalisation ... (p. 145).

With this background, it is understandable if science teachers do not grasp the notion of idealization. It is, however, somewhat surprising that philosophers of science differ so sharply on certain fundamental issues as evidenced from the above dialogue. Indeed, Elkana's (1974) reticence in not having used the editorial blue pencil, "... to polish the style of these discussions solely as an academic exercise for the community of scientists, philosophers and historians" (p. v) has provided an important pedagogical lesson.

Let us now see the other side of the coin, viz., how do scientists understand and conceptualize idealization? A recent debate about the work of Bohr and its importance for the nature of the chemical bond, provides a good illustration. The scene is set by Ogilvie (1990): "Thus this apparent success of the Bohr theory depends on the *fortuitous cancellation of two errors*, namely circular orbits and the dependence of energy on the quantum number for angular momentum; ..." (p. 281, emphasis added). Linus Pauling's (1992) response to this criticism is indeed a pedagogical masterpiece for learning philosophy of science and is worth reproducing at length:

> Ogilvie states that the great physicist Niels Bohr made two errors, which fortuitously cancelled one another, namely, treating circular orbits and using quantized angular momentum to evaluate the energy. Bohr, in his remarkable contribution to quantum theory, introduced two innovative ideas. One idea is that only a few of the infinity of states of a system according

to classical dynamics are allowed: these are the quantized energy levels.... Moreover, Bohr calculated the energy levels for H and He$^+$ by a quantum method (quantizing the angular momentum) that he had devised. Wilson and Sommerfeld soon showed that for an elliptical orbit in H and He the energy is independent of the eccentricity. Bohr had taken the eccentricity to be zero (spherical orbits), and had got results in essentially exact agreement with the spectra. When quantum mechanics was developed, 12 years later, it was found that the eccentricity is never zero. *This fact does not justify the derogation of Bohr as having committed errors* (p. 519, emphasis added).

In retrospect, some philosophers of science consider Newton to have made false assumptions (see dialogue above, Elkana, 1974) and some scientists consider Bohr to have committed errors. Given these antecedents, freshman students' responses after having studied the topic of atomic structure, to the following questions (see Items 9 and 11 of the questionnaire in chap. 6) are comprehensible: a) If Rutherford's experiments changed Thomson's model of the atom entirely, in your opinion did Thomson make mistakes while doing his experiments? Of the 171 students, 24 (14%) responded that Thomson had made mistakes in his experiments. Interestingly, 47 (27%) students did not respond; and b) If Bohr's experiments changed Rutherford's model of the atom, in your opinion did Rutherford make mistakes while doing his experiments? Of the 171 students, 19 (11%) responded that Rutherford had made mistakes in his experiments. Again, 52 (30%) students did not respond, which shows the complexity of the issues involved.

According to Kuhn (1977) thought experiments facilitated the work of great 'weavers of new conceptual fabrics' such as, Galileo, Descartes, Einstein and Bohr, as they can enable the scientist to use, "... as an integral part of his knowledge what that knowledge had previously made inaccessible to him" (p. 263). With this background it is easier to understand why, "Idealization in science has been recognized as one of the major stumbling blocks to meaningful learning of science" (Matthews, 1994, p. 211).

Finally, it is suggested that the following aspects can be utilized by the teachers to design better teaching strategies:

1.  Looking for the core beliefs (cf. 'hard core', Lakatos, 1970) of the students in a topic can be an appropriate starting point for a teaching strategy.

2.  Exploration of the relationship between core beliefs and student alternative conceptions (misconceptions) could be the next step. In order to implement this, it is essential that students' alternative conceptions not be considered as wrong responses, but instead interpreted within an epistemological perspective, viz., as models, perhaps in the same sense as used by scientists to simplify the complexity of a problem. According to Strike and Posner (1992): "... a misconception is not merely a mistake or a false belief. Either it must also play the kind of organizing role in cognition that paradigms play, or it must be dependent on such organizing concepts .... A misconception, thus, may become a candidate for change" (p. 153). Similarly, Clement, Brown, and Zietsman (1989) consider students' alternative conceptions as 'creative constructions' (p. 555).

3.  The cognitive complexity of the core belief can be broken down into a series of related and probing questions (cf. Teaching Experiments 1 and 2 in chap. 9). This can be facilitated by identifying the core beliefs (hard core), which are more resistant

to change and the soft core of student beliefs (see criteria for classification in chap. 3).

4. Students resist changes in their core beliefs (e.g., the rate of the forward reaction increases with time in chemical equilibrium, see chap. 9) more strongly than those in other related aspects of a topic (cf. Chinn & Brewer, 1993). 'Auxiliary hypotheses' used by students to defend their core beliefs can provide clues and guidance for the construction of novel teaching strategies.

5. In spite of the similarities between Strike and Posner (1992) model of conceptual change and our model, it is essential to point out an important difference. Strike and Posner consider students' misconceptions as similar to paradigms in the Kuhnian (Kuhn, 1970) sense, and hence their resistance to change. On the other hand, we consider students' misconceptions as alternative conceptions (theories) that compete with the present scientific theories (and at times recapitulate theories that the scientists held in the past) in the Lakatosian sense (Lakatos, 1970). This important epistemological difference is important for educators, as Kuhnian paradigms imply the incommensurability thesis, which has been the subject of considerable controversy (cf. Barker & Gholson, 1984; Friman, et al., 1993; Lakatos, 1970; Malone, 1993; Reese & Overton, 1972; Segal & Lachman, 1972). For science educators, the crux of the issue is that according to Kuhn (1970) different paradigms are incommensurate because their core beliefs are resistant to change and that paradigms do not merge over time, rather they displace each other after periods of chaotic upheaval or scientific revolution. In a nut-shell, misconceptions interpreted as paradigms lead to situations that are not conducive to debate as Kuhn's (1970) incommensurability thesis implies that any one science can accommodate only one paradigm. A Lakatosian conceptual change teaching strategy after having identified the hard and the soft core of students' beliefs will look for 'auxiliary hypotheses' students use to protect their core beliefs and subsequently introduce/construct alternative explanations that contradict their original beliefs. On the other hand, a Kuhnian conceptual change teaching strategy would perhaps consider students' beliefs as more rigid and less conducive to change. Strike and Posner (1992, p. 169), for example, accept the criticism that their model of conceptual change does not foresee explicit instructional strategies of the sort developed in studies reported here.

# REFERENCES

Abd-El-Khalick, F., & Lederman, N.G. (2000). Improving science teachers' conceptions of nature of science: A critical review of the literature. *International Journal of Science Education, 22*, 665-701.

Achinstein, P. (1987). Scientific discovery and Maxwell's kinetic theory. *Philosophy of Science, 54*, 409-434.

Adey, P., & Shayer, M. (1994). *Really raising standards: Cognitive intervention and academic achievement.* London: Routledge.

Agassi, J. (1977). Who discovered Boyle's law? *Studies in History and Philosophy of Science, 8*(3), 189-250.

Akeroyd, F.M. (1991). Predictions and the nature of science. *School Science Review, 72*, 138-141.

Bannerjee, A.C. (1991). Misconceptions of students and teachers in chemical equilibrium. *International Journal of Science Education, 13*, 487-494.

Bannerjee, A.C., Power, C.N. (1991). The development of modules for the teaching of chemical equilibrium. *International Journal of Science Education, 13,* 355-362.

Barker, P., & Gholson, B. (1984). The history of the psychology learning as a rational process: Lakatos versus Kuhn. In H.W. Reese (Ed.) *Advances in child development and behavior* (vol. 18, pp. 227-244). New York: Academic Press.

Basili, P.A., & Sanford, J.P. (1991). Conceptual change strategies and cooperative group work in chemistry. *Journal of Research in Science Teaching, 28*, 293-304.

Beck, M.T., & Kauffman, G.B. (1994). Scientific methodology and ethics in university education. *Journal of Chemical Education, 71*(11), 922-924.

Beilin, H. (1985). Dispensable and indispensable elements in Piaget's theory: On the core of Piaget's research program. In T.S. Evans (Ed.) *Genetic epistemology: Yesterday and today* (pp. 107-125). New York: City University of New York.

Beilin, H. (1990). Piaget's theory: Alive and more vigorous than ever. *Human Development, 33*(6), 362-365.

Ben-Zvi, R., Eylon, B., & Silberstein, J. (1986). Is an atom of copper malleable? *Journal of Chemical Education, 63,* 64-66.

Bergquist, W., & Heikkinen, H. (1990). Student ideas regarding chemical equilibrium. *Journal of Chemical Education, 67,* 1000-1003.

Berthollet, C.L. (1809). *Researches into the laws of chemical affinity.* Baltimore, MD: Philip H. Nicklin & Co.

Bidell, T. (1988). Vygotsky, Piaget and the dialectic of development. *Human Development, 31*, 329-348.

Blanco, R., & Niaz, M. (1997). Epistemological beliefs of students and teachers about the nature of science: From 'Baconian inductive ascent' to the 'irrelevance' of scientific laws. *Instructional Science, 25*, 203-231.

Blanco, R., & Niaz, M. (1998). Baroque tower on a gothic base: A Lakatosian reconstruction of students' and teachers' understanding of structure of the atom. *Science and Education, 7*, 327-360.

Brainerd, C.J. (1978). The stage question in cognitive developmental theory. *Behavioral and Brain Sciences, 2*, 173-213.

Brickhouse, N.W. (1989). The teaching of the philosophy of science in secondary classrooms: Case studies of teachers' personal theories. *International Journal of Science Education, 11*, 437-449.

Brown, D.E. (1992). Using examples and analogies to remediate misconceptions in physics: Factors influencing conceptual change. *Journal of Research in Science Teaching, 29*, 17-34.

Brown, D.E. (1993). Refocusing core intuitions: A concretizing role for analogy in conceptual change. *Journal of Research in Science Teaching, 30*, 1273-1290.

Brown, D.E., & Clement, J. (1987). Misconceptions concerning Newton's law of action and reaction: The underestimated importance of the Third law. Proceedings of the Second International Seminar on Misconceptions and Educational Strategies in Science and Mathematics, 3, 39-53. Ithaca, NY: Cornell University.

Brown, J.R. (1990). Proof and truth in Lakatos's masterpiece. *International Studies in the Philosophy of Science, 4*(2), 117-130.

Brown, T.L., & LeMay, H.E. (1987). *Chemistry: The central science* (Spanish edition). México, D.F.: Prentice-Hall Hispanoamericana.

Brush, S.G. (1976). *The kind of motion we call heat: A history of the kinetic theory of gases in the nineteenth century* (Book 1). New York: North-Holland.

Brush, S.G. (1978). Why chemistry needs history – and how it can get some. *Journal of College Science Teaching, 7*, 288-291.

Burbules, N.C., & Linn, M.C. (1991). Science education and philosophy of science: Congruence or contradiction? *International Journal of Science Education, 13*, 227-241.

Camacho, M., & Good, R. (1989). Problem solving and chemical equilibrium: Successful versus unsuccessful performance. *Journal of Research in Science Teaching, 26*, 251-272.

Carey, S. (1985). *Conceptual change in childhood*. Cambridge, MA: MIT Press.

Carey, S. (1986). Cognitive science and science education. *American Psychologist, 41*, 1123-1130.

Carey, S., Evans, R., Honda, M., Jay, E., & Unger, C. (1989). 'An experiment is when you try it and see if it works': A study of grade 7 students' understanding of the construction of scientific knowledge. *International Journal of Science Education, 11*, 514-529.

Carey, S., & Smith, C. (1993). On understanding the nature of scientific knowledge. *Educational Psychologist, 28*, 235-251.

Cartwright, N. (1983). *How the laws of physics lie*. Oxford, UK: Clarendon.

Cartwright, N. (1989). *Nature's capacities and their measurement*. Oxford, UK: Clarendon Press.

Cartwright, N. (1991). Can wholism reconcile the inaccuracy of theory with the accuracy of prediction? *Synthese, 89*, 3-13.

Champagne, A.B., Klopfer, L.E., & Gunstone, R.F. (1982). Cognitive research and the design of science instruction. *Educational Psychologist, 17*, 31-53.

Chi, M.T.H. (1992). Conceptual change within and across ontological categories: Examples from learning and discovery in science. In R.N. Giere (Ed.), *Cognitive models of science* (pp. 129-186). Minneapolis, MN: University of Minnesota Press.

Chi, M.T.H., Feltovich, P.J., & Glaser, R. (1981). Categorization and representation of physics problems by experts and novices. *Cognitive Science, 5*, 121-152.

Chiappetta, E.L., Sethna, G.H., & Fillman, D.A. (1991). A quantitative analysis of high school chemistry textbooks for scientific literacy themes and expository learning aids. *Journal of Research in Science Teaching, 28*(10), 939-951.

Chinn, C.A., & Brewer, W.F. (1993). The role of anomalous data in knowledge acquisition: A theoretical framework and implications for science instruction. *Review of Educational Research, 63*, 1-49.

Chomsky, N. (1995). Language and nature. *Mind, 104*, 1-61.

Christie, M. (1994). Philosophers versus chemists concerning 'Laws of Nature.' *Studies in History and Philosophy of Science, 25*, 613-629.

Clement, J. (1987). Overcoming students' misconceptions in physics: The role of anchoring intuitions and analogical validity. Proceedings of the Second International Seminar on Misconceptions and Educational Strategies in Science and Mathematics (vol. 3, pp. 84-96). Ithaca, NY: Cornell University.

Clement, J., Brown, D.E., & Zietsman, A. (1989). Not all preconceptions are misconceptions: Finding 'anchoring conceptions' for grounding instruction on students' intuitions. *International Journal of Science Education, 11*, 554-565.

Cleminson, A. (1990). Establishing an espistemological base for science teaching in the light of contemporary notions of the nature of science and of how children learn science. *Journal of Research in Science Teaching, 27*, 429-445.

Cobb, P., & Steffe, L. (1983). The constructivist researcher as theory and model builder. *Journal for Research in Mathematics Education, 14*, 83-94.

Cobern, W.W. (1996). Worldview theory and conceptual change in science education. *Science Education, 80*, 579-610.

Conant, J.B. (1947). *On understanding science*. New Haven, CT: Yale University Press.

Conant, J.B. (1957). Ed. *Harvard case histories in experimental science* (2 vols). Cambridge, MA: Harvard University Press.

Cooley, W.W., & Klopfer, L.E. (1961). *Manual for the test on understanding science*. Princeton, NJ: Educational Testing Service.

Cowan, R., & Sutcliffe, N.B. (1991). What children's temperature predictions reveal of their understanding of temperature. *British Journal of Educational Psychology, 61*, 300-309.

Dagher, Z.R. (1994). Does the use of analogies contribute to conceptual change? *Science Education, 78*, 601-614.

D'Ambrosio, B.S., & Campos, T.M.M. (1992). Preservice teachers' representation of children's understanding of mathematical concepts: Conflicts and conflict resolution. *Educational Studies in Mathematics, 23*, 213-230.

De Berg, K.C. (1989). The emergence of quantification in the pressure-volume relationship for gases: A textbook analysis. *Science Education, 73*(2), 115-134.

De Berg, K.C. (1992). Mathematics in science: The role of the history of science in communicating the significance of mathematical formalism in science. *Science and Education, 1*(1), 77-87.

Delamont, S. (1990). A paradigm shift in research on science education? *Studies in Science Education, 18,* 153-177.

Demastes, S.S., Good, R.G., & Peebles, P. (1995). Students' conceptual ecologies and the process of conceptual change in evolution. *Science Education, 79,* 637-666.

di Sessa, A. (1982). Unlearning Aristotelian physics: A study of knowledge-based learning. *Cognitive Science, 6,* 37-75.

di Sessa, A. (1993). Toward an epistemology of physics. *Cognition and Instruction, 10*(2&3), 105-225.

Driver, R. (1981). Pupils' alternative frameworks in science. *European Journal of Science Education, 3,* 93-101.

Driver, R., & Easley, J. (1978). Pupils and paradigms: A review of literature related to concept development in adolescent science students. *Studies in Science Education, 5,* 61-84.

Duhem, P. (1954). *The aim and structure of physical theory* (trans. P.P. Wiener). Princeton, NJ: Princeton University Press. (Original work published 1914).

Duschl, R.A. (1990). *Restructuring science education.* New York: Teachers College Press.

Duschl, R.A. (1994). Research on the history and philosophy of science. In D.L. Gabel (Ed.) *Handbook of research on science teaching* (pp. 443-465). New York: MacMillan.

Duschl, R.A., & Gitomer, D.H. (1991). Epistemological perspectives on conceptual change: Implications for educational practice. *Journal of Research in Science Teaching, 28,* 839-858.

Duschl, R.A., Wright, E. (1989). A case of high school teachers' decision making models for planning and teaching science. *Journal of Research in Science Teaching, 26,* 467-501.

Dykstra, D.I., Boyle, C.F., & Monarch, I. A. (1992). Studying conceptual change in learning physics. *Science Education, 76*(6), 615-652.

Einstein, A., & Infeld, L. (1971). *The evolution of physics.* Cambridge, UK: Cambridge University Press (original work published 1938).

Eisner, E.W. (1992). Are all causal claims positivistic? A reply to Francis Schrag. *Educational Researcher, 21,* 8-9.

Elkana, Y. (1974). Boltzmann's scientific research program and its alternatives. In Y. Elkana (Ed.) *The interaction between science and philosophy* (pp. 243-279). Atlantic Highlands, NJ: Humanities Press.

Elkana, Y., Ed. (1974). *The interaction between science and philosophy.* Atlantic Highlands, NJ: Humanities Press.

Ellis, B.D. (1991). Idealization in science. In C. Dilworth (Ed.), *Idealization IV: Intelligibility in science.* Amsterdam: Rodopi.

Erickson, F. (1992). Why the clinical trial doesn't work as a metaphor for educational research: A response to Schrag. *Educational Researcher, 21,* 9-11.

Erickson, G.L. (1979). Children's conceptions of heat and temperature. *Science and Education, 63,* 221-230.

Erickson, G.L. (1980). Children's viewpoints of heat: A second look. *Science Education, 64,* 323-336.

Ernest, P. (1994). The dialogical nature of mathematics. In P. Ernest (Ed.), *Mathematics, education and philosophy: An international perspective* (pp. 33-48). London: The Falmer Press.

Eylon, B., & Linn, M.C. (1988). Learning and instruction: An examination of four research perspectives in science education. *Review of Educational Research, 58*(3), 251-301.

Favrholdt, D. (1992). *Niels Bohr's philosophical background.* Copenhagen: Royal Danish Academy of Sciences and Letters.

Festinger, L. (1957). *A theory of cognitive dissonance.* New York: Harper.

Feyerabend, P.K. (1975). *Against method.* London: Verso.

Feynman, R. (1967). *The character of physical law.* Cambridge, MA: MIT Press.

Finley, F., Allchin, D., Rhees, D., & Fifield, S. (1995). Proceedings of the Third International History, Philosophy and Science Teaching Conference (2 volumes). Minneapolis, MN: University of Minnesota.

Franco, C., & Colinvaux-de-Dominguez, D. (1992).Genetic epistemology, history of science, and science education. *Science and Education, 1*(3), 255-271.

Friman, P.C., Allen, K.D., Kerwin, M.L.E., & Larzelere, R. (1993). Changes in modern psychology: A citation analysis of the Kuhnian displacement thesis. *American Psychologist, 48*(6), 658-664.

Furió Mas, C.J., Hernández Pérez, J., & Harris, H.H. (1987). Parallels between adolescents' conception of gases and the history of chemistry. *Journal of Chemical Education, 64*(7), 616-618.

Furth, H.G. (1981). *Piaget and knowledge: Theoretical foundations.* Chicago: University of Chicago Press.

Gabel, D.L., Sherwood, R.D., & Enochs, L. (1984). Problem-solving skills of high school chemistry students. *Journal of Research in Science Teaching, 21*, 221-233.

Gallagher, J.J. (1991). Prospective and practicing secondary school science teachers' knowledge and beliefs about the philosophy of science. *Science Education, 75*, 121-133.

Garber, E., Brush, S., & Everitt, C.W.F., Eds. (1986). *Maxwell on molecules and gases.* Cambridge, MA: MIT Press.

Garcia, R. (1987). Sociology of science and sociogenesis of knowledge. In B. Inhelder, D. Caprona, & A. Cornu-Wells (Eds.) *Piaget today* (pp. 127-140). Hove, UK: Erlbaum.

Garnett, P.J., Garnett, P.J., & Hackling, M.W. (1995). Students' alternative conceptions in chemistry: A review of research and implications for teaching and learning. *Studies in Science Education, 25*, 69-95.

Garrison, J.W. (1986). Husserl, Galileo, and the processes of idealization. *Synthese, 66*, 329-338.

Garrison, J.W., & Bentley, M. (1990). Science education, conceptual change, and breaking with everyday experience. *Studies in Philosophy and Education, 10*, 19-36.

Giere, R.N. (1988). *Explaining science: A cognitive approach.* Chicago: University of Chicago Press.

Giere, R.N. (1999). *Science without laws.* Chicago: University of Chicago Press.

Gibbs, A., & Lawson, A.E. (1992). The nature of scientific thinking as reflected by the work of biologists & biology textbooks. *American Biology Teacher, 54*(3), 137-152.

Gil Pérez, D., & Carroscosa Alis, J. (1985). Science learning as a conceptual and methodological change. *European Journal of Science Education, 7*(3), 231-236.

Gilbert, J.K., & Swift, D.J. (1985). Towards a Lakatosian analysis of the Piagetian and alternative conceptions research programs. *Science Education, 69,* 681-696.

Good, R. (1991). The many faces of constructivism. Paper presented at the Bergamo Conference, Dayton, OH, October.

Gorin, G. (1994). Mole and chemical amount. *Journal of Chemical Education, 71*(2), 114-116.

Gorodetsky, M., & Gussarsky, E. (1987). The roles of students and teachers in misconceptualization of aspects in 'chemical equilibrium.' Proceedings of the Second International Seminar on Misconceptions and Educational Strategies in Science and Mathematics, *3,* 186-192. Ithaca, NY: Cornell University.

Gottlieb, G. (1987). The developmental basis of evolutionary change. *Journal of Comparative Psychology, 101,* 262-271.

Gould, S.J. (1977). *Ontogeny and phylogeny.* Cambridge, MA: Harvard University Press.

Gruber, H.E. (1981). *Darwin on man: A psychological study of scientific creativity* (2nd ed.). Chicago: University of Chicago Press.

Guilford, J.P., & Fruchter, B. (1978). *Fundamental statistics in psychology and education* (6th ed.). New York: McGraw-Hill.

Gunstone, R.F., Robin Gray, C.M., & Searle, P. (1992). Some long-term effects of uninformed conceptual change. *Science Education, 76*(2), 175-197.

Gunstone, R.F., & White, R. (1981). Understanding of gravity. *Science Education, 65,* 291-299.

Gussarsky, E., & Gorodetsky, M. (1988). On the chemical equilibrium concept. Constrained word associations and conception. *Journal of Research in Science Teaching, 25,* 319-333.

Hacking, I. (1979). Imre Lakatos's philosophy of science. *British Journal for the Philosophy of Science, 30,* 381-410.

Hackling, M.W., & Garnett, P.J. (1985). Misconceptions of chemical equilibrium. *European Journal of Science Education, 7,* 205-214.

Hameed, H., Hackling, M.W., & Garnett, P.J. (1993). Facilitating conceptual change in chemical equilibrium using a CAI strategy. *International Journal of Science Education, 15,* 221-230.

Hanson, N.R. (1958). *Patterns of discovery.* Cambridge, UK: Cambridge University Press.

Hanson, N.R. (1970). A picture theory of meaning. In R.G. Colodny (Ed.) *The nature and function of scientific theories* (pp. 233-249). Pittsburgh: University of Pittsburgh Press.

Harrison, A.G., & De Jong, O. (2005). Exploring the use of multiple analogical models when teaching and learning chemical equilibrium. *Journal of Research in Science Teaching, 42,* 1135-1159.

Heilbron, J.L., & Kuhn, T.S. (1969). The genesis of the Bohr atom. *Historical Studies in the Physical Sciences, 1,* 211-290.

Helm, H., & Novak, J.D. Eds., (1983). Proceedings of the international seminar on misconceptions in science and mathematics. Ithaca, NY: Cornell University.

Hempel, C.G. (1970). Fundamentals of concept formation in empirical evidence. In O. Neuroth (Ed.) *Foundations of the unity of science* (p. 695). Chicago: University of Chicago Press.

Herget, D.E., Ed. (1989). The history and philosophy of science in science teaching. Tallahassee, FL: Florida State University.

Herron, J.D. (1990). Research in chemical education: Results and directions. In M. Gardner, J.G. Greeno, F. Reif, A.H. Schoenfeld, A. di Sessa, & E. Stage (Eds.) *Toward a scientific practice of science education* (pp. 31-54). Hillsdale, NJ: Erlbaum.

Hewson, P.W. (1981). A conceptual change approach to learning science. *European Journal of Science Education, 3*(4), 383-396.

Hewson, P.W., & Hewson, M.G. (1984). The role of conceptual conflict in conceptual change and the design of science instruction. *Instructional Science, 13*, 1-13.

Hewson, P.W., & Thorley, N.R. (1989). The conditions of conceptual change in the classroom. *International Journal of Science Education, 11*, 541-553.

Hills, S., Ed. (1992). The history and philosophy of science in science education (2 volumes). Kingston, Ontario: Queen's University.

Hodson, D. (1982). Is there a scientific method? *Education in Chemistry, 19*(4), 112-116.

Hodson, D. (1985). Philosophy of science, science, and science teaching. *Studies in Science Education, 12*, 25-57.

Hodson, D. (1988). Toward a philosophically more valid science curriculum. *Science Education, 72*, 19-40.

Hodson, D. (1993a). In search of a rationale for multicultural science education. *Science Education, 77*(6), 685-711.

Hodson, D. (1993b). Philosophic stance of secondary school science teachers, curriculum experiences, and children's understanding of science: Some preliminary findings. *Interchange, 24*, 41-52.

Holton, G. (1952). *Introduction to concepts and theories in physical science.* New York: Addison-Wesley.

Holton, G. (2003). The project physics course, then and now. *Science & Education, 12*, 779-786.

Holton, G., & Brush, S.G. (2001). *Physics, the human adventure: From Copernicus to Einstein and beyond* (3$^{rd}$ ed.) New Brunswick, NJ: Rutgers University Press.

Holtzclaw, H.F., & Robinson, W.R. (1988). *General chemistry* (8th ed.). Lexington, MA: Heath.

Hooykaas, R. (1948). The first kinetic theory of gases. *Archives Internationales d'Histoire des Sciences, 27*, 180-184.

Hoyningen-Huene, P. (1993). *Reconstructing scientific revolutions: Thomas S. Kuhn's philosophy of science* (trans. A.T. Levine). Chicago: University of Chicago Press.

Hunt, S.D. (1994). A realist theory of empirical testing: Resolving the theory-ladenness/objectivity debate. *Philosophy of the Social Sciences, 24*(2), 133-158.

Hynd, C.R., McWhorter, J.Y., Phares, V.L., & Suttles, C.W. (1994). The role of instructional variables in conceptual change in high school physics topics. *Journal of Research in Science Teaching, 31*, 933-946.

Inhelder, B., & Piaget, J. (1958). *The growth of logical thinking from childhood to adolescence.* New York: Basic Books.

Jammer, M. (1966). *The conceptual development of quantum mechanics.* NewYork: McGraw-Hill.

Johnstone, MacDonald, J.J., & Webb, G. (1977). Chemical equilibrium and its conceptual difficulties. *Education in Chemistry, 14*, 169-171.

Karmiloff-Smith, A., & Inhelder, B. (1976). If you want to get ahead, get a theory. *Cognition, 3*, 195-212.

Keeports, D., & Morier, D. (1994). Teaching the scientific method. *Journal of College Science Teaching, 24*(1), 45-50.

Kesidou, S., & Duit, R. (1993). Students' conceptions of the second law of thermodynamics – An interpretive study. *Journal of Research in Science Teaching, 30*, 85-106.

Kilborne, B. (1992). Positivism and its vicissitudes: The role of faith in the social sciences. *Journal of the History of the Behavioral Sciences, 28*, 352-370.

Kimball, M.E. (1967). Understanding the nature of science: A comparison of scientists and science teachers. *Journal of Research in Science Teaching, 5*, 110-120.

Kitchener, R.F. (1985). Genetic epistemology, history of science, and genetic psychology. *Synthese, 65*, 3-31.

Kitchener, R.F. (1986). *Piaget's theory of knowledge: Genetic epistemology and scientific reason.* New Haven, CT: Yale University Press.

Kitchener, R.F. (1987). Genetic epistemology, equilibration, and the rationality of scientific change. *Studies in History and Philosophy of Science, 18*, 339-366.

Kitchener, R.F. (1993). Piaget's epistemic subject and science education: Epistemological versus psychological issues. *Science & Education, 2*, 137-148.

Kitcher, P. (1993). *The advancement of science: Science without legend, objectivity without illusions.* Oxford, UK: Oxford University Press.

Kitcher, P.(1995). Précis of *The advancement of science. Philosophy and Phenomenological Research, 55*(3), 611-617.

Klapper, M.H. (1995). Beyond the scientific method. *Science Teacher, 62*(6), 36-40.

Klee, R. (1992). Anomalous monism, *ceteris paribus* and psychological explanation. *British Journal for the Philosophy of Science, 43*, 389-403.

Klopfer, L.E. (1969). The teaching of science and the history of science. *Journal of Research in Science Teaching, 6*, 87-95.

Koulaidis, V., & Ogborn, J. (1988). Use of systematic networks in the development of a questionnaire. *International Journal of Science Education, 10*, 497-509.

Koulaidis, V., & Ogborn, J. (1989). Philosophy of science: An empirical study of teachers' views. *International Journal of Science Education, 11*, 173-184.

Koyré, A. (1968). *Metaphysics and measurement.* Cambridge, MA: Harvard University Press.

Krishnan, S.R. (1994). The mole concept. *Journal of Chemical Education, 71*(8), 653-655.

Kuhn, T.S. (1962/1970). *The structure of scientific revolutions.* Chicago: University of Chicago Press.

Kuhn, T.S. (1971). Notes on Lakatos. In R.C. Buck & R.S. Cohen (Eds.) *Boston Studies in the Philosophy of Science* (vol. 8, pp. 137-146). Dordrecht, The Netherlands: Reidel

Kuhn, T.S. (1977). *The essential tension.* Chicago: University of Chicago Press.

Laburú, C.E., & Niaz, M. (2002). A Lakatosian framework to analyze situations of cognitive conflict and controversy in students' understanding of heat energy and temperature. *Journal of Science Education and Technology, 11*, 211-219.

Lakatos, I. (1970). Falsification and the methodology of scientific research programmes. In I. Lakatos & A. Musgrave (Eds.) *Criticism and the growth of knowledge* (pp. 91-195). Cambridge, UK: Cambridge University Press.

Lakatos, I. (1971). History of science and its rational reconstructions. In R.C. Buck & R.S. Cohen (Eds.) *Boston Studies in the Philosophy of Science* (Vol. VIII, pp. 91-136). Dordrecht, Holland: Reidel.

Lakatos, I. (1974). The role of crucial experiments in science. *Studies in History and Philosophy of Science, 4*(4), 309-325.

Lakatos, I. (1976). *Proofs and refutations: The logic of mathematical discovery.* Cambridge, UK: Cambridge University Press.

Langer, J. (1988). A note on the comparative psychology of mental development. In S. Strauss (Ed.) *Ontogeny, phylogeny, and historical development* (pp. 68-85). Norwood, NJ: Ablex.

Larkin, J.H. (1981). Cognition of learning physics. *American Journal of Physics, 49*(6), 534-541.

Larkin, J.H., McDermott, J., Simon, D.P., & Simon, H.A. (1980). Expert and novice performance in solving physics problems. *Science, 208*(20), 1335-1342.

Laudan, L. (1977). *Progress and its problems.* Berkeley, CA: University of California Press.

Laudan, L. (1990). *Science and relativism.* Chicago: University of Chicago Press.

Laudan, R., Laudan, L., & Donovan, A. (1988). Testing theories of scientific change. In A. Donovan, L. Laudan, & R. Laudan (Eds.) *Scrutinizing science: Empirical studies of scientific change* (pp. 3-44). Dordrecht, The Netherlands: Kluwer.

Lawler, J. (1975). Dialectical philosophy and developmental psychology: Hegel and Piaget on contradiction. *Human Development, 18,* 1-17.

Lawson, A.E. (1991). Is Piaget's epistemic subject dead? *Journal of Research in Science Teaching, 28*(7), 581-591.

Lawson, A.E. (1993). The resurrection of Piaget's epistemic subject?: A further reply to Niaz. *Journal of Research in Science Teaching, 30*(7), 813.

Lawson, A.E., Abraham, M.R., & Renner, J.W. (1989). *A theory of instruction: Using the learning cycle to teach science concepts and thinking skills.* Cincinnati, OH: NARST Monograph.

Lawson, A.E., & Worsnop, W.A. (1992). Learning about evolution and rejecting a belief in special creation: Effects of reflective reasoning skill, prior knowledge, prior belief, and religious commitment. *Journal of Research in Science Teaching, 29,* 143-166.

Lederman, N.G. (1986). Relating teaching behavior and classroom climate to changes in students' conceptions of the nature of science. *Science Education, 70,* 3-19.

Lederman, N.G. (1992). Students' and teachers' conceptions of the nature of science: A review of the research. *Journal of Research in Science Teaching, 29,* 331-359.

Lederman, N.G., & O'Malley, M. (1990). Students' perceptions of tentativeness in science: Development, use, and sources of change. *Science Education, 74,* 225-239.

Lederman, N.G., & Zeidler, D.L. (1987). Science teachers' conceptions of the nature of science: Do they really influence teaching behavior? *Science Education, 71,* 721-734.

Levin, I., & Druyan, S. (1993). When sociocognitive transaction among peers fails: The case of misconceptions in science. *Child Development, 64,* 1571-1591.

Levin, I., Siegler, R.S., & Druyan, S. (1990). Misconceptions about motion: Development and training effects. *Child Development, 61,* 1544-1557.

Levin, I., Siegler, R.S., Druyan, S., & Gardosh, R. (1990). Everyday and curriculum based physics concepts: When does short-term training bring change where years of schooling have failed to do so? *British Journal of Developmental Psychology, 8,* 269-279.

Lewin, K. (1935). The conflict between Aristotelian and Galilean modes of thought in contemporary psychology. In *A dynamic theory of personality: Selected papers* (pp. 1-42). New York: McGraw-Hill.

Lewis, E.L. (1996). Conceptual change among middle school students studying elementary thermodynamics. *Journal of Science Education and Technology, 5*, 3-31.

Lewis, E.L., & Linn, M.C. (1994). Heat energy and temperature concepts of adolescents, adults, and experts: Implications for curricular improvements. *Journal of Research in Science Teaching, 31*, 657-677.

Lickliter, R., & Berry, T.D. (1990). The phylogeny fallacy: Developmental psychology's misapplication of evolutionary theory. *Developmental Review, 10*, 348-364.

Lindauer, M.W. (1962). The evolution of the concept of chemical equilibrium from 1775 to 1923. *Journal of Chemical Education, 39*, 384-390.

Linder, C.J. (1993). A challenge to conceptual change. *Science Education, 77*, 293-300.

Linn, M.C., & Songer, N.B. (1991a).Teaching thermodynamics to middle school students: What are appropriate cognitive demands? *Journal of Research in Science Teaching, 28*, 885-918.

Linn, M.C., & Songer, N.B. (1991b). Cognitive and conceptual change in adolescence. *American Journal of Education, 99*, 379-417.

Lorsbach, A., & Tobin, K. (1992). Constructivism as a referent for science teaching. *Narst News, 34*(3), 10-12.

Loving, C.C. (1991). The scientific theory profile: A philosophy of science models for science teachers. *Journal of Research in Science Teaching, 28*, 823-838.

Machamer, P., Pera, M., & Baltas, A. (2000). Scientific controversies: An introduction. In P. Machamer, M. Pera & A. Baltas (Eds.) *Scientific controversies: Philosophical and historical perspectives* (pp. 3-17). New York: Oxford University Press.

MacMillan, C.J.B., & Garrison, J.W. (1984). Using the new philosophy of science in criticizing current research traditions in education. *Educational Researcher, 13*, 15-21.

Mager, R.F. (1962). *Preparing instructional objectives*. Palo Alto, CA:Fearon Publishers Inc.

Mahan, B.M.(1968). *University chemistry*. Bogotá: Fondo Educativo Interamericano (Addison-Wesley).

Mahan, B.M., & Myers, R.J. (1990). *University Chemistry* (4th edition, Spanish). Wilmington, Delaware: Addison-Wesley.

Malone, M.E. (1993). Kuhn reconstructed: Incommensurability without relativism. *Studies in History and Philosophy of Science, 24*(1), 69-93.

Margenau, H. (1950). *The nature of physical reality*. New York: McGraw-Hill.

Martin, J., & Sugarman, J. (1993). Beyond methodolatry: Two conceptions of relations between theory and research in research on teaching. *Educational Researcher, 22*, 17-24.

Maskill, R., & Cachapuz, A.F.C. (1989). Learning about the chemistry topic of equilibrium: The use of word association tests to detect developing conceptualizations. *International Journal of Science Education, 11*, 57-69.

Mason, L. (1994). Cognitive and metacognitive aspects in conceptual change by analogy. *Instructional Science, 22*, 157-187.

Masterton, W.L., Slowinski, E.J., & Stanitski, C.L. (1985). *Chemical Principles* (5th ed., Spanish). Philadelphia: Saunders.

Matthews, M.R. (1987). Experiment as the objectification of theory: Galileo's revolution. Proceedings of the Second International Seminar on Misconceptions and Educational Strategies in Science and Mathematics (vol. 1, pp. 289-298). Ithaca, NY: Cornell University.

Matthews, M.R. (1990). History, philosophy, and science teaching: A rapprochement. *Studies in Science Education, 18*, 25-51.

Matthews, M.R. (1994). *Science teaching: The contribution of history and philosophy of science.* New York: Routledge.

Maxwell, J.C. (1860). Illustrations of the dynamical theory of gases. *Philosophical Magazine* (January & July). Reproduced in Scientific Papers (pp. 377-409), 1965. New York: Dover.

McCann, H.G. (1978*). Chemistry transformed: The paradigmatic shift from phlogiston to oxygen.* Norwood, NJ: Ablex.

McCloskey, M. (1983). Naive theories of motion. In D. Gentner & A. Stevens (Eds.), *Mental models* (pp. 299-324). Hillsdale, NJ: Erlbaum.

McCloskey, M., Caramazza, A., & Green, B. (1980). Curvilinear motion in the absence of external forces: Naive beliefs about motion of objects. *Science, 210*, 1139-1141.

McMullin, E. (1985). Galilean idealization. *Studies in History and Philosophy of Science, 16*, 247-273.

Mendoza, E. (1975). A critical examination of Herapath's dynamical theory of gases. *British Journal for the History of Science, 8*, 155-165.

Mendoza, E. (1990). The lattice theory of gases: A neglected episode in the history of chemistry. *Journal of Chemical Education, 67*, 1040-1042.

Merz, J.T. (1904). *A history of european thought in the nineteenth century* (vol. 1). London: William Blackwood & Sons.

Middleton, W.E.K. (1965). Jacob Hermann and the kinetic theory. *British Journal for the History of Science, 2*(7), 247-250.

Millar, R., & Driver, R. (1987). Beyond processes. *Studies in Science Education, 14*, 33-62.

Miller, S.I., & Fredericks, M. (1991). Postpositivistic assumptions and educational research: Another view. *Educational Researcher, 20*, 2-8.

Mischel, T. (1971). Piaget: Cognitive conflict and the motivation of thought. In T. Mischel (Ed.) *Cognitive development and epistemology* (pp. 311-355). New York: Academic Press.

Moberg, D.W. (1979). Are there rival, incommensurable theories? *Philosophy of Science, 46*, 244-262.

Mortimer, C.E. (1983). *Chemistry* (5th ed.). Belmont, CA: Wadsworth.

Mortimer, E.F. (1995). Conceptual change or conceptual profile change? *Science and Education, 4*(3), 267-285.

Musgrave, A. (1976). Why did oxygen supplant phlogiston? Research programmes in the chemical revolution. In C. Howson (Ed.), *Method and appraisal in the physical sciences: The critical background to modern science, 1800-1905* (pp. 181-209). Cambridge, UK: Cambridge University Press.

Nakhleh, M.B. (1993). Are our students conceptual thinkers or algorithmic problem solvers? *Journal of Chemical Education, 70*, 52-55.

Nakhleh, M.B., & Mitchell, R.C. (1993). Concept learning versus problem solving. *Journal of Chemical Education, 70*, 190-192.

Needham, P. (1991). Duhem and Cartwright on the truth of laws. *Synthese, 89*, 89-109.

Neressian, N.J. (1989). Conceptual change in science and in science education. *Synthese, 80*, 163-183.

Newton-Smith, W.H. (1981). *The rationality of science.* London: Routledge & Kegan Paul.

Niaz, M. (1987). Relation between M-space of students and M-demand of different items of general chemistry and its interpretation based upon the neo-Piagetian theory of Pascual-Leone. *Journal of Chemical Education, 64*, 502-505.

Niaz, M. (1988). Manipulation of M-demand of chemistry problems and its effect on student performance: A neo-Piagetian study. *Journal of Research in Science Teaching, 25*, 643-657.

Niaz, M. (1989a). The relationship between M-demand, algorithms, and problem solving: A neo-Piagetian analysis. *Journal of Chemical Education, 66*, 422-424.

Niaz, M. (1989b). Dimensional analysis: A neo-Piagetian evaluation of M-demand of chemistry problems. *Research in Science and Technological Education, 7*(2), 153-170.

Niaz, M. (1991a). Role of the epistemic subject in Piaget's genetic epistemology and its importance for science education. *Journal of Research in Science Teaching, 28*, 569-580.

Niaz, M. (1991b). Correlates of formal operational reasoning: A neo-Piagetian analysis. *Journal of Research in Science Teaching, 28*(1), 19-40.

Niaz, M. (1992). From Piaget's epistemic subject to Pascual-Leone's metasubject: Epistemic transition in the constructivist-rationalist theory of cognitive development. *International Journal of Psychology, 27*(6), 443-457.

Niaz, M. (1993a). Progressive 'problemshifts' between different research programs in science education: A Lakatosian perspective. *Journal of Research in Science Teaching, 30,* 757-765.

Niaz, M. (1993b). Competing research programs in science education: A Lakatosian interpretation. *Interchange, 24*, 181-190.

Niaz, M. (1993c). If Piaget's epistemic subject is dead, shall we bury the scientific research methodology of idealization? *Journal of Research in Science Teaching, 30*(7), 809-812.

Niaz, M. (1994a). Enhancing thinking skills: Domain specific/domain general strategies – A dilemma for science education. *Instructional Science, 22*, 413-422.

Niaz, M. (1994b). Más allá del positivismo: Una interpretación Lakatosiana de la enseñanza de las ciencias. *Enseñanza de las Ciencias, 12*, 97-100.

Niaz, M. (1994c). Pascual-Leone's theory of constructive operators as    an    explanatory construct in cognitive development and science achievement. *Educational Psychology, 14*(1), 23-43.

Niaz, M. (1994d). From quantitative to qualitative: A better understanding of the behaviour of gases? *School Science Review, 76*(274), 87-88.

Niaz, M. (1995a). Progressive transitions from algorithmic to conceptual understanding in student ability to solve chemistry problems: A Lakatosian interpretation. *Science Education, 79*, 19-36.

Niaz, M. (1995b). Chemical equilibrium and Newton's third law of motion: Ontogeny/phylogeny revisited. *Interchange, 26*, 19-32.

Niaz, M. (1995c). Cognitive conflict as a teaching strategy in solving chemistry problems: A dialectic-constructivist perspective. *Journal of Research in Science Teaching, 32*(9), 959-970.

Niaz, M. (1995d). Relationship between student performance on conceptual and computational problems of chemical equilibrium. *International Journal of Science Education, 17*(3), 343-355.

Niaz, M. (1995e). Piaget's epistemic subject: A reply to Shayer. *Journal of Research in Science Teaching, 32*(9), 1003-1005.

Niaz, M. (1996). Reasoning strategies of students in solving chemistry problems as a function of developmental level, functional M-capacity, and disembedding ability. *International Journal of Science Education, 18,* 525-541.

Niaz, M. (1998a). Epistemological significance of Piaget's developmental stages: A Lakatosian interpretation. *New Ideas in Psychology, 16,* 47-59.

Niaz, M. (1998b). A Lakatosian conceptual change teaching strategy based on student ability to build models with varying degrees of conceptual understanding of chemical equilibrium. *Science and Education, 7,* 107-127.

Niaz, M. (2000a). Gases as idealized lattices: A rational reconstruction of students' understanding of the behavior of gases. *Science and Education, 9,* 279-287.

Niaz, M. (2000b). A framework to understand students' differentiation between heat energy and temperature and its educational implications. *Interchange, 30,* 1-20.

Niaz, M. (2001). Response to contradiction: Conflict resolution strategies used by students in solving problems of chemical equilibrium. *Journal of Science Education and Technology, 10,* 205-211.

Niaz, M. (2005). The quantitative imperative vs the imperative of presuppositions. *Theory & Psychology, 15,* 247-256.

Niaz, M. (2006). Can the study of thermochemistry facilitate students' differentiation between heat energy and temperature? *Journal of Science Education and Technology, 15,* 269-276.

Niaz, M., Abd-El-Khalick, F., Benarroch, A., Cardellini, L., Laburù, C.E., Marìn, N., Montes, L.A., Nola, R., Orlik, Y., Scharmann, L.C., Tsai, C., & Tsaparlis, G. (2003). Constructivism: Defense or a continual critical appraisal. *Science Education, 12,* 787-797.

Niaz, M., Aguilera, D., Maza, A., & Liendo, G. (2002). Arguments, contradictions, resistances, and conceptual change in students' understanding of atomic structure. *Science Education, 86,* 505-525.

Niaz, M., & Logie, R.H. (1993). Working memory, mental capacity, and science education: Towards an understanding of the 'working memory overload hypothesis.' *Oxford Review of Education, 19,* 511-525.

Niaz, M., & Robinson, W.R. (1992a). From 'algorithmic mode' to 'conceptual gestalt' in understanding the behavior of gases: An epistemological perspective. *Research in Science and Technological Education, 10,* 53-64.

Niaz, M., & Robinson, W.R. (1992b). Manipulation of logical structure of chemistry problems and its effect on student performance. *Journal of Research in Science Teaching, 29,* 211-226.

Niaz, M., & Robinson, W.R. (1993). Teaching algorithmic problem solving or conceptual understanding: Role of developmental level, mental capacity, and cognitive style. *Journal of Science Education and Technology, 2*(2), 407-416.

Novak, J.D. (1977). *A theory of education.* Ithaca, NY: Cornell University Press.

Novak, J.D., Ed. (1987). Proceedings of the second international seminar on misconceptions and educational strategies in science and mathematics (3 vols.). Ithaca, NY: Cornell University.

Novak, J.D. (1988). Learning science and science of learning. *Studies in Science Education, 15,* 77-101.

Novick, S., & Nussbaum, J. (1978). Junior high school pupils understanding of the particulate nature of matter: An interview study. *Science Education, 62,* 273-281.

Nugayev, R. (1991). The fundamental laws of physics can tell the truth. *International Studies in the Philosophy of Science, 5,* 79-87.

Nurrenbern, S.C., & Pickering, M. (1987). Concept learning versus problem solving: Is there a difference. *Journal of Chemical Education, 64,* 508-510.

Nussbaum, J. (1989). Classroom conceptual change: Philosophical perspectives. *International Journal of Science Education, 11,* 530-540.

Ogborn, J. (1995). Recovering reality. *Studies in Science Education, 25,* 3-38.

Ogilvie, J.F. (1990). The nature of the chemical bond – 1990: There are no such things as orbitals! *Journal of Chemical Education, 67*(4), 280-289.

Osborne, R.J., & Wittrock, M.C. (1983). Learning science: A generative process. *Science Education, 67,* 489-508.

Overton, W.F. (1984). World views and their influence on psychological theory and research: Kuhn - Lakatos - Laudan. In H.W. Reese (Ed.) *Advances in child development and behavior* (vol. 18, pp. 191-226). New York: Academic Press.

Oxtoby, D.W., Nachtrieb, N.H., & Freeman, W.A. (1990). *Chemistry: Science of change.* Philadelphia: Saunders.

Papineau, D. (1979). *Theory and meaning.* Oxford, UK: Clarendon.

Papineau, D. (1991). Correlations and causes. *British Journal for the Philosophy of Science, 42,* 397-412.

Pascual-Leone, J. (1970). A mathematical model for the transition rule in Piaget's developmental stages. *Acta Psychologica, 32,* 301-345.

Pascual-Leone, J. (1976). A view of cognition from a formalist's perspective. In K.F. Riegel & J.A. Meacham (Eds.) *The developing individual in a changing world* (vol. 1, pp. 89-100). The Hague: Mouton.

Pascual-Leone, J. (1978). Compounds, confounds, and models in developmental information processing: A reply to Trabasso and Foellinger. *Journal of Experimental Child Psychology, 26,* 18-40.

Pascual-Leone, J. (1987). Organismic processes for neo-Piagetian theories: A dialectical causal account of cognitive development. *International Journal of Psychology, 22,* 531-570.

Pascual-Leone, J., & Burtis, P.J. (1974). FIT: Figural Intersection Test: A group measure of M-capacity. Unpublished manuscript, York University, Toronto.

Pascual-Leone, J., & Sparkman, E. (1980). The dialectics of empiricism and rationalism: A last methodological reply to Trabasso. *Journal of Experimental Child Psychology, 29,* 88-101.

Pauling, L. (1992). The nature of the chemical bond – 1992. *Journal of Chemical Education, 69*(6), 519-521.

Perrin, C.E. (1988). The chemical revolution: Shifts in guiding assumptions. In A. Donovan, L. Laudan., & R. Laudan (Eds.) *Scrutinizing science: Empirical studies of scientific change* (pp. 105-124). Dordrecht, The Netherlands: Kluwer.

Pfundt, H., & Duit, R. (1994). *Bibliography of students' alternative frameworks and science education* (4 ed.). Kiel, Germany: Institute of Science Education.

Phillips, D.C. (1983). After the wake: Postpositivistic educational thought. *Educational Researcher, 12*(5), 4-12.

Phillips, D.C. (1985). Can scientific method be taught? *Journal of College Science Teaching, 14,* 95-101.

Phillips, D.C. (1987). *Philosophy, science and social inquiry.* Oxford: Pergamon.

Phillips, D.C. (1990). Subjectivity and objectivity: An objective inquiry. In E.W. Eisner & A. Peshkin (Eds.) *Qualitative inquiry in education: The continuing debate.* New York: Teachers College Press.

Phillips, D.C. (1994). Positivism, antipositivism, and empiricism. In T. Husén & T.N. Postlethwaite (Eds.) *The International Encyclopedia of Education* (2nd ed., pp. 4630-4634). Oxford, UK: Pergamon.

Phillips, D.C. (1995). The good, the bad, and the ugly: The many faces of constructivism. *Educational Researcher, 24*(7), 5-12.

Piaget, J. (1970). The place of the sciences of man in the system of sciences. In *Main trends of research in the social and human sciences.* Paris/The Hague: Mouton (UNESCO).

Piaget, J. (1971a). *Biology and knowledge: An essay on the relations between organic regulations and cognitive processes.* Chicago: University of Chicago Press.

Piaget, J. (1971b). *Genetic epistemology* (E. Duckworth, trans.). New York: Norton.

Piaget, J. (1980). *Adaptation and intelligence.* Chicago: University of Chicago Press.

Piaget, J., & Garcia, R. (1989). *Psychogenesis and the history of science.* New York: Columbia University Press.

Pickering, M. (1990). Further studies on concept learning versus problem solving. *Journal of Chemical Education, 67,* 254-255.

Piquette, J.S., & Heikkinen, H.W. (2005). Strategies reported used by instructors to address student alternate conceptions in chemical equilibrium. *Journal of Research in Science Teaching, 42,* 1112-1134.

Poincaré, H. (1908). *The foundations of science* (trans. G.B. Halsted). Lancaster, PA: The Science Press.

Pólya, G. (1962). The teaching of mathematics and the biogenetic law. In I.J. Good (Ed.) *The scientist speculates* (pp. 352-356). London: Heinemann.

Pomeroy, D. (1993). Implications of teachers' beliefs about the nature of science: Comparison of the beliefs of scientists, secondary science teachers, and elementary teachers. *Science Education, 77,* 261-278.

Popper, K.R. (1959). *The logic of scientific discovery.* London: Hutchinson.

Popper, K.R. (1962). *Conjectures and refutations: The growth of scientific knowledge.* New York: Basic Books.

Popper, K.R. (1976). *Unended quest.* La Salle, Il: Open Court.

Porter, T.M. (1981). A statistical survey of gases: Maxwell's social physics. *Historical Studies in Physical Sciences, 12,* 77-116.

Porter, T.M. (1994). From Quetelet to Maxwell: Social statistics and the origins of statistical physics. In I.B. Cohen (Ed.) *Boston Studies in the Philosophy of Science* (vol. 150, pp. 345-362). Dordrecht, The Netherlands: Kluwer.

Posner, G.J., Strike, K.A., Hewson, P.W., & Gertzog, W.A (1982). Accommodation of a scientific conception: Toward a theory of conceptual change. *Science Education, 66,* 211-227.

Power, C.N. (1976). Competing paradigms in science education research. *Journal of Research in Science Teaching, 13*(6), 579-587.

Psillos, S. (1994). A philosophical study of the transition from the caloric theory of heat to thermodynamics: Resisting the pessimistic meta-induction. *Studies in History and Philosophy of Science, 25*, 159-190.

PSSC: Physical Science Study Committee (1960). *Physics*. Boston: Heath & Co.

Quílez-Pardo, J., Solaz-Portolés, J. (1995). Students' and teachers' misapplication of LeChatelier's principle: Implications for the teaching of chemical equilibrium. *Journal of Research in Science Teaching, 32*, 939-957.

Quine, W.V.O. (1951). Two dogmas of empiricism. *The Philosophical Review, 60*, 20-43.

Reese, H.W. (1982). A comment on the meaning of 'dialectics.' *Human Development, 25*, 423-429.

Reese, H.W., & Overton, W.F. (1972). On paradigm shifts. *American Psychologist, 27*, 1197-1199.

Reisch, G.A. (1991). Did Kuhn kill logical empiricism. *Philosophy of Science, 58*, 264-277.

Rey, J. (1630). Essays on an enquiry into the cause wherefore tin and lead increase in weight on calcination. Alembic Club Reprints No. 11, 1953.

Riegel, K.F. (1979). *Foundations of dialectical psychology*. New York: Academic Press.

Roadrangka, V., Yeany, R.H., & Padilla, M.J. (1983). The construction and validation of Group Assessment of Logical Thinking (GALT). Paper presented at the Annual Conference of the National Association for Research in Science Teaching (NARST), Dallas, April.

Robinson, J.T. (1969a). Philosophy of science: Implications for teacher education. Journal of Research in Science Teaching, 6, 99-104.

Robinson, J.T. (1969b). *The nature of science and science teaching*. Belmont, CA: Wadsworth.

Rogan, J.M. (1988). Development of a conceptual framework of heat. *Science Education, 72*, 103-113.

Rojas de Astudillo, L., & Niaz, M. (1996). Reasoning strategies used by students to solve stoichiometry problems and its relationship to alternative conceptions, prior knowledge, and cognitive variables. *Journal of Science Education and Technology, 5*, 131-140.

Rollnick, M., & Rutherford, M. (1993). The use of a conceptual change model and mixed language strategy for remediating misconceptions on air pressure. *International Journal of Science Education, 15*(4), 363-381.

Roth, W.-M., & Roychoudhury, A. (1994). Physics students' epistemologies and views about knowing and learning. *Journal of Research in Science Teaching, 31*, 5-30.

Rowell, J.A. (1983). Equilibration: Developing the hard core of the Piagetian research program. *Human Development, 26*, 61-71.

Rowell, J.A. (1989). Piagetian epistemology: Equilibration and the teaching of science. *Synthese, 80*, 141-162.

Rowell, J.A., & Cawthron, E.R. (1982). Images of science: An empirical study. *European Journal of Science Education, 4*, 79-94.

Rowell, J.A., & Dawson, C.J. (1985). Equilibration, conflict and instruction: A new class-oriented perspective. *European Journal of Science Education, 7*, 331-344.

Rubba, P.A., & Anderson, H.O. (1978). Development of an instrument to assess secondary school students' understanding of the nature of scientific knowledge. *Science Education, 62*, 449-458.

Rutherford, E. (1915). The constitution of matter and the evolution of the elements. Annual Report of the Smithsonian Institution. (pp. 167-202). Washington, D.C.

Ryan, A.G., & Aikenhead, G.S. (1992). Students' preconceptions about the epistemology of science. *Science Education, 76*, 559-580.

Samarapungavan, A. (1992). Children's judgements in theory choice tasks: Scientific rationality in childhood. *Cognition, 45*, 1-32.

Sawrey, B.E. (1990). Concept learning versus problem solving: Revisited. *Journal of Chemical Education, 67*, 253-254.

Scheffler, I. (1967). *Science and subjectivity.* Indianapolis, IN: Bobbs-Merrill.

Scheffler, I. (1986). *Inquiries: Philosophical studies of language, science, and learning.* Indianapolis, IN: Hackett.

Scheffler, I. (1992). Philosophy and the curriculum. *Science and Education, 1*(4), 385-394.

Schrag, F. (1992). In defense of positivist research paradigms. *Educational Researcher, 21*, 5-8.

Schwab, J.J. (1962). *The teaching of science as enquiry.* Cambridge, MA: Harvard University Press.

Schwab, J.J. (1974). The concept of the structure of a discipline. In E.W. Eisner & E. Vallance (Eds.) *Conflicting conceptions of curriculum* (pp. 162-175). Berkeley, CA: McCutchan Publishing Corp.

Schwab, J.J. (1978). *Science, curriculum, and liberal education.* Chicago: University of Chicago Press.

Segal, E.M., & Lachman, R. (1972). Complex behavior or higher mental process: Is there a paradigm shift. *American Psychologist, 27*, 46-55.

Shapere, D. (1985). Objectivity, rationality, and scientific change. In P. Asquith & P. Kitcher (Eds.), Proceedings of the 1984 Biennial Meeting of the Philosophy of Science Association (Vol 2, pp. 637-662). East Lansing, MI: Philosophy of Science Association.

Shayer, M. (1993). Piaget: Only the Galileo of cognitive development? Comment on Niaz and Lawson on genetic epistemology. *Journal of Research in Science Teaching, 30*(7), 815-818.

Shayer, M., & Wylam, H. (1981). The development of the concepts of heat and temperature in 10-13 year-olds. *Journal of Research in Science Teaching, 18*, 419-434.

Shulman, L.S. (1986). Those who understand: Knowledge growth in teaching. *Educational Researcher, 15*, 4-14.

Shulman, L.S. (1992). On research on teaching: A conversation with Lee Shulman. *Educational Leadership, 49*(7), 14-19.

Siegel, H. (1978). Kuhn and Schwab on science texts and the goals of science education. *Educational Theory, 28*(4), 302-309.

Siegel, H. (1985). Relativism, rationality, and science education. *Journal of College Science Teaching, 15*(2), 102-105.

Siegel, H. (1987). *Relativism refuted.* Dordrecht, The Netherlands: D. Reidel.

Simon, D.P., & Simon, H.A. (1978). Individual difference in solving physics problems. In R.S. Siegler (Ed.) *Children's thinking: What develops?* Hillsdale, NJ: Erlbaum.

Smith, C., Carey, S., & Wiser, M. (1985). On differentiation: A case study of the development of size, weight, and density. *Cognition, 21*, 177-237.

Smith, C., Snir, J., & Grosslight, L. (1992). Using conceptual models to facilitate conceptual change: The case of weight-density differentiation. *Cognition and Instruction, 9,* 221-283.

Smith, E.L., Blakeslee, T.D., & Anderson, C.W. (1993). Teaching strategies associated with conceptual change learning in science. *Journal of Research in Science Teaching, 30,* 111-126.

Solomon, J., Duveen, J., Scott, L., & McCarthy, S. (1992). Teaching about the nature of science through history: Action research in the classroom. *Journal of Research in Science Teaching, 29,* 409-421.

Songer, C.J., & Mintzes, J.J. (1994). Understanding cellular respiration: An analysis of conceptual change in college biology. *Journal of Research in Science Teaching, 31,* 621-637.

Staver, J.R., & Lumpe, A.T. (1993). A content analysis of the presentation of the mole concept in chemistry textbooks. *Journal of Research in Science Teaching, 30,* 321-337.

Staver, J.R., & Lumpe, A.T. (1995). Two investigations of students' understanding of the mole concept and its use in problem solving. *Journal of Research in Science Teaching, 32,* 177-193.

Sternberg, R.J. (1989). Domain-generality versus domain-specificity: The life and impending death of a false dichotomy. *Merrill-Palmer Quarterly, 35*(1), 115-130.

Stewart, J., Finley, F.N., & Yarroch, W.L. (1982). Science content as important consideration in science education research. *Journal of Research in Science Teaching, 19,* 425-432.

Stinner, A. (1992). Science textbooks and science teaching: From logic to evidence. *Science Education, 76*(1), 1-16.

Stofflett, R.T. (1994). The accommodation of science pedagogical knowledge:The application of conceptual change constructs to teacher education. *Journal of Research in Science Teaching, 31,* 787-810.

Stofflett, R.T., & Stoddart, T. (1994). The ability to understand and use conceptual change pedagogy as a function of prior content learning experience. *Journal of Research in Science Teaching, 31,* 31-51.

Strauss, S., Ed. (1988). *Ontogeny, phylogeny, and historical development.* Norwood, NJ: Ablex.

Strike, K.A., & Posner, G.J. (1992). A revisionist theory of conceptual change. In R.A. Duschl & R.J. Hamilton (Eds.) *Philosophy of science, cognitive psychology, and educational theory in practice* (pp. 147-176). Albany, NY: State University of New York Press.

Suppe, F. (1977). *The structure of scientific theories* (2nd ed.). Chicago: University of Chicago Press.

Suchting, W.A. (1992). Constructivism deconstructed. *Science and Education, 1*(3), 223-254.

Taber, K.S. (1995). Time to be definitive? *Education in Chemistry, 32*(3), 56.

Thagard, P. (1990). The conceptual structure of the chemical revolution. *Philosophy of Science, 57,* 183-209.

Thagard, P. (1992). Analogy, explanation, and education. *Journal of Research in Science Teaching, 29*(6), 537-544.

Thorley, N.R., & Stofflet, R.T. (1996). Representation of the conceptual change model in science teacher education. *Science Education, 80,* 317-339.

Tiles, J.E. (1992). Experimental evidence vs. experimental practice? *British Journal for the Philosophy of Science, 43*(1), 99-109.

Tobias, S. (1993). What makes science hard? A Karplus lecture. *Journal of Science Education and Technology, 2*(1), 297-304.

Tobin, K., & Tippins, D.J. (1996). Metaphors as seeds for conceptual change and the improvement of science teaching. *Science Education, 80*, 711-730.

Toulmin, S. (1961). *Foresight and understanding.* Bloomington, IN: Indiana University Press.

Treagust, D.F., Harrison, A.G., Venville, G.J., & Dagher, Z. (1996). Using an analogical teaching approach to engender conceptual change. *International Journal of Science Education, 18*, 213-229.

Tsaparlis, G. (1998). Dimensional analysis and predictive models in problem solving. *International Journal of Science Education, 20*, 335-350.

Tsaparlis, G., Kousathana, M., & Niaz, M. (1998). Molecular-equilibrium problems: manipulation of logical structure and of M-demand, and their effect on student performance. *Science Education, 82*, 437-454.

Van't Hoff, J.H. (1896). *Studies in chemical dynamics* (T. Evans, trans.). Easton, PA: Chemical Publishing Co.

Venville, G.J., & Treagust, D.F. (1996). The role of analogies in promoting conceptual change in biology. *Instructional Science, 24*, 295-320.

Viennot, L. (1979). Spontaneous reasoning in elementary dynamics. *European Journal of Science Education, 1*, 205-221.

Villani, A. (1992). Conceptual change in science and science education. *Science Education, 76*(2), 223-237.

von Glasersfeld, E. (1987). Learning as a constructivist activity. In C. Janvier (Ed.) *Problems of representation in the teaching and learning of mathematics* (pp. 3-17). Hillsdale, NJ: Erlbaum.

von Glasersfeld, E. (1989). Cognition, construction of knowledge, and teaching. *Synthese, 80*, 121-140.

Vonéche, J., & Bovet, M. (1982). Training research and cognitive development: What do Piagetians want to accomplish? In S. Modgil & C. Modgil (Eds.) *Jean Piaget: Consensus and controversy* (pp. 83-94). New York: Praeger.

Vosniadou, S., & Brewer, W.F. (1987). Theories of knowledge restructuring in development. *Review of Educational Research, 57*, 51-67.

Vosniadou, S., & Brewer, W.F. (1994). Mental models of the day/night cycle. *Cognitive Science, 18*, 123-183.

Vuyk, R. (1981). *Overview and critique of Piaget's genetic epistemology 1965-1980.* New York: Academic Press.

Vygotsky, L.S. (1978). *Mind in society: The development of higher psychological processes.* Cambridge, MA: Harvard University Press.

Wade, N. (1977). Thomas S. Kuhn: Revolutionary theorist of science. *Science, 197*, No. 4299, 143-145.

Wandersee, J.H. (1985). Can the history of science help science educators anticipate students' misconceptions? *Journal of Research in Science Teaching, 23*(7), 581-597.

Wandersee, J.H. (1993). Guest editorial: The declared research interests of NARST members: An analysis of the 1992 NARST directory of members. *Journal of Research in Science Teaching, 30,* 319-320.

Wandersee, J.H., Mintzes, J.J., & Novak, J.D. (1994). Research on alternative conceptions in science. In D.L. Gabel (Ed.) *Handbook of Research on Science Teaching* (pp. 177-210). New York: Macmillan.

Weckert, J. (1986). The theory-ladenness of observations. *Studies in History and Philosophy of Science, 17*(1), 115-127.

Wheeler, A.E., & Kass, H. (1978). Student misconceptions in chemical equilibrium. *Science Education, 62,* 223-232.

Whewell, W. (1856). *On the philosophy of discovery.* New York: Franklin.

White, B.Y. (1993). ThinkerTools: Causal models, conceptual change, and science education. *Cognition and Instruction, 10*(1), 1-100.

White, R.T. (1988). *Learning science.* Oxford, UK: Basil Blackwell.

Whitten, K.W., Gailey, K.D., & Davis, R.E. (1992). *General Chemistry* (3rd ed., Spanish). New York: McGraw-Hill.

Williams, H. (1994). A critique of Hodson's 'In search of a rationale for multicultural science education'. *Science Education, 78*(5), 515-519.

Winchester, I. (1993). Science is dead. We have killed it, You and I – How attacking the presuppositional structures of our scientific age can doom the interrogation of nature. *Interchange, 24*(1-2), 191-198.

Wiser, M. (1988). The differentiation of heat and temperature: History of science and novice-expert shift. In S. Strauss (Ed.) *Ontogeny, phylogeny, and historical development* (pp. 28-48). Norwood, NJ: Ablex.

Wiser, M., & Carey, S. (1983). When heat and temperature were one. In D. Gentner & A. Stevens (Eds.) *Mental models* (267-297). Hillsdale, NJ: Erlbaum.

Witkin, H.A., Oltman, P.K., Raskin, E., & Karp, S.A. (1971). *A manual for the embedded figures test.* Palo Alto, CA: Consulting Psychologists Press.

Zohar, A., & Aharon-Kravetsky, S. (2005). Exploring the effects of cognitive conflict and direct teaching for students of different academic levels. *Journal of Research in Science Teaching, 42,* 829-855.

Zoller, U., Dori, Y.J., & Lubezky, A. (2002). Algorithmic, LOCS and HOCS (chemistry) exam questions: Performance and attitudes of college students. *International Journal of Science Education, 24,* 185-203.

Zoller, U., & Tsaparlis, G. (1997). Higher and lower-order cognitive skills: The case of chemistry. *Research in Science Education, 27,* 117-130.

# INDEX

## A

access, 117
accommodation, 15, 27, 158
accuracy, 143
achievement, 141, 152
acquisition of knowledge, 12, 14, 98
adaptation, 79, 128
adolescence, 147, 150
adolescents, 145, 150
adults, 14, 150
age, 63, 75, 86, 100, 160
algorithm, 111, 114
alternative(s), vii, 4, 10, 14, 16, 20, 27, 33, 34, 41,
    43, 44, 48, 49, 53, 55, 65, 66, 68, 72, 73, 80, 83,
    85, 86, 88, 89, 90, 93, 95, 98, 99, 108, 109, 113,
    114, 119, 129, 130, 138, 139, 144, 145, 146, 154,
    156, 160
alters, 22
antecedent variables, 15
anxiety, 46
argument, 13, 34, 76, 114
Aristotle, 2
assignment, 100
assumptions, 7, 10, 11, 12, 18, 32, 62, 63, 71, 73, 99,
    100, 135, 136, 137, 138, 151, 154
atomic theory, 1, 2, 7, 17, 118, 119, 120, 127
atoms, 4, 11, 17, 23, 24, 25, 31, 34, 45, 47, 49, 59,
    60, 70, 73, 123, 127
attention, 6, 30
attitudes, 160
attractiveness, 77
attribution, 94
authority, 59, 62
awareness, 13

## B

barium, 29
behavior, 9, 55, 59, 63, 66, 70, 71, 130, 141, 149,
    153, 154, 157
*Behaviorism*, 1
beliefs, vii, 15, 20, 22, 32, 34, 35, 55, 72, 73, 80, 81,
    82, 83, 98, 99, 105, 107, 108, 117, 118, 122, 126,
    129, 131, 138, 139, 142, 145, 151, 155
blocks, 138
Bohr, 2, 3, 4, 7, 10, 11, 20, 22, 37, 38, 39, 40, 41, 42,
    50, 51, 52, 54, 55, 57, 62, 120, 137, 138, 146
boils, 78
Boyle's law, 3, 59, 60, 63, 68, 141
buffer, 88, 91
burning, 4

## C

California, 149
carbon, 31
carbon dioxide, 31
caricatures, 4
case study, 157
cast, 59, 107
catalyst, 97
celestial bodies, 2
Ceteris paribus, 10
chaos, 51, 70
chaotic behavior, 62
charge density, 46, 47, 48
chemical reactions, 85, 93
Chicago, 145, 146, 147, 148, 149, 155, 157, 158
child development, 141, 154
childhood, 142, 147, 157
children, 12, 13, 14, 28, 71, 73, 143, 147

chlorine, 64
chromium, 31, 32
chunking, 25, 134
Cincinnati, 149
classes, 21
*Classic positivism*, 1
classical electrodynamics, 11, 54
classification, 20, 41, 99, 121, 127, 139
classroom(s), 17, 20, 21, 30, 32, 35, 37, 46, 54, 55, 57, 63, 67, 73, 75, 78, 80, 82, 98, 114, 115, 142, 147, 149, 158
classroom practice, 21, 115
CO2, 64, 87, 90
cognition, 16, 138, 154
cognitive ability, 100
cognitive development, 13, 21, 142, 152, 154, 157, 159
cognitive developmental theory, 142
cognitive dissonance, 145
cognitive process, 155
cognitive psychology, 15, 158
cognitive style, 12, 153
cognitive variables, 24, 63, 66, 156
college students, 23, 77, 160
collisions, 60, 69, 85, 91, 136
combustion, 5, 15
communication, 15
community, 15, 137
competence, 12
competition, 5, 6, 14, 47, 134
complexity, 18, 20, 26, 27, 28, 42, 48, 62, 70, 71, 97, 115, 135, 136, 137, 138
complications, 135
components, 62, 121
composition, 45
compounds, 23, 24, 29, 33, 34
concentration, 47, 86, 88, 89, 94, 95, 97, 98, 100, 101, 103, 106, 107, 110, 112
conception, 14, 46, 85, 89, 90, 94, 95, 97, 98, 107, 108, 109, 113, 114, 123, 129, 145, 146, 155
conceptual model, 158
conceptualization, 5, 34, 37, 47, 51, 68, 70, 72, 77, 97, 98, 115, 124, 125, 129, 133
concrete, 22, 48, 52, 79
confidence, 3
configuration, 17
conflict, 15, 24, 26, 27, 28, 29, 31, 34, 54, 77, 100, 108, 109, 114, 128, 130, 133, 143, 147, 148, 149, 151, 152, 156, 160
conflict resolution, 143
confrontation, 6, 47, 134
consensus, 5, 117, 120
conservation, 44, 60, 124, 128, 129

constraints, 90, 93
construction, vii, 6, 13, 21, 46, 54, 55, 72, 115, 139, 142, 156, 159
content analysis, 158
control, 29, 31, 32, 33, 93, 100, 102, 105, 106, 107
control group, 29, 31, 32, 33, 100, 102, 105, 106, 107
conversion, 15
cooling, 82
Copenhagen, 145
copper, 141
correlation(s), 63, 71
cotton, 42, 123
course content, 55, 78
creativity, 146
credentials, 9, 129
credit, 24, 56, 67, 68, 88, 93, 102
criticism, 2, 59, 137, 139
curiosity, 27
curriculum, vii, 47, 147, 149, 157

## D

death, 136, 158
decision making, 144
decisions, 5
defense, 53, 157
definition, 21, 35, 124, 126, 128
demand, 66, 85, 91, 152, 159
density, 13, 32, 46, 49, 60, 61, 64, 157, 158
dependent variable, 66
developmental psychology, 149
differentiation, 78, 153, 157, 158, 160
discipline, 18, 37, 157
disequilibrium, 112
displacement, 15, 145
dissatisfaction, 107
dissociation, 110, 133
distribution, 46, 62, 65, 69, 75, 77, 78
diversity, 62, 137
division, 73
domain-specificity, 158

## E

earth, 2, 33, 126
ecology, 15
education, vii, 1, 2, 5, 6, 10, 13, 14, 16, 17, 19, 28, 34, 37, 38, 54, 79, 102, 118, 133, 134, 141, 142, 143, 144, 145, 146, 147, 148, 149, 150, 151, 152, 153, 154, 155, 156, 157, 158, 159, 160
educational research, 117, 144, 151

educators, 117, 139
Einstein, 82, 128, 138, 144, 147
elaboration, 38, 41, 120, 125, 133
elasticity, 59
electric charge, 46
electricity, 40, 128
electrochemistry, 75
electromagnetic, 50
electromagnetism, 11
electron(s), 11, 17, 38, 40, 42, 43, 44, 45, 46, 47, 50, 51, 52, 56, 57, 123, 128
electronic structure, 4
elementary teachers, 155
emission, 3, 11, 51, 56, 57
emotional state, 126
*Empiricism*, 1
endothermic, 95, 96, 104
energy, 1, 4, 48, 50, 51, 61, 69, 70, 73, 74, 76, 78, 80, 81, 82, 83, 123, 128, 129, 130, 137, 148, 150, 153
England, 60
environment, 28
epistemological constructions, 9, 130
epistemology, 10, 11, 13, 137, 141, 144, 145, 148, 151, 152, 155, 156, 157, 159
equality, 94, 97, 115
equilibrium, 27, 60, 75, 85, 86, 87, 88, 89, 90, 91, 92, 93, 94, 95, 96, 97, 98, 99, 100, 101, 102, 103, 104, 106, 107, 108, 111, 112, 113, 114, 115, 131, 139, 141, 142, 146, 147, 150, 152, 153, 155, 156, 159, 160
equipment, 49
ethics, 141
evidence, 10, 14, 20, 32, 34, 38, 39, 41, 48, 49, 51, 52, 62, 71, 81, 92, 93, 95, 98, 109, 115, 118, 120, 125, 130, 133, 146, 158, 159
evolution, 13, 17, 32, 53, 86, 95, 97, 106, 115, 127, 144, 149, 150, 157
exclusion, 22
execution, 79
exercise, 137
experimental condition, 44, 90, 104, 136
expertise, 17, 25

**F**

faith, 148
false belief, 16, 138
feedback, 54
females, 63
Feynman, 9, 129, 145
flavor, 4, 53
fluid, 59

foils, 47
food, 81
formal reasoning, 80
fossil, 32
fruits, 47

**G**

gas phase, 75, 91
gases, 3, 40, 44, 45, 59, 60, 61, 62, 63, 66, 67, 68, 70, 71, 72, 76, 77, 87, 125, 130, 131, 134, 142, 143, 145, 147, 151, 152, 153, 155
gene, 3, 6, 119, 133
generalization, 9, 63, 129
generation, 27, 62, 109
Geneva, 136
Germany, 154
glass, 74, 76, 77
glasses, 73, 74, 76, 77
goals, 157
God, 125, 126
gold, 47, 48, 49
gravitation, 3, 9, 125, 129
gravitational force, 10
gravity, 13, 146
Greeks, 129
grounding, 143
group work, 141
groups, 21, 31, 33, 34, 70, 75, 80, 100, 105
growth, 10, 11, 28, 117, 147, 148, 155, 157
guidance, 21, 139
guidelines, 19, 21, 22, 29

**H**

harm, 127
harmony, 127
Harvard, 143, 146, 148, 157, 159
heat, 13, 60, 73, 74, 75, 76, 77, 78, 79, 80, 81, 82, 83, 95, 96, 104, 130, 142, 144, 148, 153, 156, 157, 160
heat capacity, 79
heat loss, 79
high school, 16, 17, 23, 35, 39, 118, 119, 124, 136, 143, 144, 145, 147, 154
Honda, 142
hostility, 1
human development, 27
human sciences, 155
hydrogen, 3, 4, 11, 31, 38, 50, 51, 55, 56, 64, 65, 69, 70
hydrogen gas, 64, 69

hypothesis, 2, 3, 4, 11, 12, 22, 47, 53, 59, 60, 62, 63, 77, 98, 99, 109, 115, 127, 128, 130, 136, 153
hypothetico-deductive, 3, 20

## I

idealization, 9, 10, 11, 12, 18, 62, 130, 135, 136, 137, 145, 151, 152
identification, 21
illusions, 148
imagination, 129
inclusion, 11
independent variable, 66
indication, 33
indicators, 53
individual development, 12
induction, 3, 118, 156
information processing, 25, 66, 85, 154
inheritance, 10
injury, iv
insight, 14, 17, 20, 38, 50, 71, 83, 134
inspiration, 38, 61, 134
instability, 51
instruction, 11, 16, 32, 54, 75, 98, 143, 145, 147, 149, 156
instructors, 16, 155
instruments, 46
integration, 12, 131
intelligence, 155
intensity, 56, 57
intentions, 126
interaction, 45, 54, 97, 126, 130, 134, 144
interpretation, 3, 4, 10, 32, 43, 45, 47, 50, 51, 59, 95, 96, 97, 104, 106, 129, 131, 152, 153
interrelationships, 28
intervention, 107, 141
interview, 122, 154
introspection, 1
ions, 44

## J

justification, 24, 52, 56, 67, 69, 76, 77, 96

## K

kinetic model, 82
knowledge acquisition, 13, 143
knowledge restructuring, 159

## L

language, 156, 157
lanthanum, 88
lattices, 70, 153
laws, 1, 3, 9, 10, 17, 19, 35, 40, 50, 51, 59, 60, 62, 63, 68, 71, 124, 125, 128, 129, 130, 131, 133, 135, 137, 141, 142, 145, 151, 154
learners, 28
learning, 16, 27, 71, 81, 85, 92, 115, 133, 134, 137, 138, 141, 143, 144, 145, 146, 147, 149, 151, 153, 154, 155, 156, 157, 158, 159
liberal education, 157
links, 12
liquids, 76
literacy, 46, 143
literature, vii, 3, 5, 6, 12, 13, 14, 18, 20, 27, 28, 32, 54, 66, 79, 83, 97, 102, 113, 114, 117, 130, 133, 134, 136, 141, 144
*Logical positivism*, 1

## M

Mach, E., 1
magnetic field, 44
males, 63
manipulation, 63, 66, 71, 72, 82, 90, 159
mathematics, 13, 69, 75, 81, 145, 146, 153, 155, 159
measurement, 142, 148
medicine, 128
memory, 12, 153
men, 2, 11, 12, 54
mental capacity, 24, 63, 134, 153
mental development, 149
mercury, 59
metals, 4
metaphor, 144
methane, 31
microscope, 123
Minnesota, 143, 145
misconceptions, vii, 16, 20, 73, 98, 106, 138, 139, 142, 143, 146, 149, 153, 156, 159, 160
mixing, 74, 77, 85, 88, 98, 115
models, vii, 2, 10, 11, 12, 18, 19, 20, 23, 25, 26, 28, 37, 41, 43, 46, 47, 48, 49, 50, 53, 54, 55, 56, 57, 62, 66, 67, 72, 79, 80, 83, 97, 115, 119, 123, 124, 128, 134, 135, 137, 138, 143, 144, 146, 150, 151, 153, 154, 159, 160
modules, 141
mole, 23, 25, 26, 30, 64, 130, 134, 148, 158
molecules, 4, 24, 25, 60, 61, 62, 64, 65, 66, 69, 70, 127, 136, 145

momentum, 7, 21, 39, 60, 137
monograph, vii
motion, 40, 60, 61, 62, 73, 82, 86, 94, 95, 97, 106, 111, 136, 142, 149, 151, 152 ·
motivation, 151
motives, 21
movement, 50, 51, 60, 61, 62, 69, 70, 76, 136
multiculturalism, 17
multiple regression analysis, 24, 66

**N**

Na⁺, 88
NaCl, 88
natural science(s), 5
natural selection, 62
Netherlands, 148, 149, 154, 155, 157
neutrons, 123
New York, 141, 142, 144, 145, 146, 147, 149, 150, 151, 154, 155, 156, 158, 159, 160
Newton' law, 9
Newtonian theory, 3, 125
Niels Bohr, 4, 137, 145
nitrogen, 24
nucleus, 11, 38, 40, 46, 47, 48, 49, 50, 51, 52, 55, 123

**O**

objectification, 150
objectivity, 5, 48, 126, 147, 148, 155
observations, 2, 3, 4, 5, 41, 49, 53, 63, 71, 117, 119, 121, 122, 126, 128, 136, 160
ontogenesis, 12, 13, 97
orbit, 11, 135, 138
organization, 28
orientation, 42
Ostwald, W., 1
overload, 153
oxidation, 53
oxides, 5
oxygen, 14, 15, 23, 24, 29, 31, 151r

**P**

paradigm shift, 144, 156, 157
Paris, 155
parroting, 82
particles, 38, 39, 40, 42, 43, 45, 46, 47, 48, 49, 53, 55, 59, 60, 61, 62, 134
pedagogy, 18, 158
peers, 43, 149

perceptions, 149
performance, 12, 24, 28, 33, 34, 56, 63, 65, 66, 77, 78, 79, 80, 81, 83, 86, 90, 91, 92, 105, 106, 107, 109, 142, 149, 152, 153, 159
permit, 51
personal, 142
personality, 149
pH, 88
phenomenology, 2
philosophers, 1, 2, 3, 5, 9, 32, 50, 117, 133, 134, 135, 136, 137, 138
phosphorus, 4, 23, 24
phylogenesis, 12, 13, 97
physical chemistry, 1
physical sciences, 151
physics, 1, 7, 9, 10, 11, 16, 17, 20, 38, 40, 50, 51, 54, 55, 61, 75, 82, 130, 136, 142, 143, 144, 147, 149, 154, 155, 157
Piagetians, 159
planets, 11, 123, 135
planning, 144
plausibility, 62, 110
PM, 64
Poincaré, 13, 155
poor, 33, 45, 65, 78, 80, 131
poor performance, 65, 78
population, 61
positivism, 1, 5, 51
power, vii, 7, 12, 18, 19, 25, 26, 47, 50, 51, 56, 77, 83, 97, 115
prediction, 18, 91, 143
predictor variables, 66
pressure, 59, 60, 61, 62, 64, 66, 67, 68, 69, 70, 71, 87, 90, 91, 103, 143, 156
prestige, 60
primacy, 122
*Principia*, 59
prior knowledge, 24, 149, 156
probability, 125
problem solving, 6, 17, 21, 23, 26, 29, 30, 31, 33, 37, 85, 100, 102, 109, 151, 152, 153, 154, 155, 157, 158, 159
problem-solving behavior, 85
problem-solving strategies, 31, 33
production, 91, 94, 95, 105, 110, 113
program, 6, 7, 10, 11, 14, 18, 20, 21, 32, 39, 42, 47, 52, 54, 62, 73, 76, 78, 83, 85, 141, 144, 156
proliferation, 6, 134
proportionality, 64, 66
proposition, 20, 129, 130
protons, 123
psychological phenomena, 28
psychological processes, 159

psychology, 12, 14, 141, 145, 146, 148, 149, 150, 156
pupil, 37

## Q

quality of life, 128
quantum mechanics, 50, 138, 147
quantum theory, 40, 50, 51, 137

## R

radiation, 50
range, 45, 62
rational reconstruction, 10, 11, 13, 28, 37, 67, 70, 118, 133, 148, 153
rationality, 148, 151, 157
reactant(s), 34, 85, 89, 90, 93, 95, 97, 98, 101, 106, 107, 111, 112, 113, 115
reaction rate, 86, 87, 89, 90, 99, 100, 101, 102, 104, 105, 108, 109, 110, 111, 114
reading, 52, 61
reality, 28, 41, 45, 51, 119, 127, 128, 150, 154
reasoning, 6, 12, 22, 25, 44, 61, 63, 66, 70, 76, 77, 82, 85, 88, 91, 94, 95, 101, 105, 121, 122, 128, 129, 149, 152, 159
recall, 2, 40, 134
recalling, 79
recognition, 62, 63
reconcile, 4, 143
reconstruction, 4, 11, 12, 15, 18, 19, 26, 37, 63, 130, 134, 142
reduction, 125
regression, 66
regression analysis, 66
regression equation, 66
regulations, 28, 155
rejection, 21
relationship(s), vii, 3, 4, 6, 12, 14, 17, 20, 25, 31, 37, 44, 45, 47, 52, 54, 68, 78, 80, 89, 104, 115, 118, 128, 131, 138, 143, 152, 156
relevance, 4
replication, 96
research design, 94
resistance, 20, 82, 98, 108, 139
resolution, 71, 91, 109, 110, 120, 122, 153
respiration, 158
restructuring, 13, 14, 78, 83, 98, 99
reverse reactions, 86, 94, 95, 97, 98, 106, 111, 112, 114, 115
Revolutionary, 159
rhetoric, 38, 57

rote learning, 19, 37
Royal Society, 60
Rutherford, 2, 4, 11, 37, 38, 39, 40, 41, 42, 46, 47, 48, 49, 50, 51, 52, 53, 55, 57, 121, 138, 156, 157

## S

salt, 88
sample, 24, 29, 71, 78, 82
scattering, 39
school, 2, 37, 133, 145, 147, 150
schooling, 149
science educators, 9, 10, 13, 15, 17, 19, 37, 38, 61, 66, 117, 139, 159
science teaching, 133, 143, 144, 146, 147, 150, 151, 156, 158, 159
scientific knowledge, 1, 35, 38, 39, 118, 124, 142, 155, 156
scientific method, 5, 6, 42, 48, 117, 124, 126, 128, 147, 148, 155
scientific progress, 5, 10, 19, 38, 41, 45, 47, 49, 52, 120, 130, 133
scientific theory, 9, 119, 124, 125, 128, 129, 131, 150
scores, 80
search, 147, 160
secondary school students, 156
selecting, 91
series, 3, 18, 19, 20, 38, 51, 60, 73, 83, 88, 97, 115, 117, 121, 123, 134, 137, 138
shape, 126
sharing, 14
silver, 82
similarity, 4, 28, 128
skills, 68, 145, 149, 152, 160
social sciences, 5, 61, 148
society, 159
sodium, 88
solar system, 123
solubility, 88, 91
special creation, 33, 149
species, 12
specific heat, 76, 79, 80
specific knowledge, 23, 37, 80
spectrum, 3, 4, 11, 50, 51, 55, 56
speed, 64, 66
spin, 11, 55
stability, 4, 11, 38, 39, 50, 51, 52
stages, 10, 21, 134, 153, 154
standard deviation, 64
standards, 5, 141
stars, 129
statistics, 62, 146, 155

steel, 64

stimulus, 28

stoichiometry, 29, 33, 34, 35, 90, 108, 130, 131, 156

strategies, vii, 7, 12, 16, 18, 19, 20, 21, 23, 25, 26, 54, 55, 56, 67, 68, 83, 85, 86, 96, 99, 102, 105, 108, 109, 113, 114, 134, 139, 141, 152, 153, 156, 158

stress, 17

stroke, 136

subjectivity, 121, 122, 157

sugar, 22

sulfur, 31

surprise, 9, 27

switching, 55

symbiosis, 11

symbols, 66

synthesis, 62

systems, 11

## T

teachers, 1, 9, 13, 16, 17, 19, 30, 37, 39, 43, 46, 48, 50, 51, 52, 53, 54, 55, 65, 71, 75, 78, 83, 85, 99, 117, 118, 119, 120, 127, 128, 129, 130, 133, 134, 136, 137, 138, 141, 142, 143, 144, 145, 146, 147, 148, 149, 150, 155, 156

teaching, 1, 4, 16, 19, 20, 21, 27, 28, 29, 30, 31, 34, 38, 39, 42, 49, 54, 66, 80, 82, 83, 86, 99, 100, 101, 102, 105, 106, 107, 115, 119, 138, 139, 141, 142, 144, 145, 146, 148, 149, 150, 151, 152, 153, 155, 156, 157, 159, 160

teaching experience, 39, 119

teaching strategies, 19, 21, 54, 83, 107, 138, 139

temperature, 13, 61, 62, 64, 65, 67, 69, 70, 71, 73, 74, 76, 77, 78, 79, 80, 81, 82, 83, 86, 87, 95, 96, 100, 101, 102, 103, 104, 108, 130, 143, 144, 148, 150, 153, 157, 160

tension, 2, 148

textbooks, 2, 4, 5, 7, 11, 13, 16, 22, 38, 39, 42, 45, 46, 47, 48, 49, 50, 59, 85, 92, 93, 100, 102, 105, 107, 115, 130, 131, 133, 134, 143, 145, 158

thermodynamics, 73, 75, 76, 78, 80, 81, 148, 150, 156

thinking, 16, 17, 20, 26, 27, 28, 42, 53, 54, 61, 70, 76, 90, 93, 97, 99, 113, 122, 126, 128, 130, 131, 145, 147, 149, 152, 157

Thomson, 37, 38, 39, 40, 41, 42, 43, 44, 45, 46, 47, 49, 50, 51, 52, 54, 55, 57, 61, 121, 128, 131, 134, 138

threshold, 17, 56, 57, 77

time, 4, 15, 17, 29, 30, 31, 40, 46, 47, 50, 52, 57, 68, 82, 85, 88, 93, 98, 99, 102, 105, 107, 108, 120, 139

tin, 156

tracking, 107

tradition, 15, 48, 57, 133

training, 17, 19, 105, 149

transformations, 28, 79, 88

transition(s), 4, 10, 18, 19, 23, 25, 26, 37, 42, 55, 56, 57, 62, 67, 68, 72, 83, 92, 97, 113, 115, 118, 130, 133, 134, 152, 154, 156

translation, 61

trend, 42, 91

trial, 144

## U

UK, 142, 144, 145, 146, 148, 149, 151, 154, 155, 160

uncertainty, 127

UNESCO, 155

uniform, 40, 46, 47, 61, 62

universe, 119, 125, 126, 129

university education, 141

## V

vacuum, 136

validation, 156

validity, 50, 53, 135, 143

values, 55, 56, 68, 90

variable(s), 12, 24, 63, 66, 68, 71, 72, 100, 130, 134, 147

variance, 24, 66

variation, 71

vector, 128

vehicles, 38

velocity, 56, 57, 60, 61, 62

Venezuela, 23, 24, 29, 39, 56, 67, 69, 75, 86, 94, 96, 99, 109, 119, 124

vessels, 75, 78

Vienna Circle, 1

vision, 4

voice, 114

Vygotsky, 27, 142, 159

## W

wave number, 56, 57

wavelengths, 3

working memory, 34, 153

writing, 39, 69, 88, 102, 109, 118, 119